Voicing Orpheus

On Poets
and Poetry

George Franklin

Published by: Nicasio Press
                 Sebastopol, California
                 www.nicasiopress.com
Cover Design: Constance King Design

ISBN: 979-8-9864100-1-2

FOR SHEILA

Acknowledgements

I would like to thank Laura Duggan at Nicasio Press for her meticulous, painstaking, and unfailingly skillful work in editing this book and shepherding it into its final form, as well as my sister Helena for her always insightful suggestions. Thanks, too, to my friend and fellow poet Martin Edmunds for his thoughtful and encouraging reading of this text.

Table of Contents

1.

On (Mostly) Failed American Political Poetry

1.

I wish at the outset to explore a topic only tangentially broached in my previous books of criticism—the political dimension of poetry, in this case of American political poetry. Though my own poems are predominantly lyrics, albeit lyrics that often entail rudimentary narratives, or rarely, as in my poem "Talking Head," more complex ones, and though my interests as a poet devolve around my own characteristic predilections and concerns, I have not been oblivious to matters political. Indeed, I have on several occasions tried—and failed—to write poems of considerable length addressing political issues. These failures have been abject and frequent enough to lead me to ponder the causes, beyond my own incompetence, for the abortiveness of such perhaps too well-intentioned efforts.

In deciding how to organize this general survey, a useful distinction, at least for me, arose between poems that are topically political, addressing contemporaneous political realities or those of the recent past, and those that attempt to envisage a kind of ideal polis. William Carlos Williams' "Patterson" and Charles Olson's "Maximus" poems, both of which concretely focus on their respective hometowns, are attempts to imagine such ideal polities as well as their susceptibility to that which continually threatens to cheapen and undercut them—in "Patterson," primarily the thinness of American culture, a culture with which Williams had a profound love/hate relationship, and whose history he reinvented in "In The American Grain"; and in Olson's work, the short-sighted rapaciousness of a ravenous capitalism that, consonant with the long Western tradition of a hypertrophied rationality stretching back to Plato and Aristotle, abstracts value from its concrete manifestations, from that with which one can be in actual contact. Both writers are profoundly influenced by and attempt to compensate for the failures of Pound's "Cantos" which, in their vast trans-historical, cross-cultural range, however eccentric, strive to create a Paradiso, itself a kind of ideal, virtual global polis, from luminous fragments gleaned from seemingly limitless strata of the past. Of course, Pound's masterwork came catastrophically, if magisterially, to grief. Olson and Williams attempted to rectify what they saw as a too-abstract quality in the "Cantos," which, divorced from any concrete, actual, temporally and spatially located polity, had become untethered and unhinged.

All three poets struggled with their attempts to produce, deploying their predominantly lyrical rather than narrative gifts, works of an epic scale. Their poems become a series of tangentially related, or suggestively juxtaposed, lyrical passages. As such, they grope, mostly unsuccessfully, for some kind of non-narrative momentum and in weaker passages succumb to inertia or to a kind of entropic aimlessness. All three grapple with seeking some alternative principle by which to order a long poem, a principle that seems to remain elusive. All experimented with a kind of spatial form. None had a teleological notion of time and of history—of history, in particular, as dynamically progressing in accordance with some providential plan, or through an immanent dialectical process, or through some collective unfolding of human consciousness itself, toward some determinate end. Accordingly, their long poems do not lend themselves to closure, but simply keep on keeping on—in the case of all three lyric/epics, mostly with diminishing returns. Such poems are perhaps the poetical version of utopian communities. They begin with, and sustain for awhile, considerable excitement but seem doomed to ultimate disappointment and dissolution.

Hart Crane's "The Bridge" is another a noble failure. Crane, with his eccentric, hybrid brand of mysticism, had few affinities with the figures mentioned above. Reacting against the pessimism of Eliot, and against the squalor and cheapness of an age that yet held forth great promise, he sought to create a grand, synoptic, mythical vision of America. Crane constantly worried over and strove to find some adequate structure for "The Bridge," but when he attempted to describe that prospective structure to his patron Otto Khan and others, it always feels as though he is trying to force his poem into a preconceived mold. In truth, he had set for himself a task that was impossible on two grounds. First, the attempt to meld mythical with historical material results in the poem's overly schematized yet still eccentric movement through time and space. Crane, like Pound, Williams, and Olson, seems to have no poetically generative notion of history, which in Crane is trumped by his deeper concern with myth. Secondly, the increasingly atomized America of the early twentieth century was not Whitman's America. It was an exuberantly and rapaciously capitalist America that found its preeminent mythographer in Fitzgerald, not in Crane.

"The Bridge," like the "Cantos," "Patterson," and the "Maximus" poems, is essentially a congeries of more or less effective lyrical passages. Among these are passages that address political issues, including slavery, enforced vagabondage, poverty, and the alcoholism that destroyed Edgar Allen Poe, as it would later destroy Crane himself. Dealing with such harsh political realities seems to uncomfortably divert Crane from his primary idiom, from his vaunting, vaulting, extravagant, at times exquisite, Neo-Elizabethan language, a language that is oddly akin in spirit to that of Whitman's grand arias. Crane's failures are more frequent and conspicuous than his successes, but the latter, mostly predating "The Bridge" but including its magnificent "Proem: To The Brooklyn Bridge," and, finally his last poem, "The Broken Tower," are among the most enthralling lyric poems in English.

Wallace Stevens was, like Crane, predominantly a post- or Neo-romantic poet, a successor of Keats and Shelley as well as of Emerson and Whitman. His poems are not, however, instances of the organic form touted by Coleridge and occasionally by others of what used to be called the Major Romantics. When I speak of Stevens' long poems, I am speaking of poems that are no longer than about thirty pages. Stevens had the sense of decorum not to push his own collations of lyrics to an unsustainable length. His two longest poems, "Notes Toward a Supreme Fiction" and "An Ordinary Evening in New Haven," are virtually identical in format and length. Where they begin and end has been arbitrarily predetermined. The movement of Stevens' poetry tends, as I have noted elsewhere, to be additive and reiterative rather than dialectical, and to proceed by the multiplication of increasingly apposite analogies. Both of the poems just cited, for all of their virtues, have, like the long poems of Pound, Williams, and Olsen, little propulsive force. They are primarily concerned with means rather than ends, with process rather than product. Their subject is the simultaneous tracking and recording of their unfolding within the poet's mind. They display little direct interest in the political and the historical.

And yet Stevens was more deeply engaged with and troubled by the vicissitudes of his time, which included both the Great Depression and the Second World War, than is generally realized. The Second World War in particular was constantly on Stevens' mind. It was for him a prime instance of what he called "the pressure of reality," a reality against which the imagination must constantly contend.

In the extended essay on Stevens in my book *Some Segments of a River,* I have discussed how in another of his longer poems, "Esthetique du Mal," he addressed the horrors of the war by a strategy of indirection, by attempting to create, amidst the squalor of the real, a work of the imagination that embodies and reimagines the saving graces, however fraught, of the beautiful and the sublime.

In closing this section, I would like to suggest that there is one American political poem that entirely succeeds in achieving both a complex narrative and mythic and symbolic coherence—but only if we commit a hopefully not too egregious act of poetic license and consider Melville's *Moby Dick* a kind of grand, encyclopedic, epic poem, as well as, at times, a dramatic one.

The crew of the *Pequod* is both racially and culturally a heterogenous polis, a microcosm of the United States. However, far from being a democracy, it is lorded over, entranced by a despot who is repellent yet strangely charismatic. It is Ahab's monomaniacal, fixed obsession, his blasphemous attempt to replace God's will with his own, that decrees the end, the telos toward which the novel inexorably moves—his disastrous, apocalyptic confrontation with the white whale. Far from ending arbitrarily, *Moby Dick* seems to conclude at a point toward which it has been driving all along.

Melville's depiction of Ahab's monomania is a critique of an intransigent strain of Puritanism, with its moral rigidity, with its obsessive concern with the *Book of Revelation* and the final disposition, the damnation or salvation, of the soul. Ahab's quest has a metaphysical dimension of which Ahab himself seems only fleetingly aware. Melville, of course, recognized that his own spirit was in some ways akin to Ahab's. In *Moby Dick*, he keeps pressing toward some ultimate revelation of the nature of things, probing ever deeper into the metaphysical light and dark of a penetralium close to some source or end, but his driving toward that end always reaches an impasse. Reality as commonly understood is, for him, a façade, a cardboard mask that he is determined to strike through, penetrating to the revelation of whatever lies on the other side, an act that is doomed to fail—perhaps fortunately, as there may well be nothing at all on the other side. Ahab ultimately both fails and succeeds in his quest: he meets and wreaks vengeance upon the leviathan who is his nemesis but is also destroyed by him. The apocalypse that he engenders is neither revelatory nor redemptive; it is the work of a tragically self-destructive anti-messiah who brings down all others with him. Melville himself never got beyond the metaphysical impasse he reached in *Moby Dick* and, his spirit largely broken, gave up trying to confront it further—before somehow, in a kind of miraculous, exquisite coda, producing *Billy Budd*.

Moby Dick, a testament recording an impasse which, for Melville the man, constituted a tragic obsession, is itself anything but a failure. For Olson, whose "Call Me Ishmael" was a groundbreaking and revelatory assessment of Melville, *Moby Dick* is a stage upon which metaphysical ideas and conceits dramatically work themselves out. It is as allusive as Pound's "Cantos." Its chapter "The Whiteness of the Whale," to cite one of many examples, is a tour de force, an encyclopedic tissue of far-flung allusions that steadily builds toward a visionary intensity. But *Moby Dick's* most important allusions are to the Bible, with its teleological view of history, and to Shakespeare. It ranges extraordinarily widely not only, like the United States, spatially, but also spiritually, metaphysically, politically, racially, and ethnographically. It is not only epic and dramatic but also, again, as instantiated by its notorious chapter on cetology, encyclopedic. Reflecting the heterogeneity of its crew, it encompasses multiple genres and cannot be confined to one.

And yet, that crew is entirely cut off from half of the human race, from women. As a result the enterprise to which the crew is consigned is monozygotic and sterile, destined not to prosper or propagate. Indeed, by the time Melville wrote *Moby Dick*, whaling was already an industry in decline.

As for the United States, its future, too, seemed uncertain. *Moby Dick* paints a remarkably vivid picture of an American polis headed toward an apocalyptic civil war. Ahab can be seen as a dark parody of an uncompromising Puritan metaphysician as well as a representative of the ravenous ruthlessness of an emergent, monomaniacal, secular capitalism, its only motive the profit motive. That capitalism is, in effect, a kind of Puritanism stripped of its spiritual and metaphysical dimensions, though it still feeds, as have countless politicians, on shopworn Puritan rhetoric such as the rote and monotonous citing of John Winthrop's depiction of the Puritan's project as the creation of a shining "city upon a hill"—a virtual city that has for many, throughout its history, been a hellish, all too real penal colony.

In *Moby Dick*, the *Pequod*—with its infernal industrial tryworks, a furnace topped by iron try-pots used to render oil from blubber, spouting fire and dense smoke—is depicted, particularly at night, as a kind of hell. The virtual indentured servitude of most of its crew is loosely analogous to the status of slaves on slave ships, which, like whalers, were fueled by the profit motive. And it is the young black sailor Pip who, having been almost lost at sea, becomes mad, as the rest of the crew do not, in response to a maddening situation, and who thereafter, like Lear's fool, speaks uncommon sense. Though lowest on the Pequod's pecking order, restricted to janitorial duties and to providing light entertainment to the crew, Pip has an odd kind of eccentric centrality. His madness links him to Ahab, and his near-death experience aligns him with Ishmael.

In addition, Melville wrote the brilliant, vexed, still strangely unsettling short story *Benito Cereno*, which is based on the slave revolt on the Spanish ship *Amistad* orchestrated by the Congolese chief Cinquez, a revolt that also plays a major role in Robert Hayden's remarkable poem "The Middle Passage." In *Benito Cereno*, both the captain of the ship, who is held hostage, and Cinquez himself, seem locked in a ghastly charade that is all too real and that dehumanizes both.

In Melville, the pluribus and the unum, the heterogenous and singular, never coalesce as they do in Whitman, but at best coexist in an uneasy truce. Melville, a luminously dark angel to Whitman's bright one, was, in addressing the ever-changing polis that is the United States, an equally essential and foundational writer.

2.

The second type of political poetry alluded to above is more directly topical, attempting to respond immediately and forcefully to exigent political realities that are either current or recently past. It is here, in particular, that American poetry hits few high notes. Even Whitman succeeded in writing only one great poem on the Civil War, his elegy for Lincoln, "When Lilacs Last in the Dooryard Bloomed." Melville's poems on the war are distant and stiff. It is a novelist to whom we must turn to find a convincing account of the horrors of the Great War. I am speaking of Stephen Crane's now too-little-read *Red Badge of Courage*. Remarkably, no—*astonishingly*—Crane was a non-combatant. His novel is an almost impossible to account for *tour de force* of the sympathetic imagination.

Moving quickly on to World War I, where are the American equivalents of Wilfred Owen, Rupert Brooke, Siegfried Sassoon? Where are her great poetic chroniclers of World War II? And what of the innumerable poetic responses to the Vietnam War? Even the best of these, by poets like Robert Bly, W. S. Merwin, Denise Levertov, Allen Ginsberg and others, now seem almost embarrassingly dated, indifferently written, and beside the point. None of these poets experienced war first-hand, and so their poems tend to feel hollow and histrionic as well as gratingly self-righteous and sanctimonious.

The fact that there are precious few good topically political poems written by Americans does not, of course, mean that there are none. I have chosen three exemplars of successfully topical American political poems. The first is written by a poet of the generation of remarkable poets that immediately succeeded the major Modernist writers; the second by a figure who was herself a major Modernist; the third by a member of my own much maligned generation, the baby boomers. This sequence, though not chronological, has, I hope, a logic of a different kind.

The first of my exemplary poems is Anthony Hecht's harrowing "More Light! More Light!" As a very young man, Hecht was drafted into the army and served in several fronts of the European theater. His company was among the first to liberate a concentration camp. These experiences were permanently seared into Hecht's consciousness. He suffered from what is now termed PTSD, and throughout his life, he occasionally woke up screaming in the middle of the night. Like many World War II veterans, he did not speak of his wartime experience. Clearly, Hecht found in poetry a much needed sense of control and mastery, which perhaps held his demons at bay, resulting in his penchant for writing in elaborate, traditional forms. Though his poems are formidable and impressive, there is something detached, distanced, and difficult to warm up to about many of them.

However, in two exceptional instances Hecht did write poems that brilliantly and painfully reflected his wartime experience. "It Out-Herod's Herod. Pray You, Avoid It" and "More Light! More Light!" are his two masterpieces, unequalled by anything else in his poetic oeuvre. Here are the concluding stanzas of the latter:

> We move now to outside a German wood.
> Three men are there commanded to dig a hole
> In which the two Jews are ordered to lie down
> And be buried by the third, who is a Pole.
>
> Not light from the shrine at Weimar beyond the hill
> Nor light from heaven appeared. But he did refuse.
> A Lüger settled back deeply in its glove.
> He was ordered to change places with the Jews.

Much casual death had drained away their souls.
The thick dirt mounted toward the quivering chin.
When only the head was exposed the order came
To dig him out and to get back in.

No light, no light in the blue Polish eye.
When he finished a riding boot packed down the earth.
The Lüger hovered lightly in its glove.
He was shot in the belly and in three hours bled to death.

No prayers or incense rose up in those hours
Which grew to be years, and every day came mute
Ghosts from the ovens, sifting through crisp air,
And settled upon his eyes like a black soot.

Hecht's normally assured, elegant cadences are here deliberately roughed up, as is his diction. The usually perspicuous literal level of Hecht's poetry, particularly of his narrative poetry, becomes, likewise, atypically opaque. The events recounted by the poem took me several readings to piece together into a coherent narrative.

The line "much casual death had drained away their souls" could easily be from the *Iliad*, a poem that is uncompromisingly graphic in its depiction of violence. But in "More Light! More Light!" unlike in *The Iliad,* death is entirely unheroic. It takes the Pole three hours, shot unceremoniously not in the head nor heart but in the unheroic, colloquial belly, to bleed out and die. In movies and television, characters who are shot almost always seem to die instantly. Decades ago, the ending of *Bonnie and Clyde,* whose bodies dance spasmodically as they are riddled by machine-gun fire, caused considerable controversy, while years after that the relatively realistic scene of the chaotic landing of allied forces at Normandy in *Saving Private Ryan* drew considerable praise.

Then and now, however, we prefer our depictions of violent death either neat or, as in Tarantino's movies, stylishly fetishized into a species of absurdist humor. We, of course, also want death to have some kind of meaning, metaphysical or otherwise. The "light" in the poem is the light of Goethe's shrine at Weimar, memorializing a preeminently lucid and civilized poet and scientist whose last words were "more light, more light," words, which become brutally ironic when used by Hecht as his poem's title. Here neither the light of poetry, nor of science, nor the metaphysical light of heaven offer any consolation. All have been extinguished, reduced to a black soot that settles on the eyes of the still-living speaker as though he, too, were as good as dead or blind.

Finally, one senses that much casual death has drained away the speaker's soul, that survival, for him, is not altogether a boon. "More Light! More Light!" recounts an event that Hecht did not personally witness but might as well have. It is a poem of witness that manages to speak of the unspeakable.

In "More Light! More Light!" the dead die, like Gloucester on the storm-ravaged heath in *King Lear*, receiving no last rites, unaccompanied by either prayers or incense. Lear speaks for all of the dispossessed characters in the play, as well as for all soldiers who suffered the trauma of World War II, and perhaps most for those who were subjected to genocide, when he proclaims:

> Poor naked wretches, whereso'er you are,
> That bide the pelting of this pitiless storm,
> How shall your houseless heads and unfed sides,
> Your looped and windowed raggedness defend you
> From seasons such as these?

"What Are Years?", a poem written by Marianne Moore, herself a major Modernist poet, also with World War II in mind, is a kind of counterpoint to Hecht's poem. Her perspective on the war, as a civilian, was, of course, very different from Hecht's. The poem is quite strikingly unlike most of Moore's poems, which are written almost entirely in syllabics. They tend to be spiky, both rough-grained and elegant, eccentric in their rhythms, usually disciplined by a close and exacting examination of various actually existent phenomena, particularly the flora and fauna of a nature that seems to resist being tamed even by so close and strict an observer as Moore. Moore's poems are structured in such a way that we as readers feel this resistance. The halting movement of many of her poems, which at times seem arbitrarily enjambed, reflected by their eccentric, often jagged look on the page, is one way in which this resistance is registered. Her tentative, careful, exacting, rigorously formulated and reformulated approach to her subjects is another. Moore seems to have had a particular aversion to the emptily rhetorical and to the abstract and generalizing.

"What are Years?", by contrast, although written in syllabics, has a fluid, propulsive, free-verse rhythm commensurate with Moore's evident passion for her subject. Uncharacteristically, it contains only two concrete images, the chasm and the cock, and its language is to a highly unusual degree, for her, both abstract and generalizing. "What Are Years?" is clearly a meditation on courage and heroism in a time of war, qualities that can be embraced and exhibited by both combatants and non-combatants. The poem itself seems to enact the acceptance of constraints, and in particular, paradoxically, the exhilarating, bracing, even joyful rising up of the spirit within the self, like water rising in a narrow chasm, as well as the "surrendering" and "continuing" that result from the acceptance of such constraints, not least of which is an acceptance of the ultimate constraint, that of death itself.

WHAT ARE YEARS?

What is our innocence,
what is our guilt? All are
        naked, none is safe. And whence
is courage: the unanswered question,
the resolute doubt—
dumbly calling, deafly listening—that
in misfortune, even death,
        encourage others
        and in its defeat, stirs

        the soul to be strong? He
sees deep and is glad, who
        accedes to mortality
and in his imprisonment rises
upon himself as
the sea in a chasm, struggling to be
free and unable to be,
        in its surrendering
        finds its continuing.
        So he who strongly feels,
behaves. The very bird,
        grown taller as he sings, steels
his form straight up. Though he is captive,
his mighty singing
says, satisfaction is a lowly
thing, how pure a thing is joy.
        This is mortality,
        this is eternity.

Set side by side with Hecht's poem, "What are Years?" might seem facile in its idealisms. However, it was as rooted in the reality of Moore's experience as "More Light! More Light!" was in the reality of Hecht's. Indirectly, it gives voice to the extraordinary contribution of women, who, of course, could not be combatants, to the war effort. We know, too, how far from her usual theater of operations Moore has ventured in creating this poem which, with respect to her canon as a whole, is a conspicuous outlier. In confronting horrific circumstances, poems of appalled witness to brute realities and of a hard-earned respect for genuine heroism both have their place.

As my third and final exemplar, I have chosen the title poem from James Tate's first book, *The Lost Pilot*, written before his turn toward the habitual, and habitually engaging, absurdist humor that characterizes his later poetry. "The Lost Pilot" registers, in perfectly enjambed free-verse stanzas, the effect that wartime deaths can have upon the succeeding generation or generations. In the poem, Tate addresses his father, a pilot killed during World War II, whom Tate imagines as trapped in a kind of limbo, constantly and pointlessly orbiting overhead. I quote from the poem's last lines, to which I will append no superfluous commentary. Much of the beauty of the poem involves the way it builds toward these lines, so I would suggest looking it up on the web.

> ... All I know
> is this: when I see you,
> as I have seen you at least
>
> once every year of my life,
> spin across the wilds of the sky
> like a tiny, African god,
>
> I feel dead. I feel as if I were
> the residue of a stranger's life,
> that I should pursue you.
>
> My head cocked toward the sky,
> I cannot get off the ground
> and, you, passing over again,
>
> fast, perfect, and unwilling
> to tell me that you are doing
> well, or that it was a mistake
>
> that placed you in that world,
> and me in this; or that misfortune
> placed these worlds in us.

3.

If our political and topical poetry tends to be tame—the three counter instances adduced above notwithstanding—during periods of unusual crisis and upheaval, it is tamer still in relatively uneventful periods. Perhaps in democratic societies in which the right to free speech is protected, political concerns, in such relatively placid interregnums, tend to fade and become insufficiently pressing to be given urgent voice.

I recently read an interesting interview in which Czeslaw Milosz suggested that the political oppression inflicted by repressive, authoritarian regimes casts everything that the poet writes in a political light. It is not only political poems that overtly criticize such a regime that raise red flags. Poems, and specifically lyric poems, that are seemingly apolitical, that address themselves to simple existential truths or that celebrate the sensual beauty or sublimity of the world, come under an even greater scrutiny. They are too subtle, too ungovernable, too difficult to characterize, and are suspected of harboring hidden messages. Surviving as an artist under authoritarian regimes requires a constant vigilance and alertness to political realities and the development of strategies of expression that ward off the always present threat of being altogether silenced. In such a situation, with survival at stake, Milosz suggests, there is no room for the irony, for the persistent strain of self-alienation—let alone for language games, or for the various kinds of self-referential meta-discourse—that have taken root in the poetry of the United States and that of other liberal democracies.

Of course, in all supposedly liberal democracies, and especially in our own, there are the voices of the unjustly marginalized, often with a vital political agenda, struggling to be heard, with varying degrees of success. Their right to be heard, to speak their truths, is at least theoretically, constitutionally respected. Unfortunately, that right has never been simply granted. Over and over again, it has been fought for.

With respect to American political poetry produced by members of historically and currently disenfranchised groups, whether by blacks, latinos, Native Americans, gays, or women, I of course, while recognizing that not all forms of oppression are created equal, do not discount the value of poems with a strong political agenda. I suspect, and hope, that they will be heard, heard for their music and for their message, polemical or otherwise, just as inspired, impeccably crafted political messages, whether "The Gettysburg Address" or "Letter from a Birmingham Jail," will always need to be crafted and heard.

Many black poets in particular are engaged in the urgent business of rediscovering, reclaiming, refashioning, and projecting forward historical narratives and cultural legacies that have for too long been repressed. In the past, and still in the present, with respect to its black citizens, the United States has in fact been, and in large measure remains, a totalitarian, hegemonic, brutalizing society, necessitating the imaginative modeling of new polities, whether within or outside of the at-once abstract and all-too-real polity of a state that ironically can only be productively transformed by being subverted.

At the same time, one needn't and shouldn't insist that poets who happen to be members of historically oppressed groups *ought* to write political poetry, in the way that all poets were expected during the Vietnam War to write protest poems, leading some, like John Ashbery, to be routinely castigated for not doing so. The degree to which an artist decides to identify with a given group should be entirely up to him or her. Elizabeth Bishop's refusal to be published in anthologies of poetry by women still seems to me a perfectly honorable position, certainly as honorable, as legitimately feminist, as Adrienne Rich's refusal, for a time, to allow men to attend her poetry readings.

With respect to political poems written by those with no history of being systematically oppressed, are they now likely to be more successful as *literature* than, say, the anti-war poems of the sixties written by those with no experience of the Vietnam War? Merely by asking such a value-laden question, I am doubtless proving myself to many to be the wrong person to answer it. The category of the literary has come to seem perniciously patriarchal and passé not only to some among habitually oppressed groups but also to many academic critics. While admitting that there is some justice to this position, I am one of a dwindling few who deem it essential that at least *some* poetry concern itself with what used to be considered specifically literary values and hope that it will remain at least one among the kinds of poetry that will continue to be written.

Still, I am myself an unreconstructed child of the sixties, a period of political and cultural upheaval that saw a re-evaluation and recuperation, after the strictures of Eliot and the New Criticism, of the reputation of the English Romantic poets who have always laid a strong claim on my own imagination—all of whom responded to the political ferment of their own time, and some of whom, in particular Blake, Shelley, and the early Coleridge, were themselves, in some of their poetry and in much of their prose, gifted polemicists. There is, I concede, no clear-cut line between the literary and the polemical.

4.

I will now briefly discuss the political as dealt with by two poets who would seem to have little in common, George Oppen and Allen Ginsberg, both of whom, like Hecht, are of the generation subsequent to that of the great high Modernists.

Oppen published one book, *Discrete Series*, as a young man—a fledgling and aggressively thorny effort allied with Luis Zukofsky's Objectivism—after which he abandoned poetry for a life of political activism as a socialist, and perhaps for a brief time as a communist. He and his wife worked as what might now be called community organizers. They eventually fled the United States for Mexico during the McCarthy era and remained there, feeling unhappily alienated, for most of a decade. Finally they felt it safe to return to the United States, specifically to New York.

After a twenty-five-year hiatus, Oppen began, with a startling energy and conviction, to write poetry again. He soon gravitated to writing short, lyrical poems as parts of larger series, though never, fortunately, on anything like an epic scale. The most well-known of these long lyric sequences is Oppen's book-length poem *Of Being Numerous,* its title perhaps evoking a kind of subliminal pun in which *numerous* can be replaced with *numinous*. Poetic feet, the building blocks of meter, are also occasionally referred to as *numbers*. The lyrics that comprise this work are spare, elliptical, austere, and surprisingly abstract, although New York City remains vitally present in many of them. They have the virtue of being distinctive, of sounding like no one else. The political dimension of this poem—like that of all of Oppen's books, beginning with *The Materials*, written after his long hiatus from poetry—is likewise surprisingly abstract and is never in any overt way topical. Ultimately, Oppen's poems are no longer restricted to New York City but assume an almost global dimension. His poems address what might pretentiously be called our being-together-in-the-world, in a shared social, political, geographical, and ecological space, and how best to comport ourselves in that space.

My echo of the rhetoric of Heidegger in the previous sentence is deliberate. Shortly after his reemergence as a poet, Oppen became, surprisingly to some, a devoted and insightful student of Heidegger. Even more surprisingly, a work of the Catholic theologian Jacques Maritain, *Creative Intuition in Art and Poetry*, provided a vitally important impetus to Oppen's reimagining of his poetic project. His poetic sequences, unlike the more apparently ambitious efforts of his Modernist forebears, have a unity of style and structure, and move dynamically with a quite powerful feeling of momentum and forward propulsion, perhaps because Oppen was a rigorous thinker-in-poems whose distinctly dialectical habit of mind was reflected in his work. The inextricably embedded, strategically situated nature of the usually brief numbered lyrics in the dynamic flow of the larger contexts of Oppen's sequences makes it difficult, without violence, to quote any one or even several of such lyrics as exemplary instances of his work.

But Oppen also wrote poems that were not parts of sequences. The poem below is a love poem to Oppen's wife—in no obvious way political. Oppen dealt with a wide range of subjects. He wrote, for example, not only poems that powerfully evoke urban environments but also a number of poems set in natural landscapes that can only be called ecological in their awareness; they remind us that if we fail to recognize and respect the integrity and untamed otherness of the natural world even as we appropriate it for our uses, we will desecrate both that world and ourselves. The poem below is set in that mysteriously beautiful world. It has a kind of delicate ungainliness that is characteristic of Oppen, of the distinctive, slightly halting sound unlike that of anyone else referred to above.

THE FORMS OF LOVE

Parked in the fields
All night
So many years ago,
We saw
A lake beside us
When the moon rose.
I remember

Leaving the ancient car
Together. I remember
Standing in the white grass
Beside it. We groped
Our way together
Down-hill in the bright
Incredible light

Beginning to wonder
Whether it could be lake
Or fog
We saw, our heads
Ringing under the stars. We walked
To where it would have wet our feet
Had it been water.

Some feel that Oppen abandoned the political altogether. But the title *Of Being Numerous* itself suggests a conception of America as an ideal polity, again as an *e pluribus* that constantly approaches and constantly resists becoming *unum*.

Oppen's poems run the risk, for me, of becoming too relentlessly austere and thereby of courting a kind of monotony. They lack, too, something of the ambition and scope of the work of Pound, Williams, and Olson—a lack that is, however, intrinsic to their strength as well as reflective of Oppen's innate sense of proportion and of decorum. Oppen's poems can feel inhibited, lacking in sensuous immediacy, hedged about by an excessive scrupulousness. Regardless, his poetry is consistently characterized by a high integrity of purpose and design, and remains, despite a recent uptick of critical attention, too-little read.

Allen Ginsberg was a far more complicated, cultivated, and interesting figure, both as a poet and a man, than is generally realized. He was as much a learned rabbi as a revolutionary. Here I will focus strictly on "Howl," written in 1955, leaving aside his later poems on the Vietnam War, of which "Wichita Vortex Sutra" is the most successful. Is "Howl" a poem that imagines an ideal polis or polity, or is it a poem of a more topical kind, dealing with some important contemporaneous or nearly contemporaneous political issue? My answer is that it manages to be both, while at the same time being typical of neither.

With respect to the first question, whether or not Ginsberg is concerned with an ideal polity, one need initially proceed no further than the poem's first line, "I saw the best minds of my generation..." The generation referred to soon became known as the Beat Generation. The core group of Beats became Ginsberg, William Burroughs, and Jack Kerouac, but in "Howl," "my generation" refers largely to a group of petty and not so petty criminals with literary pretensions with whom a naïve Ginsberg had become enmeshed while a student at Columbia. Neal Cassady would later become the supreme embodiment of such a figure, a male muse and sometime lover to both Ginsberg and Kerouac. Taken literally, the "best minds of my generation" were a fairly negligible bunch. But Ginsberg remained committed to promoting the myth of the Beat Generation as a kind of ideal, utopian polity even as he must have realized that like most utopian polities, it had come to grief. There must have been an essential sadness to Ginsberg's life, though he never, except in the harrowing "Kaddish," fully expresses it. Everyone most closely associated with him, beginning with his psychotic mother, lacked Ginsberg's essential sanity, his hard-won psychic and spiritual autonomy, and descended, horribly disfigured by various addictions, despite his best efforts, into their own private mental and physical hells. Ginsberg was a savior who ultimately failed to save.

And yet Ginsberg, who cast himself in the prophetic mode of his two chosen poetic forebears, Blake and Whitman, managed to write in "Howl" a poem that is addressed not only to the small group of writers and misfits whom it mythologizes and memorializes, but also to the American polity as a whole. It seems uncannily to anticipate the counter-culture that flourished in the late sixties and seventies, with respect to which Ginsberg came to be a key figure.

To what extent, if any, was "Howl" a topical poem addressing the exigencies of the political and cultural realities of its day? The poem is a frontal assault on what Ginsberg saw as the complacent, conformist society of the fifties. Though it shrewdly does not advance any kind of specific political program, surely it does address, and in fact contributed in some part to changing, the very culture that it condemns. Finally, when Ginsberg was indicted and put on trial for its purported obscenity, "Howl" became something of a political *cause celebre*, and Ginsberg's acquittal was one of the few vindications of what were considered and prosecuted as dangerously antinomian movements, whether political or cultural, during the fifties. As such it was one of the few harbingers of the changing times that were to come more than a decade later. Considerable courage was required on the part of Ginsberg to both produce and promote the poem, a courage that was perhaps, along with his generosity to his literary, political, and spiritual confreres, and ultimately even to his detractors, the most prominent aspect of his character.

A final, vital question remains: to what extent is "Howl" successful as a literary artifact, as a poem? Though "Kaddish," an almost unbearably heartbreaking account of Ginsberg's relationship with his mother, is his most fully and most powerfully realized poem, "Howl" remains a formidable and still vital, rhetorical performance. It is a poem that grabs one's attention immediately, and its propulsive force, enabled by a powerful use of repetition, and of brief, telegraphic, often aphoristic phrases, seldom flags. Its use of language, including its striking juxtaposition of seemingly incompatible words, has a genuine freshness and vitality. Though not as ambitious as, nor on the scale of, some of the other poems I have discussed, and though not a great poem, it is surely a successful one and not, blessedly, yet another noble failure.

Ginsberg's period of peak productivity, like Whitman's, was relatively brief. His later poems are shadows of his earlier ones. Yet he remained in other arenas—both in his continued political activism, and in his immersion in and quiet evangelizing on behalf of Tibetan Buddhism—an engaged and productive figure. The last line of his hilarious and poignant poem "America"—"America, I'm putting my queer shoulder to the wheel"—serves well as his epitaph.

5.

By way of completing this brief survey, I would like to come full circle, to address a political document by an American poet that *does*, like *Moby Dick*, have great force and imperishable pertinence. I am speaking again, of course, of *Leaves of Grass*.

First, however, I will address a more peripheral document, Whitman's diaries during the Civil War years. They provide, crucially, an unfiltered picture of Whitman the man, not merely the poet. In contrast to the lesser of his declamatory, relentlessly optimistic, and sometimes self-mythologizing poems, they have a pure, raw, emotional force. The diaries contain voluminous entries chronicling Whitman's work in hospitals, tending to wounded and dying Union soldiers, often visiting certain favorites every day, bearing little gifts, offering company and comfort, sometimes helping them to write letters home. It is difficult to describe how moving some of these entries are. Whitman became quickly and deeply attached to many of the young men whom he took care of, most of whom eventually died in the hospital. In a short time, he learned the intimate details of their lives. There was something about Whitman that inspired trust in these soldiers, that made him the welcome bearer of such confidences. Too many of Whitman's visits involved long vigils that culminated with his paying witness to the death of one of his beloved boys, after which he wrote consolatory letters to parents, wives, or girlfriends, assuring all that death was painless and swift.

The emotional and physical burden Whitman chose to carry was enormous. His visits put him in considerable physical danger. The hospitals he frequented were breeding grounds for numerous infectious diseases. And yet without fail, for several hours a day every day, even after full days of clerical work, Whitman went on his self-appointed rounds. There is no question that this vocation took a great toll on Whitman. His friends, visiting him from New York, were alarmed at his physical appearance. In two years, he seemed to have aged more than a decade.

Toward the end of his time in Washington, Whitman recounted in his diary an incident in which he, while walking to work, suddenly saw Lincoln's carriage approach. As it slowly passed, Lincoln caught and held Whitman's glance in what felt to Whitman like a profound moment of mutual recognition. For me, this apparent moment of acknowledgement between perhaps our greatest political figure and our greatest poet has a kind of mythical resonance.

Not long after the end of the Civil War, Whitman suffered a debilitating stroke that failed, typically, to eclipse his habitual good cheer. Eventually, the house to which he moved in Camden, New Jersey, became a pilgrimage site for those who admired his poems, many of whom came to feel that there was a kind of magnetic, galvanizing spiritual force emanating from the ruddy, white-maned old man.

Ultimately, it seems to me that the diaries that I have been describing are, in a unique way, a political document. They are evidence of Whitman's response, both personal and political, to the Civil War. He rightly considered his time spent at the hospitals as the most active and committed contribution he could have made to the war effort.

Whitman had previously attempted, largely successfully, to write a great personal and yet mythic "poem of these states" in his sprawling, ever-expanding volume *Leaves of Grass*. Whitman imagines the entire nation as a polis bound together by a kind of filial love which he termed "adhesiveness." In *Leaves of Grass*, he witnesses all that he beholds with a kind of unconditioned positive regard and empathy—"I am the man, I suffered, I was there." As always "both in the game and out of it," Whitman is both one with his fellow citizens as constituting a polis, and also their epitome, the truly representative man, the macrocosm with respect to whom all others are the microcosm. Whitman created a kind of myth of America, with himself daringly at its center. That he largely succeeded, again, is the result of the literary merit, the linguistic force, flexibility, and inventiveness of the new free-verse form that he had created.

It strikes me that, unlike all of his contemporaries and, indeed, in one way or another, unlike almost all of his successors—with Ginsberg, a self-avowed disciple of Whitman, being perhaps the sole exception—there is precious little in Whitman to offend our current academic valorization of diversity in all of its forms, our avowal of multiculturalism, of feminism, of ecological sensitivity and awareness, and of a fluid and open conception of gender and of sexuality. Somehow, Whitman got there, or here, before we did, and feels strangely undated, contemporary. His myth, with its unconditional respect for and identification with all human others, regardless of their class or race, with its regard for women as the equals of men, with its daring evocations of what was once considered a sexuality so deviant that it lacked a name, and finally with his identification with all living things, with the minutiae of the natural world, remains for many our preferred myth.

Where there is the occasional use of now-offensive terms, such as the "red squaw" referred to in the "The Sleepers," it is almost immediately redeemed by the dignified and respectful treatment bestowed upon its referent. The red squaw is depicted in a colloquy with Whitman's mother in which they are seen as equals. For Whitman, his mother was the archetypal exemplar of unconditional love, a love she bestowed on him and that was the precursor of his own. She was his progenitor in a more than a merely literal sense.

> A red squaw came one breakfast-time to the old homestead,
> On her back she carried a bundle of rushes for rush-bottoming chairs,
> Her hair, straight, shiny, coarse, black, profuse, half-envelop'd her face,
> Her step was free and elastic, and her voice sounded exquisitely as she spoke.
>
> My mother look'd in delight and amazement at the stranger,
> She look'd at the freshness of her tall-borne face and full and pliant limbs
> The more she look'd upon her she loved her,
> Never before had she seen such wonderful beauty and purity,
> She made her sit by the jamb of the fireplace, she cook'd food for her,
> She had no work to give her, but she gave her remembrance and fondness.
>
> The red squaw staid all the forenoon, and toward the middle of the afternoon
>   she went away,
> O my mother was loath to have her go away,
> All the week she thought of her, she watch'd for her many a month,
> She remember'd her many a winter and many a summer,
> But the red squaw never came nor was heard of there again.

The scene feels both mythic—as though it is a portrayal of a somehow ideal matriarchal society—and actual. The last line seems subtly to refer to the genocide perpetrated upon indigenous Indian nations, a genocide perpetrated by a patriarchal society run amok.

Whitman, whose myth refuses to grow obsolete, has become, more than any other figure, the mostly unacknowledged angel with whom succeeding generations of American poets have had to grapple. And yet, preferring to ignore Whitman, many claim primarily to be reacting against other figures—in the case of Pound,

Romantic and Victorian ideas and diction; in the case of Crane, Eliot; in the case of Williams and Olson, the thinness of American culture and the squalor of a rapacious capitalism. Although Whitman succeeded where many his successors failed to produce an epic out of a congeries of lyrics, he is mentioned by them only occasionally and in passing, if at all, and often to diminish him. Pound's condescending and disingenuous little poem "A Pact," which follows, is a case in point. It is one of those embarrassing instances in which a lesser poet castigates, or worse, damns with faint praise, a greater one, akin to Eliot's indictment of Shelley as an inferior craftsman.

A PACT

I make a truce with you, Walt Whitman—
I have detested you long enough.
I come to you as a grown child
Who has had a pig-headed father;
I am old enough now to make friends.
It was you that broke the new wood,
Now is a time for carving.
We have one sap and one root—
Let there be commerce between us.

It does not seem to me, despite Pound's somewhat presumptuous assertion, that he and Whitman share "one sap and one root." Even Whitman's post-Romantic successors, including Stevens and more recently, John Ashbery, have been cagily discreet in their few mentions of our preeminent native bard—if they mention him at all. Only Ginsberg, Crane, and Theodore Roethke have been exceptions to this rule.

Of course, I have been exaggerating to make a point. Whitman is not the sole sun among the galaxy of poets, whether American or foreign, around whom American poets have orbited before becoming luminaries in their own right. He is, however, the most luminous and persuasive one.

It is important to stress that Whitman wrote his share of bad, inadvertently self-parodic poems, poems that make it too easy to read him as a jingoistic populist peddling a disingenuous and falsely optimistic vision of America. He also had the limitations endemic to his time and place. Though in a general way sympathetic to black Americans, he was less sensitive to the original sin of race in America than was Melville, who on his whaling voyages had direct experience of blacks of a kind and intensity that Whitman did not. And it is worth remembering, in defense of Whitman, that what I have been calling Whitman's myth of America remains a myth, an as-yet-unrealized paradigm.

Nevertheless, Whitman retains his uncanny capacity to suggest that he is always several steps or moves ahead of us, existing elusively both in the present and in a yet-to-be-realized but much-to-be-desired future.

To cite, finally, the last lines of "Song of Myself," in which he addresses us, his future readers:

> I depart as air, I shake my white locks at the runaway sun,
> I effuse my flesh in eddies, and drift it in lacy jags.
>
> I bequeath myself to the dirt to grow from the grass I love,
> If you want me again look for me under your boot-soles.
>
> You will hardly know who I am or what I mean,
> But I shall be good health to you nevertheless,
> And filter and fibre your blood.
>
> Failing to fetch me at first keep encouraged,
> Missing me one place search another,
> I stop somewhere waiting for you.

2.
WALLACE STEVENS AND THE VOCATION OF THE POET

1.

Wallace Stevens, though fundamentally a post-Romantic poet, differs from most of the major English Romantic poets in not seeing history as dialectically progressing toward some ultimate end. Blake, proclaiming that without contraries there is no progression, was a dialectical thinker *avant la lettre*, and as a committed if eccentric Christian, he envisaged history as advancing toward a transformative apocalypse. Coleridge, having spent years in Germany, was thoroughly conversant with German idealism and embraced its dialectical habit of mind, particularly as propounded by Schelling, whom he plagiarizes in key passages of his *Biographia Literaria*. Much of Wordsworth's metaphysics was supplied by Coleridge, and *The Prelude*, in the Romantic tradition of the Bildungsroman, aims to delineate the progress of the poet's mind. Shelley's *Prometheus Unbound* moves ineluctably via the reconciliation of opposites, represented by Zeus and Prometheus, toward an extravagant apocalypse.

Only Byron and Keats among the major Romantics were consistently skeptical, like Stevens, of visions of human consciousness as collectively, progressively, moving toward some more enlightened state. Stevens did not live in what seemed to him, unlike to committed Marxists, a time when a revolutionary, ameliorative renovation of society seemed close at hand, as it once had to the major Romantic poets. To the contrary, he feared the apocalyptic rhetoric of revolution. He found the reality of his time, particularly in the years leading up to and during the Second World War, appallingly destructive and violent.

In his essay "The Noble Rider and the Sound of Words," the first of two seminal essays that open his extraordinary book of essays *The Necessary Angel,* both of which I shall be discussing here, Stevens writes of "the pressure of reality":

> I am thinking of life in a state of violence... physically violent for millions of our friends and for still more millions of our enemies and spiritually violent, it may be said, for everyone alive.

Since the role of the imagination, particularly in inauspicious times, is to resist the pressure of reality, and since Stevens characterizes the imagination as "a violence within protecting us from a violence from without," one might have expected that he would advocate confronting the brutality of war directly, with the full, violent force of the imagination. Yet Stevens writes:

> Then I am interested in the role of the poet... In this area of the subject
> I might be expected to speak of the social, that is to say the sociological
> and political, obligation of the poet. He has none.

We are, and perhaps should be, caught up short by this bald, no doubt intentionally provocative, declaration. Just as it is not the province of poetry to explicitly address the social and the political, so Stevens' poetry does not directly address ethical issues or assume a moral stance.

Equally disturbing to our contemporary sensibility is Stevens' notion that the poet necessarily addresses himself to an elite:

> Time and time again it has been said of the poet that he may not
> address himself to an elite. I think he may... The poet will continue to
> do this: to address himself to an elite even in a classless society, unless,
> perhaps, this exposes him to imprisonment or exile. In that event he is
> likely not to address himself to anyone at all.

Stevens is far from being glib or dismissive here. He was well aware that poets, particularly in the Soviet Union, had been and were continuing to be subjected to imprisonment, exile, or worse, and he was, of course, entirely in sympathy with them.

No less a poet than the revolutionary Milton himself declared that his poetry was written for a "fit audience though few." And yet the word *elite* signifies for us something to which we are no longer able, to use Stevens' terms, grant our assent. Indeed, it signifies something pernicious. The same obsolescence is true of many key words in Stevens' vocabulary, including the word *imagination* itself—and including, too, as we shall see, the idea of nobility that "The Noble Rider and the Sound of Words" is at pains to rehabilitate.

In stating that the poet does not deal directly with the sociological, the political, or the ethical, and that he addresses himself to an elite, hasn't Stevens intolerably restricted the scope and influence of poetry? Hasn't he ceded the field in advance, relegating poetry to a merely marginal status? What, finally, is the role of the poet? Stevens writes, with respect to his elite audience:

> I think his function is to make his imagination theirs and that he fulfills himself only as he sees his imagination become the light in the minds of others.

The function of poetry, finally and most fundamentally, is that it "helps people," or at least some people, "to lead their lives." Yet Stevens recognizes that the light of the poet's imagination is not likely to shine in the minds of all. Few are fully capable of receiving it. Even then it can only shine in one mind at a time. But for those in whose minds it does shine, it can clearly, in his view, have a significant, even a redemptive impact. In one of his *Adagia*, a collection of aphorisms, Stevens states, unequivocally and a bit surprisingly, that "poetry is redemption."

Stevens' view of the role of the lyric poet resonates, somewhat ironically, with that of Theodor Adorno, the Marxist social critic, a leading light of the Frankfurt school, as expressed in his influential essay "Lyric Poetry and Society." Adorno suggests that it is by refusing to address the social and political, by remaining uncontaminated by the terms of whatever oppressive ideology is ascendant in any given culture, that lyric poetry in fact has its social impact. Lyric poetry becomes a kind of cell, a site of resistance to oppressive regimes, not by engaging with the political but by refusing to engage with it. Likewise, by eschewing value judgements, it judges all the more powerfully.

Lest this sound far-fetched, it is worth pointing out that great lyric poets like Anna Akhmatova, Osip Mandelstam, and Czeslaw Milosz, to name but a few poets who wrote under repressive political regimes, were quite literally members of literary cells. They did not and could not, in good conscience, write conformist poems extolling an ascendant ideology. Likewise they did not, nor did they wish to, write poems that were overtly opposed to that ideology. Often it was their poetry's *lack* of social, political, or ideological content that made it seem subversive to authorities, who considered such poems to be written in a difficult-to-detect code (as are, in fact, most good poems, though that is another story).

Denied the means of reaching a wider audience, members of poetic cells distributed their poems in an intimate, reciprocal exchange with each other. They were each other's elite, each other's fit audience though few. Reading each other's poetry and writing their own helped them, in a very real way, to live their lives. Exchanging poems sustained their morale and their determination to keep writing. Surely we are the beneficiaries of that determination.

In assessing the adequacy of "Esthetique du Mal," a poem in which Stevens assays a response to a letter from a soldier fighting on the Italian front in the Second World War, I address, in my long essay on Stevens in *Some Segments of a River*, the beauty and sublimity of the poem's language and then explore its power of suggestion, its uncanny ability create a kind of zone of intimacy with its reader, admittedly an elite reader, who is able, as Stevens says, to do what Stevens cannot, to "receive his poetry." This power to establish a sense of shared intimacy between the poet who conceives and the reader who receives and re-conceives is surely one of lyric poetry's essential attributes and functions. Writing poems is, for the most part, a solitary not a social exercise, as is reading them. Nonetheless, the compact, the understanding, between writer and reader, when it attains the kind of intimacy I have described, is a small triumph over solitude and alienation, a triumph of a kind that occurs in spite of the coarsening, sometimes violent, sometimes insidiously impinging influences of the social and the political, and is an implicit rebuke to them.

Perhaps, then, "Esthetique du Mal" was not merely an adequate response to the exigencies of war, of social and political upheaval, was not merely a nice try, the best that Stevens could come up with. Perhaps "Esthetique du Mal" would have seemed to Adorno, or leaving Adorno aside, might still seem to us, an effective way for one whose vocation was that of a poet, and specifically that of a lyric poet, to address such exigencies. Again, as I have previously suggested, by creating an inexhaustibly suggestive poem in his strikingly singular language, only tenuously related to its prescribed subject, and by establishing a peculiar intimacy with his readers, Stevens was perhaps, in resisting writing easily consumed, easily forgotten, political boilerplate, committing a subtly subversive act. He was allowing beauty and sublimity, even in the most horrific of world historical circumstances, at precisely the time it might have seemed in bad taste, or in bad faith, or worse still, completely irrelevant, to step forth and declare, *I am alive and well. I still exist. Do not despair.* Rather than verbally grappling with the unspeakable obscenities of a war that he had not experienced and surely knew he could not imagine, Stevens composed "Esthetic du Mal" as a kind of counter example, a momentary stay against confusion and ugliness, a space of imaginative freedom in which the nightmare visions of society, no longer, for at least a brief interval, reigned supreme.

But we do not now live in the time of Stevens and Adorno. Lyric poetry now more than ever inhabits a marginal position *vis a vis* a society that increasingly has time only for the easily consumed, easily-disposed-of products of popular culture. In the meantime, the category of the "literary," one that Stevens frequently and unabashedly invoked, has become passé, as has the notion of canonical literature itself, let alone any broad notion of culture, by which in this case I mean not high culture but a culture that retains some links to its past, including its distant past.

The literary lyric, to the extent it has survived at all, while addressing the contemporaneous, as all vital poetry must, need not entirely capitulate to it. It must address, perhaps by not addressing, by not voicing or incorporating, the disposable values and pervasive, ersatz rhetoric of a debased culture that everywhere surrounds us. That culture is partly promulgated by whatever late stage of capitalism we happen to be in. Partly, and more significantly, it has been formed by the exponential growth of technologies that ostensibly help us to lead our lives, to save precious time, but which instead invite us, almost compel us, to waste time. As a result many of us, without quite knowing why, feel busier and busier, with no time to engage in activities like reading poetry, which demand extended contemplation.

Writing literary poetry in America in no way confronts its practitioner with the prospect of imprisonment or exile but exposes him instead to a kind of massive, dispiriting indifference. Lacking even the illusion of being subversive, the poet continues his peculiar enterprise largely within the no longer dangerous (to others) cell of himself. Perhaps lyric poetry is already caught in the vortex of its own destruction, with a vast and undifferentiated ocean soon to close over it, an ocean that will render up no Ishmael to tell his miraculous tale, much less an audience anxious to hear it.

I am, I confess, exaggerating my pessimism here to make a point. Certainly I am making no distinction between "high" and "low" art. Most vital art is an admixture of both. Nor am I prescriptively seeking to banish pop culture references from poetry. John Ashbery, for example, who was a keen ephebe of Stevens, uses such references with an at times gleefully exhilarating effect. He also wrote in long, beautifully cadenced and counterpointed sentences that not only enshrine what Stevens called "dear gorgeous nonsense," but also, at times—as in his exquisite "Self-Portrait in a Convex Mirror"—attain a nobility of both theme and diction. In a subsequent essay in this book, I note that Frank O'Hara's "Lunch Poems," which are replete with specific news of the day, nonetheless speak to us with a peculiar immediacy. So do those poems of Catullus, which scabrously and obscenely indict witless and pretentious politicians whose names would otherwise have been lost to oblivion. It is true of both poets that their present speaks to our present. Again, poetry must be sensitive to the contemporary. Weak poetry, including that aspiring to be "high art," is as disposable as yesterday's news. Poetry must remain news that, bridging gulfs in time, however vast, stays news. Such poetry, one hopes, will continue to be written.

"The Noble Rider and the Sound of Words" represents Stevens at perhaps his most pessimistic, at a time, in the midst of the Second World War, in which he himself felt particularly marginalized. And yet in precisely this dark time, he made his case that the writing of poetry is essentially a noble exercise.

Nobility is another word, like the word *elite*, that seems foreign to contemporary discussions of poetry. And yet in "The Noble Rider and the Sound of Words," Stevens spends considerably more time on the idea of nobility than on the sound of words. He is all too well aware that the word *nobility* may sound anachronistic and foregone. He traces some of the vicissitudes of the term, first associating it with Plato's figure of a celestial charioteer drawn heavenward by winged horses, an image that now feels too divorced from the real, to adhere too closely to the merely imaginative, for us to grant it—and the feeling of nobility it once conjured up—our assent. Other examples are given of works that fail to convey nobility by cleaving too closely, on the contrary, to the real.

Throughout "The Noble Rider and The Sound of Words," Stevens is engaging in a process of clearing a space in which the word *nobility* can be resuscitated, can once again become a viable term. He clearly felt that poetry should be both a noble and an ennobling calling, worthy of the energy, of the aspirations, of those who create it, as well as being answerable to the nobler aspirations and feelings of those who read it. This idea of nobility is clearly aligned with the notion of poetry as a vocation that requires something close to a spiritual vow, a commitment and dedication of one's whole being, in those who most truly practice it. Stevens wrote that nobility was the one quality most essential to combating the ugliness and dross of his age and yet was the one quality most conspicuously absent from its poetry. One might wonder if poets and poetry are, in our own moment, in the same plight.

Toward the end of "The Noble Rider and The Sound of Words," Stevens writes of nobility:

> I am evading a definition. If it is defined it will be fixed and it must not be fixed...Nobility resolves itself into an enormous number of vibrations, movements, changes. To fix it is to put and end to it.

We hear in this passage the privileging of the inexhaustibly dynamic over what is fixed by the mind and is therefore reified and lifeless, a notion that is a fundamental leitmotif in Stevens. Later, he writes, still with reference to nobility:

> But as a wave is a force and not the the water of which it is composed, which are never the same, so nobility is a force and not the manifestations of which it is composed, which are never the same.

Nobility is dynamic, fluid, alive, its manifestations never the same in any given epoch, and Stevens equates its power to that of the imagination itself to ennoble and uplift us by lifting from us the dead weight of a sometimes intolerable reality.

In a particularly beautiful passage, again toward the end of "The Noble Rider," Stevens writes:

> For the sensitive poet, conscious of negations, nothing is more difficult than the affirmations of nobility and yet there is nothing that he requires of himself more persistently, since in them and in their kind, alone, are to be found those sanctions that are the reasons for his being and for that occasional ecstasy, or ecstatic freedom of the mind, which is his special privilege.

In "The Figure of the Youth as Virile Poet," to which I will now turn, Stevens addresses "the sanction," the "ecstatic freedom" or "liberation" of the poet's mind as a frankly redemptive force. The sensitive reader, too, shares in the poet's liberation. The second section of Stevens' poetic *summa* in "Notes Toward A Supreme Fiction" is entitled "It Must Give Pleasure." The sanction of which Stevens writes here is a pleasure of the highest order.

2.

Clearly, Stevens had a powerful sense of vocation as a poet, a vocation that, as we shall see, he likens, but of course with a difference, to that of the saint or mystic. "The Figure of the Youth as Virile Poet," written after World War II had ended, is more confident and assertive about the role of the poet than is "The Noble Rider and the Sound of Words."

In "The Figure of the Youth as Virile Poet," Stevens is largely concerned with imagining and then briefly calling into being a prospective youthful poet. How might he most fruitfully fulfill his vocation? Toward the end of the essay, Stevens writes that such a poet, who is part of the real, must speak from and for the real, while at the same time equally respecting the demands of the imagination, which has the power to transform our experience of the real. The prospective poet, Stevens decrees, will and must choose to embrace such a dual sense of his vocation.

> Can there be the slightest doubt what the decision can be? Can we suppose for a moment that he will be content merely to make notes, merely to copy Katahdin when, with his sense of the heaviness of the world, he feels his own power to lift, or help to lift, that heaviness away? Can we think that he will elect anything except to exercise his power to the full and at its height, meaning by this as part of what is real, to rely on his imagination, to make his own imagination that of those who have none, or little?
>
> And how will he do this? ...Having made an election, he will be faithful to the election that he has made.

Stevens himself can be seen, and might, in certain moods, have seen himself, as a poet who is merely a producer of notes; after all, he entitled his aforementioned poetic summa "Notes Toward a Supreme Fiction," and much of his poetry, as I have discussed at length in *Some Segments of a River*, endlessly qualifies, elaborates, and defers. He lived at a time when poetry was becoming increasingly marginalized. His own poetry, uniquely demanding in its complexity, scarcely invited a wide readership.

Stevens wrote of Paul Valery, a poet whom he otherwise greatly admired, that he was too content to write poems that were concerned with and issued from the liminal, was too content, in effect, to be marginal. In *Some Segments of a River,* I have discussed Stevens' own proclivity for liminality. Nonetheless, there was something in him that was not content merely to write refined dispatches from the periphery but sought to find, to write from, in some way to represent, the vital communal center of human experience, to become, like Emerson, a representative man—or better still, to take as his exemplar Whitman, who outrageously deemed himself a "kosmos," and who with a boldness surpassing even that of Emerson, to a remarkable degree succeeded, even if mostly posthumously, in establishing himself as both the prophet, epitome, and embodiment of American democracy.

In "The Noble Rider and the Sound of Words," Stevens is unabashed about writing poetry for an elite, for those with the imagination to do what he cannot, to "receive his poems," whereas in "The Figure of the Youth as Virile Poet," consonant with Stevens' inclination in this essay to move from a marginal position toward a more central one, his poems are said to grant the enlivening power of the imagination not simply to an elite but also to those who have "little or no imagination."

Stevens, a lover of Cervantes, quixotically wished to reinstall poetry, and perhaps himself as a poet, to its once more prestigious, central place. Hence his evocations of "the central man," "the major man," the "thinker of the first idea," invested with the power to write "supreme fictions," fictions so powerful as to inspire assent and belief in a world now devoid of the capacity to inspire either.

Such grand ambitions aside, it is clear that Stevens' sense of his prospective poet's vocation implied, as did Emerson's and Whitman's, a project that was to a significant degree spiritual in nature. Quite deliberately spiritual language insinuates its way into the passage quoted above. Stevens writes of the young poet: "Having made an election, he will be faithful to the election he has made." Usually one thinks of the *elect* and the path they are to follow as being chosen by God. Here, however, the poet elects himself to fulfill his vocation as poet. Nonetheless, this election is powerful and binding. The poet must remain faithful to it. It demands, like any spiritual vocation, the devotion of his powers "to the full and at their height," as well as the commitment of the whole person.

Moreover, in a passage immediately prior to that cited above, Stevens demands that his prospective poet speak out, publicly, "so that we can all hear him," his poetic credo, which, by being spoken publicly, essentially has the force of a vow that cannot be lightly or easily abrogated. The prospective poet is asked to come to a decision on a crucial question, a decision upon which, Stevens says, perhaps playfully echoing Williams, for him and for us, "much depends." The question is: "At what level of the truth shall he compose his poems?" The correct answer, as noted above, is on both levels, on the levels of both the real and the imaginative. This answer is by no means entirely the youthful poet's own. He is able to read the "inscription on the portal," and he repeats, in his answer, lines that, according to Stevens, are universally applicable while at the same responsive to the nature of what his time demands. The poet speaks, yes, but like the speaker of most vows, he repeats lines, in this case lines written on the sacred, liminal space of a portal, that he himself has not composed.

However, for my purposes here, it is not so much the poet's answer but the question itself that is noteworthy. "At what level of the truth shall he compose his poems?" *Truth*, leaving aside the somewhat odd notion of levels of truth, is a word that, except when pertaining to logical propositions or matters of fact, has in our age lost its prestige. In *Some Segments of a River*, I have mentioned the scandal, from the point of view of critics of a positivist bent, caused by the concluding lines of Keats' "Ode to a Grecian Urn," "beauty is truth, truth beauty," which, though equating two abstract terms, is still a metaphor, and therefore exempt from the law of non-contradiction. Nevertheless, this line has been indicted by those who insist on seeing what for Keats was the expression of an existential truth as a failed, meaningless logical proposition. I have given Keats' use of this term a vigorous defense on my chapter on Keats in *Some Segments of a River*, an argument that I will not repeat here.

Keats, more than any other poet, had a profound influence on Stevens and is clearly the tutelary deity of Stevens' early masterpiece "Sunday Morning," in which the speaker declaims "Death is the mother of beauty, mystical." The overt thematization of beauty ceases in Stevens' later work but still runs like an underground stream that frequently resurfaces.

In one of the earlier of his extant letters, Keats writes:

> I am certain of nothing but of the holiness of the Heart's affections and the truth of Imagination. What the imagination seizes as Beauty must be truth.

The truth or truths that Stevens approaches, rather than seizes upon, as beautiful, particularly in what I have called his endlessly proliferating poems of summer, with their "intricate evasions of as," tend to be highly imaginative, elusive, unfixable, untethered to the real to a degree that might have baffled even Keats. His strategy in such poems is, in the words of Hamlet, to "by indirections find directions out." They operate in precincts that only glancingly reference a world apart from the language in which they are expressed.

Especially, however, in his more stripped down, bare, contemplative poems of winter, those more closely adhering to "the real," of which "The Snowman" is a justly celebrated example, the word *truth* attains particular force for Stevens. In "The House Was Quiet and The World Was Calm," it is the truth that the protagonist/

reader most passionately, lovingly seeks from the book that he is engrossed in reading.

Truth appears, as well, in the concluding line of "The Man on the Dump": "Where was it one first heard of the truth? The the."

"The Man on the Dump" is one of a number of poems by Stevens whose seriousness of intention gradually emerges from what seems like a comical beginning. The poem's final, peculiar, and unexpected two words catch us up short, subject us to a not-unpleasant shock of surprise.

There is something poignant in the question "Where was it one first heard of the truth?" The man on the dump is sitting not only upon a heap of trash but also upon a heap of worn-out tropes, a kind of miscellany of the banal and the outmoded. Having worked one's way through the poem, one has an appetite for something primary, something essential, that will clear away accumulated mental and linguistic debris. In Stevens, that which is temporally prior, which is first, represents a kind of "immaculate" beginning, the antithesis of the contents of the dump. Implicit in the question "When was it one first heard of the truth?" is a sense of loss, a nostalgia for origins, for something once heard that one can no longer hear.

In the typically grammatically strange concluding locution "The the," which has the look of a tautology, the second "the" becomes a kind of place filler that stands, potentially, for any number of possible analogous nouns; but more crucially, and paradoxically, the second definite article stands for something that is not propositional truth, but which, like the word *nobility*, is unfixable, indefinite, undefined, and above all ineffable and essential, that no words can grasp—and that also like the word *nobility* is more of a force than an abstract idea or ideal. However one interprets the "the," or the truth as the "the," one senses that for Stevens, as for Keats, the effort to get at the truth, however one might conceive it and however difficult it might be to grasp, or even granting the impossibility of grasping it, is not a wasted effort. Seeking to approach an undefined and undefinable truth might seem to be an activity one would associate more with a spiritual seeker than with a modernist poet, but it is just this kind of open-ended, unlikely-to-be-consummated quest that was congenial to Stevens.

Referring, on the other hand, to propositional truth as the would-be arbiter of the real, to the notion of truth as it pertains to matters of fact and to the dictates of reason, perhaps with logical positivism in mind, Stevens writes in "The Noble Rider":

> We have been a little insane about the truth. We have had an obsession. In its ultimate extension, the truth about which we have been insane will lead us beyond the truth to something in which the imagination will be the dominant complement.

Once again the truth of imagination, as a complement to the truth of reason, is, when grounded in reality, of paramount value. Stevens characteristically speaks of the complementarity of imagination with whatever lies beyond our obsession with propositional truth. The more pessimistic, agonistic formula advanced in "The Noble Rider," referring to poetry as a violence within pressing back against a violence without, is an exception to Stevens' generally preferred notion of the imagination and reality as complementary polar forces.

Toward the end of "The Figure of the Youth as Virile Poet," Stevens again explicitly likens the role of the poet to that of the saint and the mystic. The poet, according to Stevens, experiences liberation and a kind of apotheosis when, having greatly desired and aspired, he achieves, fulfills, in any given poem, whatever aim he has proposed to himself:

> If, then, when we speak of liberation, we mean an exodus, if when we speak of justification, we mean a kind of justice of which we had not known and on which we had not counted, if when we experience a sense if purification, we can think of the establishing of a self, it is certain that the experience of the poet is of no less degree than the experience of the mystic and we may be certain that in the case of poets, the peers of saints, those experiences are of no less a degree than the experiences of the saints themselves.

Here we draw close to a sense of the poem as a privileged space of enhanced freedom in which the structure of aesthetic experience is similar to that of spiritual experience, and with analogous rewards. Once again, words more associated with spirituality than poetry abound: *liberation, exodus, justification, purification.*

The goal of mystical practice is the liberation, the freedom, of the practitioner and the ecstasy that that liberation entails. Stevens likewise describes, as we have seen, the experience of the poet when he is accomplishing his purpose as entailing a feeling of liberation. He writes that the poet who adheres to the nobility of his vocation finds the "sanction" that is the reason for his being as a poet, a sanction that grants the occasional ecstasy, or ecstatic freedom of the mind, that is his special privilege. The word *sanction* has about it the aura of sanctity, suggesting, again, an analogy between the poet and the saint or mystic.

However, the two vocations that I have been describing are, as Stevens stresses, though analogous, not identical. The mystic attempts, through dedication to spiritual practice, to become one with a Consciousness that can perhaps never be fully realized, that even for the saint remains ineffable and inexplicable, and that in its spontaneity and freedom is a constant source of surprise, wonder, and delight; the poet, by contrast, *elects* himself to his vocation. He petitions, as though in prayer to himself, setting forth his purposes. He both proposes and like God, disposes, not only "petitions" but utters fiats, "harmonious decrees" in the form of poems that fulfill his purposes. Stevens, whether exploring the relationship of poetry to philosophy or to spirituality, is always keen to uphold the sovereign prerogatives of poetry.

The mystic and the poet are alike engaged in a sustained, dedicated practice that is the guarantor of their sincerity. The poet seeks the "acutest vibration" of words, a vibration that can be approximated but never fully, finally realized by language, but which, when approached, produces a rapturous feeling of rightness in the poet that is likewise a source of delight, wonder, and surprise. Both vocations, when their practitioners remain true to their vows, are noble ones.

Like the terms *election* and *faith,* the notion that the poet, in his own way, is trying to get at the truth that poetry is a noble vocation entailing a kind of vow; that the poet achieves, in particularly felicitous moments, a liberation that is also a kind of redemption; that the imagination is a kind of inner light that can be transferred from poet to reader; that the role of poetry is to help us to lead our lives—all seem to a belong to a cluster of terms or notions that one would typically associate as much with spirituality as with poetry. The use of such terms in the discussion of poetry is proscribed by current critical orthodoxy, and they are, as deployed by Stevens, treated as best passed over, ignored, or dismissed out of hand, as though they are embarrassments, instances of bad taste, that the poet of our current moment should surely wish to disavow.

3.

When I was a youthful and, in my queer way, a virile poet, I found *The Necessary Angel* and in particular the two essays I have been discussing—far more than, for example, Rilke's more dramatic, histrionic, and self-regarding *Letters to a Young Poet*—a source of great inspiration. Much of my sense of poetry as a potentially noble and ennobling vocation was both formed and quickened by Stevens' words. I felt the uncanny intimacy that Stevens can establish with his reader, felt as though his words were specifically directed to me. Several years later when, through meeting my spiritual teacher, I embraced as best I could a spiritual vocation, I found that Stevens' words spoke to, were aligned with, that vocation as well, which encouraged me, although perhaps I had no choice, to pursue both vocations and to find them in some way interrelated.

As for Stevens himself, he can be seen to have led an ascetic, almost monastic life, entirely given over to his habitual daily practices. He rose before dawn, performed his ritual ablutions in the form of a bath, and then sat quietly, meditatively, awaiting the moment when the crest of the sun rose above the horizon. Thereafter he walked to work, sometimes composing poems *en route,* and for the better part of the day submitted himself to the Jesuitically rigorous work of being a first-rate lawyer and actuary. His evenings were spent pursuing his equally rigorous but more liberating vocation as a "rabbi"/scholar/poet working alone at night in his study, trying to recover for himself and others some provisional form of a spiritual dimension that had been stripped from life.

This is not, of course, the only possible narrative. Indeed, some have embraced the counter-narrative of Stevens as the economically privileged apostle of a narcissistic hedonism, as an aging epicure and arch-consumer, ordering artistic knickknacks and gustatory treats from his various complicit foreign agents abroad, and indulging, in his poetry, in a kind of endless self-pleasuring linguistic foreplay, not only cut off from the larger sphere of the social and the political, from suffering on a grand scale, but personally cold and aloof in his interactions with others.

Certainly Stevens himself was aware of the rampant consumerism and materialism, the cheapening and coarsening of culture, the ugliness, that were a by-product of American capitalism; they were insidious instances of the pressure of reality, and he tried, in his own way, to counter them. That he did not denounce capitalism itself is unsurprising. He had the conservative but not monstrously conservative politics of the upper middle-class burgher that he was.

While admitting at least the semblance of force to the counter-narrative, I find it unnecessarily harsh and judgmental. I prefer to see Stevens in something closer to his own terms, as an older version of the young scholar in Milton's "Il Penseroso," pursuing his arcane studies late into the night, a "rose rabbi," a magus without portfolio, ever striving, through some subtle alchemy, to wed, in the alembic of his poetry, the leaden dross of the real with that lightest of elements, the imagination, and awaiting some first gleam of the golden words, the golden world, that he has every expectation will issue from their marriage.

3.

STARK DIGNITY

Notes On Two Poems By Williams

1.

Like Pound, Eliot, Stevens, and Yeats, and perhaps Crane and Frost as well, William Carlos Williams is now considered to be among the major Modernist poets. Throughout his life, however, he suffered from considerable critical condescension. Just as Stevens' austere, meditative "poems of winter," of which the prime exemplar is "The Snow Man," have been misapprehended by some critics as grim poems of imaginative poverty, so Williams' commitment to writing poems that, as we shall see, are relatively undistorted by cognitive filters, led to the widespread New Criticism charge that his poems were intellectually and structurally deficient. Most early–to–mid-century American and English critics lacked any perspective through which the stark, apparent simplicity of such poems could be considered a virtue. Only late in his life was Williams' poetry, like Stevens', accorded some measure of respect, from which a degree, however scant, of recognition and fame ensued.

Far more successfully than any other American poet, including Pound and his lesser imagist progeny, Williams wrote what might be called the poetry of the pure percept. Williams was intent on evoking the pith, the quick, the felt quality of the world as it presented itself to his consciousness, or as his consciousness presented it to him. The act of writing poems, which were often scribbled as a result of some inner imperative on scraps of paper during the course of busy days, also demanded an abiding in the quick of their unfolding. Williams' poems are an enactment, word by word, moment by moment, of the urgency of their creation, a creation in which process and product remain inextricably allied.

His poems are also expressions of value, not only of the intrinsic value of objects as immediately apprehended by consciousness, but of Williams' values, of what he prizes and cherishes, which is to say that they enshrine a kind of implicit ethic. To quote the opening line of perhaps Williams' most famous poem (one that, alas, I dislike), his poetry of the pure percept lets us know that "much depends" upon a right relationship to and apprehension of the things of this world. Williams remained unwaveringly committed to this ethic of right relationship and right apprehension at every stage of his career as a poet.

An early manifestation of this ethic was Williams' decision to become an obstetrician, to live an active life in and of the world, a life that would require of him as a whole person, not only as a poet, the cultivation of what Buddhists call "skillful means." He wanted a life that would make concrete demands on him, and he was committed to responding to those demands as conscientiously as possible.

It was important to Williams, too, that his work put him in touch with people from all strata of society. Williams could have chosen to move to Manhattan and to become a charming and affluent physician to the well-heeled. Instead, he chose to remain in Rutherford, New Jersey, his hometown, a relatively impoverished backwater of New York. At a time when babies were frequently delivered not in hospitals but at home, he chose a life in which he made irregular, peripatetic rounds, serving his patients, particularly during the Depression, whether or not they could pay him—to the understandable consternation of his more practical wife, Flossie. Williams' life as a poet and his life as a physician mutually informed each other. His work—like that of Keats, who was Williams' first and abiding poetic love, and who was also a trained physician—never loses touch with the concrete vicissitudes and joys of an embodied life apprehended in the living of it. Williams wrote poems that were, to use Keats' term, negatively capable, relatively undistorted by the designs of the ego or by rigid conceptual frameworks.

As an obstetrician, Williams ushered countless souls through the gates of life. It was something like an ideal choice of career. Among the values that Williams' poetry of the pure percept implicitly espouses is a keen appreciation of eros, of the life force itself, and particularly of its indomitable resilience, as it it expresses itself in and through the objects of the natural world.

I will take as my example of a such a poem the first, justly well-known, untitled poem in Williams' seminal volume *Spring and All*, published in 1923, which begins with the line "By the road to the contagious hospital...." The first line of the poem, which has come to serve as a kind of *ad hoc* title, is, of course, significant. I think it permissible to assume that the speaker of the poem is, like Williams, a physician, though presumably not an obstetrician, and that he is headed to a hospital in which reminders of the imminence and immanence of death abound. At the time when the poem was written, neither tuberculosis nor polio, among other contagious diseases, was curable, and the devastating Spanish flu had ravaged the country only several years before. The specter of death alluded to in the poem's first line makes the poem's evocation of the emergence of life all the more poignant.

I will proceed to quote here all but the poem's two opening stanzas.

> All along the road the reddish
> purplish, forked, upstanding, twiggy
> stuff of bushes and small trees
> with dead, brown leaves under them
> leafless vines—
>
> Lifeless in appearance, sluggish
> dazed spring approaches—

It soon becomes clear that the poem, and its depiction of the gradual advent and final arrival of spring, is based not upon a single act of observation but upon many such acts over time. Thus one can assume that the road on which the poem's speaker travels has often, perhaps routinely, been traversed by him.

Williams first presents us with the unprepossessing vegetation lining the road, with the scarcely differentiated "reddish / purplish, forked, upstanding, twiggy/... bushes and small trees" that, referred to as mere "stuff," are accorded no particular dignity. The color of the bushes, too, is scarcely differentiated, vaguely purplish and reddish, not definitively either purple or red. Likewise, we are at a kind of impossible-to-define interstitial time in which winter, still lingering in the form of "dead brown leaves" and as yet "leafless vines," is just beginning to give way to spring. In the line "lifeless in appearance, sluggish," the word "lifeless," picking up on and reinforcing the word "leafless" in the previous line, refers to an as yet moribund, "sluggish / dazed" unawakened world, but also suggests the impending advent of leaves, of the first signs of spring.

The mere stuff of unprepossessing bushes and small trees are, as spring begins to take hold, as though reborn:

> They enter the new world naked,
> cold, uncertain of all
> save that they enter. All about them
> the cold, familiar wind—

Williams was a fiercely and self-consciously American poet; the reference to the "new world" here is not accidental. At this point, as is often the case with Williams' poetry, the poem as pure percept becomes the poem as slightly-more-than-pure percept. It is, of course, not merely bushes and trees but human beings who, in being born, "enter the new world naked / cold, uncertain." Williams himself as an obstetrician was constantly reminded of the painful but exhilarating entrance of embodied souls, "one by one," into a world that is immediately inhospitable to them, and that, unlike the the warm and buffered world of the womb, is buffeted by a cold wind.

These new entrants into life are "cold," are minimally aware, unconscious "of all / save that they enter." It is this difficult entrance that ushers in the exquisite concluding stanzas of the poem:

> Now the grass, tomorrow
> the stiff curl of the wildcarrot leaf
>
> One by one objects are defined—
> It quickens: clarity, outline of leaf.

As spring takes hold, discrete, autonomous objects present themselves to the awareness of the speaker and assume definition. In this quickening world, the clarity of outline of each leaf, emerging from an heretofore undifferentiated background, is apprehended by consciousness as a pure, radiant percept, instinct with life. The emphasis here on definition, on clarity of outline, reminds me of Blake, for whom clarity of outline in art, as well as attention to "minute particulars," was something like an ethical imperative. The poem concludes:

> But now the stark dignity of
> entrance—Still, the profound change
> has come upon them: rooted, they
> grip down and begin to awaken.

The previously undignified stuff of bushes and small tress now enters into clarity with a kind of "stark dignity." "The profound change / has come upon them." What is the nature of this change? "Rooted they / grip down and begin to awaken." That which was previously sluggish, dazed, dormant in nature herself begins to awaken. But there is also a vital, implicit agent that operates as though invisibly here. The "profound change," the reawakening of life in spring, is connected to the awakening of the consciousness of the poem's speaker. Moments of spiritual insight, involving a sudden, profound change of perspective, are, of course, also, for good reason, colloquially referred to as awakenings.

Crucially, the poem ends with a kind of gripping down, a rootedness, that enables the burgeoning, phallic, "upstanding" movement of the bushes and small trees. One senses that for Williams, a similar, stubborn gripping down, an adherence or faithfulness to the rooted and the real, was essential to the implicit ethic both of his life and of his poetry. Without this gripping down, this rootedness, the mind, and specifically the mind of the poet, can become mired in lifeless abstraction or, as in the case of Pound, can become tragically untethered.

2.

I would like to turn from one of Williams' earliest mature poems to one of his latest, representative of a phase of his work that came to the fore after Williams suffered, in 1948, the first of a devastating series of strokes that would increasingly circumscribe his life both as a poet and as a physician. This late phase of Williams' work as a poet complicates any reading of Williams that takes as its touchstone his early nostrum "no ideas but in things."

Prior to his strokes, Williams had led an extraordinarily active life. He reveled in this intense activity, even when the demands of a life committed to serving two vocations could become, quite simply, too taxing, too much of a drain on his formidable energy. Williams recovered most of his powers after his first stroke, but he anticipated, correctly, that others would likely ensue. He could no longer practice medicine, and the aphasia that worsened after every stroke compromised his facility with language, which grew increasingly refractory. One cannot adequately imagine what an existential threat his strokes must have been to Williams, nor how directly they struck at the heart of all that was most essential to his life.

Williams' strokes subjected him to periods of despair and depression. The worst of these was triggered by a cruel political farce. After having been nominated to serve in the mostly ceremonial but highly prestigious role as consultant to the Library of Congress, an honor that was reflective of the increasing recognition of and respect for his poetry that Williams had long craved, his political views came under scrutiny. Williams' politics, alone among the major modernist poets, were left-wing, though never radically so. He had never felt inclined to embrace communism, let alone Stalinist communism and the repressive regimentation to which it subjected the individual. Regardless, Williams was forced by the head of the Library of Congress, as a precondition to serving as consultant, to suffer a protracted, aggressive series of interrogations about his political views. Williams was disheartened, appalled, and debilitated by this questioning of his patriotism. He spiraled into a depression for which he was hospitalized for several months; as a result, he never, in fact, reaped the reward of assuming a position he so richly deserved.

And yet, despite these and other setbacks, Williams continued to write. The question he continually faced, in Frost's words, was "what to make of a diminished thing." What he made of it included, in my view, which is a common one, some of his most moving and compelling poems, the most powerful of which is perhaps "Of Asphodel, That Greeny Flower," a long love poem to his wife, Flossie. To discuss 'Asphodel' adequately would require its own essay. The poem I will turn to here as my primary exemplar of Williams' last phase is "The Descent," which of all of Williams' poems is the one that has most consistently moved me at every phase of my life. It is a poem of old age, written after Williams had experienced the first of his strokes—yet when I first read it at the age of twenty, without knowing any details of

Williams' life, it profoundly affected me, though I would have had difficulty accounting for why I found it so moving.

I will simply reproduce, here, the entire text of the poem, which I will then briefly discuss:

> The descent beckons
> 　　　　as the ascent beckoned.
> 　　　　　　　　Memory is a kind
> of accomplishment,
> 　　　　a sort of renewal
> 　　　　　　　　even
> an initiation, since the spaces it opens are new places
> 　　　　inhabited by hordes
> 　　　　　　　　heretofore unrealized,
> of new kinds—
> 　　　　since their movements
> 　　　　　　　　are towards new objectives
> (even though formerly they were abandoned).
>
> No defeat is made up entirely of defeat—since
> the world it opens is always a place
> 　　　　formerly
> 　　　　　　　　unsuspected. A
> a world lost,
> 　　　　a world unsuspected,
> 　　　　　　　　beckons to new places
> and no whiteness (lost) is so white as the memory
> of whiteness .
>
> With evening, love wakens
> 　　　　though its shadows
> 　　　　　　　　which are alive by reason
> of the sun shining—
> 　　　　grow sleepy now and drop away
> 　　　　　　　　from desire .
>
> Love without shadows stirs now
> 　　　　beginning to awaken
> 　　　　　　　　as night
> advances.

The descent
        made up of despairs
                and without accomplishment
realizes a new awakening:
                which is a reversal
of despair.
                For what we cannot accomplish, what
is denied to love,
        what we have lost in the anticipation—
                a descent follows,
endless and indestructible .

What one first notices about the "The Descent" is how extraordinarily abstract its language is. What has happened to Williams' erstwhile poetic credo "no ideas but in things"? The single external referent in the poem is the sun. The movement of descent in the poem is at the same time a movement inward. One can well imagine that Williams' strokes, compromising his heretofore habitual modes of apprehending the world, including, quite likely, the acuity of his senses, dictated such a movement inward. The poem is in large part a valiant attempt to discover in loss, defeat, and despair a compensatory gain.

Williams, like Blake again, had never been a poet of memory. Quite to the contrary, he had been very much a poet of immersion in the present. His poems had always been minimally discursive, even minimally reflective. For Coleridge as for Blake and for the early Williams, memories are degraded copies of experience, fixed and lifeless counters, often linked together in poems by mere association and contingency. According to Coleridge, poems that rely on memory are the work of mere fancy not of the imagination, which, rooted in the present and oriented toward the future, is generative of new, heretofore unseen, unrealized possibilities.

"The Descent," however, in the first of its several movements, immediately confronts us with memory. Rather than recalling specific instances of memory, the poem considers, reflects upon, memory itself. As one ages, at some point, well past the apogee of life, one embarks upon a kind of descent, a descent that ultimately, of course, leads to death. In the meantime, one's mental balance of power shifts from the prospective to the retrospective. This shift need not be seen solely as a loss of vitality but can also be experienced as a graceful acquiescence to a necessarily changed perspective on the world. In the case of Williams, this shift was at first traumatically abrupt, then painfully protracted as his condition continued to worsen.

In considering memory, Williams' radically re-conceives it. By an act of the imagination, memory itself is seen, or realized, as imaginative. As "a sort of renewal / even / an initiation," it serves the quintessentially imaginative function of opening up, of disclosing, both new "spaces" and "new places" inhabited metaphorically by "hordes" (with "hordes" punningly evoking treasure "hoards"), "heretofore unrealized / of new kinds." The movement of the poet's mind, though retrospective, is nonetheless also prospective, entertaining the possibility of imaginatively realizing "new objectives," particularly objectives that may have been abandoned and unrealized in the past.

In what can be thought of as the poem's second movement, beginning with the declaration that "No defeat is made up entirely of defeat," it is revealed that it is defeat itself, linked to Williams' strokes, that has enabled this newly imagined conception of memory. It is defeat that, not "made up entirely of defeat," reveals "a place / formerly / unsuspected," that "beckons," in its turn, to still further unsuspected places. This second movement concludes with the somewhat cryptic and difficult lines: "And no whiteness (lost) is so white as the memory / of whiteness."

These lines conjure up for me the treatment of the color white in the extraordinary second canto of Stevens' "The Auroras of Autumn." The whole canto enacts a "farewell to an idea," a relinquishment, a divestiture, of anything that has once interposed itself between the self and its experience of reality. The whiteness of a deserted cabin on a beach "reminding, trying to remind, of a white / That was different, something else, last year / Or before." These differences, apprehended by the senses, mark time; they begin almost to vanish, to lose their vividness, as death approaches. "The season changes. A cold wind chills the beach.../ A darkness gathers though it does not fall / And the whiteness grows less vivid on the wall." The deserted cabin is a trope for the aging self and is a prelude to the poem's depiction of the solitary individual confronting his own mortality. Whiteness, Melville's "all color of nothingness," connotes not only purity and innocence but that which is so pure, so extreme in its wintry purity, that it is also deathly.

In "The Descent," "no whiteness (lost)," no past sensory apprehension of whiteness that involves, like the observations of Steven's cabin over the years, the perception of gradations, differences, changes, can equal the purity of whiteness as it is abstractly apprehended in memory. Thus memory involves, like the imagination, an intensification of experience. At the same time, Williams' evocations of a world lost, and of memories of whiteness lost, make it clear that this imaginative intensification is intimately connected with the multiple losses experienced by the aging self.

In the poem's third and final movement, as Williams proceeds from a renewed conception of memory to a renewed conception of love, the darkness of death gathers. With evening, love's "shadows," becoming more prominent as the sun declines, "grow sleepy now" and begin to "drop away," to detach themselves, "from desire." It is worth noting in this context that prior to his strokes, Williams had engaged in a number of fleeting affairs; his multiple infidelities, which as a younger man he justified to himself as the natural and libidinous prerogative of the vigorous male of the species, later subjected him to considerable guilt and remorse. "Asphodel," which is a kind of hymn to his abiding love for his wife, and which is directly addressed to her, is thus also a kind of heartfelt apologia. "On The Road to the Contagious Hospital" and poems from the same period, like "The Young Sycamore," celebrate a kind of upthrusting eros with phallic connotations, whereas "The Descent" and "Asphodel" explore a more mature experience of love that has its own kind of vitality. "Love without shadows stirs now / beginning to awaken / as night," a night that will absorb and dispel all shadows, "advances." Once again something stirring "now," some "new" conception of a love unencumbered by desire, is beginning to "awaken." In these lines, instinct with incipience, the now, the present tense of the imagination, is reinstated, reclaimed, paradoxically, by memory. Even in the face of the gathering darkness of death, "new awakenings" are still possible.

Even a descent "made up of despairs and without accomplishment," entailing the traumatic failing of Williams health and the curtailing of his accomplishments as a doctor and potentially as a poet, "realizes a new awakening: / which is a reversal / of despair." The last lines of the "The Descent" are, perhaps fittingly, the most difficult:

> For what we cannot accomplish, what
> is denied to love,
>   what we have lost in the anticipation—
>   a descent follows,
> endless and indestructible .

These lines, which I find ineffably moving, are often read as an expression of remorse; and yet it seems odd that a poem that registers throughout a reversal of despair should end on a note of endless and undying regret. Perhaps, or perhaps as I would merely like to imagine, what is being suggested here is something akin to the purport of Pound's beautiful passage in the *Pisan Cantos*, written immediately after he was arrested and imprisoned for treason toward the end of the Second World War, that begins with the lines: "what thou lovest well remains/ the rest is dross." Perhaps it is only our failings that ultimately fall away from us, while what we have accomplished in the spirit of love and of the imagination somehow remains.

I would like to conclude with a few words on form. I have mentioned that "By the Road to the Contagious Hospital" is mimetic of the arising of the pure percept, or of a series of pure percepts, from an undifferentiated context into full awareness, and of the creation of the poem itself, which at some point is finally ready for what Williams movingly calls "the stark dignity of entrance." We as readers participate in this unfolding. "The Descent" does not simply thematize the capacity of the imagination, and specifically of the imagination under the aegis of the memory of an old man, to disclose, even under the most straitened of circumstances, new modes of being, of writing, of loving. It also enacts, in its tentative, exploratory movement forwards, involving repeated reiterations and doublings back, the recursive movement of memory that is at the same time allied with the imaginative project of renewal, of projecting a viable future.

Likewise, I find Williams' use of an almost entirely abstract, non-sensory vocabulary entirely appropriate to the inward movement of consciousness that the poem enacts. Indeed, I find the poem, in essence, to be as profoundly contemplative as those of avowedly religious poets, including those of Eliot. It begins with an initiation, a word with unavoidable spiritual connotations, and ends with an awakening. The poem realizes its own faultless decorum. In "By the Road to the Contagious Hospital," a renewed physical life, though still shadowed by death, grips down and libidinously thrusts upward, tracing an ascending arc. In "The Descent," as desire drops away and the shadow of death becomes more prominent, a renewed experience of love emerges. "By the Road to the Contagious Hospital" refers, with respect to spring, to the stark dignity of entrance. "The Descent" enacts the stark dignity of an impending departure.

4.
WILLIAMS' AMERICA: NO ONE TO DRIVE THE CAR

1.

"No one to drive the car" is the last line in Williams' poem "To Elsie," which is largely known by its memorable first line, "The pure products of America go crazy." Williams, who unlike Pound or Eliot remained passionately committed to writing about his native land, had a love/hate relationship with it and wrote poems of these states that are both celebratory and condemnatory. "To Elsie" is a poem of the latter type. It is a bracing, lacerating indictment of the ugliness, squalor, and endemic immaturity that Williams regards as characteristic of American life at its most debased and pitiless. It is also a depiction of those, including the poet, who are trapped by and implicated in this squalor. The "Elsie" to whom the poem refers was a mentally challenged young woman, a ward of the state, who was sent for some time to work as a domestic servant in Williams' household. Here I will quote only the last lines of the poem, which are most relevant to the somewhat eccentric discussion which follows. Williams depicts, in "To Elsie," a hellish realm so degraded that it is:

> as if the earth the earth under our feet
> were
> an excrement of some sky
>
> and we degraded prisoners
> destined
> to hunger until we eat filth
>
> while the imagination strains
> after deer
> going by in fields of goldenrod in
>
> the stifling heat of September
> somehow
> it seems to destroy us

It is only in isolate flecks that
something
Is given off

No one
to witness
and adjust, no one to drive the car

"To Elsie" has a fierce, propulsive forward momentum, its impassioned language rising, at times, to an almost prophetic indignation. "To Elsie," however, is also animated by a painful compassion for its subject. It constitutes Williams' most extreme indictment of the thin topsoil of American culture, of its squalor and filth, as suffered by and embodied in the figure of Elsie, herself one of many who are a rebuke to the American myth of the sovereign individual. Such radically disenfranchised, at times brutalized figures are imprisoned by a dire material, linguistic, imaginative, and spiritual poverty. They have no chance from the start, are hemmed about by all that they are unable to express, are adrift in the shallowness of American culture that lacks even "peasant traditions" to shore it up and give its expressions some redeeming, communal character. To be devoid of linguistic, imaginative, and spiritual resources is to become the passive victim of one's experiences, is to experience sex, for example, as something to which one submits "without / emotion / save numb terror." Even so-called consensual sex, in such a context, is tantamount to rape.

Crucially and typically, when fate in the form of the state throws Elsie up on Williams' doorstep, he recognizes that he is implicated in her predicament. Not only she, but *we* are "prisoners / destined to hunger / until we eat filth." The poem's speaker, who is inescapably a participant in this "we," specifically identifies himself, like Elsie, as a prisoner. One notes that "To Elsie," for all its propulsive power, is in some ways, like Elsie herself, strangely inarticulate. It consists of a single, run-on sentence slapped together by a promiscuous use of dashes, a sentence whose syntax is fractured, its connective tissue elided. Its very forward motion seems in danger of careening out of control as the poem drives headlong toward its conclusion. Its speaker is himself oddly inarticulate about a predicament to which he struggles to give voice. He merely briefly, indefinitely exclaims that "somehow / it seems to destroy us," a statement in which the referent of *it* remains indeterminate.

In "To Elsie," however, it is from imaginative poverty, in part, that the deadening malaise to which the poem struggles to give voice arises. It is the imagination that strains to envisage some kind of alternative reality, some glimpse of beauty. It is through the imagination in the form of language that we propose to ourselves, that we articulate to ourselves, new possibilities, new modes of being in the world, which have the potential to be realized by us. It is the imagination that, enshrined in language, orients us toward a meaningful future, and therefore liberates us from time as the experience of a mere undifferentiated blank duration. Without it we have no possibility of further development, are given over to the experience of time as a series of random moments that do not pertain to us in any meaningful way.

Imaginative literature, of course, like the imagination itself, proposes and disposes, articulates new ways of being in the world, propositions that suggest a project or projects that we can choose to realize, thereby transfiguring our worlds, transforming them into arenas in which we do not merely passively suffer but *act*, in which we make our reality our own—but only, and this is a crucial caveat, if we are *not*, like Elsie, given no chance from the start, whether due to lack of intrinsic or a bare minimum of extrinsic resources.

As it is with individuals, so it is with those societies and cultures that either repress or devalue the imagination, which includes the moral imagination. They tend to be becalmed, or embalmed, in a kind of moribund, lifeless, terminal immaturity—before, at worst, succumbing to an atavistic barbarism. In Williams' time, as in our own, Blake's specter, the unrecognized shadow of an American culture that prides itself on being vibrant, open to the new, instead threatens to seal off all avenues of genuine expression.

Sadly, in the impoverished world of "To Elsie," the imagination, straining for some vision or experience of beauty, glimpses it only in "isolate flecks" that never cohere or attain anything like a critical mass. We, too, are isolate flecks, lonely parodies of the American myth of the sovereign individual, our contracted identities, what Blake would call our Selfhood, left to career headlong into a future that is no future, with "no one / to witness / and adjust, no one to drive the car."

The squalor so brilliantly anathematized by Williams has, of course, periodically irrupted, in the course of American history, into the political sphere, often in the form of paranoid conspiracy theories conjoint with an aggressive nativist strain of know-nothingness. McCarthyism was one such irruption—of which Williams himself became, to his great consternation, due to some innocent political associations as a young man, an unlikely target.

2.

In once again pondering "To Elsie," and particularly its last two lines, I experienced what Wallace Stevens calls an "ecstasy of associations" in the form of several figures flashing almost simultaneously across or within my mind—including the protagonists of one poem, two novels, a film, and two historical figures, one a mythologized character whose actual life was impoverished and tragically attenuated, the other a great American artist whose sudden fame likewise inflated him, without his consent, into a kind of mythological figure, a role he was ill-equipped to play. These protagonists, whether fictional or real or both, are all in fact *not* protagonists, free agents, but are passive victims of the strain of ugliness and immaturity in American culture to which Williams was so sensitive. Their stories are quite literally associated with the vehicular ("no one to drive the car").

Let me stipulate from the outset that our bodies are vehicles, poems are vehicles, triumphal chariots are vehicles, and that the Biblical prophets beheld sublime vehicles bearing the presence of an unseen God. My own focus, perforce, will be far narrower. My chosen texts will involve more modest vehicles, never taking flight, but instead carrying us over particularly dispiriting stretches of specifically and indigenously American psychic and cultural terrain.

Several of my vehicular texts are associated with the supposedly conformist fifties, in which the consequences of the mass commodification of culture, with its attendant shallowness, were growing ever more apparent—and by which time the interstate highway system, so hospitable to vehicles, had been completed. And yet it is in the fifties, too, the decade of my birth, that rebellious voices begin to speak, making the much-vaunted sixties, in retrospect, seem not a break from the fifties but in many ways an extension of them.

3.

Robert Creeley's justly well-known poem "I Know A Man" was, I am convinced, directly influenced by, and is a riff on, the last lines of "To Elsie."

> I KNOW A MAN
>
> As I sd to my
> friend, because I am
> always talking,—John, I
>
> sd, which was not his
> name, the darkness sur-
> rounds us, what
>
> can we do against
> it, or else, shall we &
> why not, buy a goddamn big car,
>
> drive, he sd, for
> christ's sake, look
> out where yr going.

Creeley was associated with the Black Mountain school of poetry, and particularly with his role as minimus to Charles Olson's "Maximus," before he embarked on his own, unique, experimental excursions or incursions into both poetry and, increasingly, prose. In his early poetry, with its brief lines, many of them ending in prepositions, that are cut, as it were, against the bias, and with his tendency toward compression and concision, he seems more a student of Williams than of Olson. Indeed, Williams himself wrote that of all of the younger poets whom he had read or encountered, it was Creeley whose aesthetic was closest to his own.

What is distinctive in Creeley's early poems, particularly in his remarkable early collection "For Love," an extended suite of love/anti-love poems, is their cognitive and affective dissonance. Creeley's combination of disenchantment and residual enchantment, his sometimes frank evocations of sexuality as well as his attraction to the idealizing tendencies of romance, his sardonic irony, his mordant, sometimes comically rueful humor, tilt the emotional tenor of his poems from any familiar, recognizable axis.

The sheer weightiness, the specific gravity, with which humorless critics have freighted the remarkably nimble and quick-witted little poem cited above is quite astonishing. One reading of the poem, which caused Creeley particular dismay, took as its cue the names *John* and *Christ,* and disregarding the fact that the latter appears flippantly in lower case, and that his name is clearly taken in vain, managed to turn the poem into kind of allegory of the relationship between Christ and John the Baptist.

More often, the poem has been taken to be a solemn, existential pronouncement on the darkness and destructiveness of American consumerist culture, so alienating that its protagonists do not even know each other's names—a darkness whose only antidote is consumption on a still grander and more self-destructive scale.

And yet the poem is nothing if not funny. Its humor lies largely in the speaker's repeated, quirkily endearing qualifications of his assertions: "I sd..., *as I am always talking*"; "John, I sd......*which was not his name*"; "shall we... *and why not.*" To which can be added the speaker calling one whom he identifies as a friend by the wrong name, which is in humorous and ironic apposition to the assertion, "I Know a Man," which is the poem's title. The obsessive chatter of the poem's speaker seems not only a whistling in the dark, but a means of precluding any confrontation with that darkness and with the vastness of the indifferent space in which he is embedded. Is something also being suggested here about the shallow and *ad hoc* nature of friendships, and particularly of male friendships, but by extension of all human connections, in an increasingly mobile society that has only grown more mobile since?

In the poem's last stanza, we finally, unceremoniously and precipitously, find our protagonists plunked down in the car, which has heretofore only been spoken of, but which now, in the space of little more than a line, has been instantly procured, stolen, or miraculously materialized, as though conjured by the very words that pronounce it. The poem ends with a form of vehicular slapstick, with the likely drunken command "Drive, he sd... / look out where yr going."

It seems to me that there are two equally valid readings of the poem. On the one hand, the poem's more solemn critics are onto something. It is typical of Creeley's often complex irony that the poem requires that we read it not merely as comical, that we register its more serious existential undertow as well. To possibly drive drunk, and in this case, to set forth aimlessly, is to drive with "no one to witness and adjust." It is to give oneself over to a benumbed and occluded present that is a dark parody of the mystic's valorization of living in the present. The result, of course, can be disastrous.

On the other hand, when surrounded by and stuck in darkness, doing something, *anything* proactive to escape it, including driving a car, seems a perfectly reasonable solution, a kind of typically American pulling up of stakes and moving on —if only to feel soon enough the need to move on, pointlessly, aimlessly, yet again. The problem, of course, to cadge a phrase from AA, or perhaps from some title of one of the many currently proliferating simplifications of Buddhist tracts, is that "wherever you go, there you are": changes of scene, although briefly salubrious, ultimately do nothing to keep the darkness at bay.

4.

Jack Kerouac's *On The Road* is of interest to me here not as a novel, though I am susceptible to its charm, but for its portrayal of Dean Moriarty, who in real life was Neal Cassady, mythologized by both Ginsberg and Kerouac as a kind of sexual archangel and a quintessentially American free spirit. Cassady, in fact, was an intriguing and complicated character. Both Kerouac and Ginsberg considered him their undoubted superior with respect to raw, native intelligence. His speech consisted of an improvised pastiche of both inspired and incoherent riffs or rants. He aspired, prompted by the example of Ginsberg and Kerouac, to be a writer, but throughout his childhood he had been shunted around from foster home to foster home and had received no formal education to speak of.

Cassady's vision as a writer, had he had one, would have been foredoomed to founder on the shoals of his inarticulateness, or rather of the impossibility of translating his articulateness from the spoken to the written word, a deficit which it was too late to remedy. Cassady would never have the means to develop beyond the bounds of his fictional incarnation. His once-fetishized body aged, his marriage failed, he succumbed to addictions and ultimately receded into the scarcely differentiated shadows of the underside of American life. Remaining a sadly rootless soul, he drifted from odd job to odd job and died alone. His body, the victim of an overdose, was eventually found draped across an abandoned railroad track in Mexico. At least no oncoming train would disfigure his once worshipped form.

He was, in many ways, one of Williams' pure products of America, which is doubtless at least in part why the bookish Kerouac and Ginsberg were drawn to him. He remained, for Ginsberg, although even before his death necessarily *in absentia*, mythically alive in the guise of *puer aeternus,* as "angel-headed hipster" and phallic demigod. Whether or not Cassady himself, a brilliant and sensitive manic-depressive who lacked the wherewithal to make himself or his life cohere, would have wished to be memorialized in such a way, we will never know.

5.

Bonnie and Clyde, in which being on the road, at any rate as portrayed in the typically cheery Hollywood road movie, takes a pathological turn, moved me more than any other film I encountered during my rocky and benighted adolescence. Outlaws on the run have become, in our shining and perishing republic, particularly during periods of economic or cultural duress, figures upon whom romantic fantasies are projected. Set during the Great Depression, *Bonnie and Clyde* reflects the anti-establishment, anti-Vietnam War ethos of the late sixties. But here, our romantic hero is impotent, our heroine terminally bereft. The two are as children—with the exception of one late scene of sexual consummation that seems almost as miraculous as the Virgin birth. Even had they settled down into a life of unglamorous domesticity, they would likely have remained childless, futureless.

The movie's score, provided in part by a jauntily twanging bluegrass banjo, keeps things moving at a brisk pace. *Ah, to escape, to keep escaping, miraculously, just one step ahead of the law!* Whatever stolen car our protagonists and their increasing brood of poor relations commandeer—and cars, not only one car but a parade of them, have if not starring then featured roles in the film, providing flashes of color in an otherwise monochromatic environment—its tires kick up the dust in a landscape at once a sterile wasteland and itself somehow, because empty, undefined, susceptible to romantic projections.

Our protagonists go through the fated, increasingly bloody stations of what has become not a spiritual but a capricious and pointless ordeal. As a premature death tracks them down, Bonnie—something of an artist, it seems—writes a ballad to ensure the survival of their names, or to ensure a lasting infamy whose currency, then as now, seemed interchangeable with that of fame.

The famous, in our culture, become quasi-mythological figures upon whom our fantasies are projected. They are typically inflated, then torn down. The line between fame and infamy is often a tenuous one. For those who choose to embrace fame, whether out of naïveté or out of cynicism, bad publicity is often almost as good as good publicity. Others upon whom the mantle of fame is thrust are often tragically ill-suited to assume it. Many die young, becoming sacrificial figures, which further augments, although posthumously, their mythological status.

At some point toward the end of Bonnie and Clyde, there is a dreamy, gauzily shot, sotto voce scene, a strange and haunting interlude in which Bonnie reconnects with her mother for the last time. Far gone into senility, her mother barely recognizes her. The illusion of home, too, has been foreclosed. Bonnie seems in danger of not living on, even in her mother's memory.

Why did this movie affect me so? I longed, like so many adolescents of my generation, to be a romantic rebel, a role which I felt painfully ill-suited to play. In the guileful guise of deconstructing the myth of the romantic outlaw, *Bonnie and Clyde* is in fact one of its purest expressions. By the end of the film, its protagonists have undergone an apotheosis and become almost saintly. Romance seems almost to encroach upon a different genre, the tragic.

In the movie's final scene, their luck having run out, Bonnie and Clyde are trapped in a fatal, final ambush, their bodies riddled with bullets, as is the car against which they are pinned and with which they become, at last, cruelly incorporate. Their two bodies jerk spasmodically in slow motion like puppets on invisible strings, enacting a convulsive, carefully rehearsed choreography.

What does it matter that Bonnie and Clyde are in fact pathetic animals cornered at the predestined point at which all further options, in a society in which few options are available, are terminally foreclosed?

At least they have died, like the beautiful, slain demigods of Greek myth, before having to endure the insult of maturity. At least their pitiful legend, with the help of Bonnie's ballad, and abetted by the film itself, has endured, if only for a time.

6.

In Nabokov's *Lolita*, the title character, an entrancing nymphet, no longer a child, not yet a woman, is in part the fictional embodiment of the dangerous seductiveness of a still immature, and perhaps terminally immature, American culture. Humbert Humbert, like Nabokov, is a cultured European, or rather is a parody of such a European, and is slated, as the novel opens, to be a visiting professor at a small New England college. His encounter with Lolita, while briefly staying at an inn run by her mother, occasions, to say the least, a change in plans. He and Lolita, like Kerouac and Cassady, like Bonnie and Clyde, and like the nameless protagonists of "I Know a Man," wind up indulging in the quintessentially American act of hitting the road—at Humbert's uncontrollable criminal behest. As I have argued elsewhere, literary evocations of America, with its wide-open spaces, with its relatively brief history, and with its attenuated historical horizon, tend to stress the spatial over the temporal.

The "road picture" was by this point a kind of sunny staple of Hollywood movies. With Nabokov at the wheel, however, the genre, which is in fact as venerable as the Odyssey itself, takes a "bend sinister." Humbert and Lolita wander aimlessly from motel to motel as they traverse the mostly desolate and undifferentiated hinterlands of the newly created American interstate highway system.

Their squalid escapade is in no way exhilarating for its protagonists, nor is it titillating for the reader. Although *Lolita* retains elements of the picaresque, they are darkly inflected. We are amused, at though despite ourselves, by the transgressive. We laugh at what we imagine should not engender laughter and fail to surmise that we should perhaps be laughing, along with Nabokov, at ourselves.

At some point during his peregrinations with Lolita, Humbert succumbs to the apparently paranoid fantasy that they are being followed by a man in a red car. Eventually, as usual making a point of being touchingly solicitous, deeply concerned with the well-being of his charge, who is in fact a far hardier specimen than he, Humbert checks Lolita into a mental hospital (one of the many madhouses that crop up in, or are referred to, in the course of the novel), whereupon his paranoid fantasy proves to be no fantasy at all. Lolita is kidnapped by Clare Quigly, a playwright, pedophile, and child pornographer who is Humbert's doppelgänger, and who has indeed been following Humbert and Lolita in a red car, waiting patiently for his moment to pounce and to kidnap Humbert's precious charge.

We are informed that it takes Humbert two hapless, wasted years to finally track down his beloved no-longer-nymphet. After having appeared in a few of Quigly's underground, pornographic films, Lolita, now at the overripe age of seventeen, already and prematurely no longer desirable, has settled down, appropriately, in Hollywood, city of aborted phantasies, celluloid or otherwise, to a dull and impoverished life with a husband as nondescript as herself. Like a child star who has outgrown her stardom, she is without interest, value (which in America often means monetary value) or utility. Quigly has long since discarded her. Her own possibilities of further development, her prospects, are less than meager. She seems destined to live a life of simple, domesticated squalor.

Upon her reunion with Humbert, Lolita, resorting to emotional blackmail, becomes an extortionist, a novice capitalist, draining Humbert of his meager remaining funds. Never the most sensitive of creatures, Lolita blithely informs Humbert that she had always, in fact, been in love with Quigly, with whom she had had a prior relationship, and had never had any feelings for Humbert himself—thus dealing a fateful and fatal blow to his fragile narcissism.

Though no longer sexually attracted to Lolita, Humbert nonetheless has never relinquished his emotional claim on her, nor has he been released from her claim on him. Enraged not only by Quigly's perfidy but by his preeminence in Lolita's impoverished imagination, Humbert tracks Quigly down, the pursued becoming the pursuer, and murders him in the oddly surreal confines of his home. By killing his doppelgänger, Humbert is in effect killing himself, terminally foreclosing his own future. Lolita, impassive as ever, has at least survived their misadventure, but Humbert is destroyed by it. At the novel's end, he is interred for life in a prison for the criminally insane.

The futures of all of the characters in *Lolita* are terminally foreclosed, admit no possibility of further development. Nabokov's vision of America seems that of a soulless madhouse without walls, in which a great deal of movement, almost all of it aimless, without purpose, takes place; in which mobility seldom involves upward mobility; in which all abide in a kind of pseudo-present, heedless of the past, careless of the future. And yet, like a good Hollywood movie, America still has the power to manipulate and seduce, to entrance the spellbound spectator with the fantasy of never having to mature, let alone to grow old. Quigly, Humbert, Lolita, even Lolita's mother—all have been exercising, however perversely, that strangest and most problematic American right, the usually futile pursuit of an elusive happiness that will find us only in its own good time, if it finds us at all.

As for their creator, Nabokov—the author as transgressive tantric master, verbal magician and prestidigitator, inducer of shamanic trances; as inscrutable Slavic Sphinx; as fearless flouter of a prudish and therefore prurient American Protestantism; as sworn enemy of the dull, of the "oh so dull," of the unspeakably and unpardonably dull; as exiled chess hustler without portfolio, always not one but many steps ahead of his stupefied and bedazzled reader; as master translator, linguistic double agent, speaking in tongues and miraculously, the master and servant of a foreign tongue, running rhetorical circles around the naïve offerings of its native speakers, trouncing them at their own game; and finally, most importantly, as indefatigable lepidopterist, dusted by butterflies' wings, discoverer, anointer, and perhaps conjurer of one of the rarest and most elusive of the species—was and remains a figure who is impossible to pin down.

Lolita, upon its publication in the benighted fifties, was denounced, as Nabokov surely would have anticipated, as obscene. It was an act of bravery, or at least of gleeful effrontery, to have written and published such a book. The scandal that it created was greater even than that occasioned by Ginsberg's "Howl." Nabokov was well-regarded as man of letters. Surely he should have felt grateful to the nation that had so generously adopted him. Instead, he had mocked and betrayed it. Perhaps it required an outsider, more aristocratic, ironic, and resourceful than de Tocqueville, to so savagely and (perhaps) lovingly anatomize the culture of a land that he would never more than temporarily adopt as his own.

7.

Born in Wyoming, Jackson Pollock was brought up in Southern California, where he was repeatedly expelled from various high schools. He would never graduate. Eventually, under the auspices of the WPA, he moved to New York and studied art under Thomas Hart Benton, a mannerist mythographer of the American West.

It can certainly not be said of Pollock's work that it failed to display imaginative development. He soon broke free of his mentor and experimented with looser, freer forms of representation. He gravitated toward artists who were likewise experimenting in search of a radically new painterly idiom.

However, as a laconic man with little education, operating in a milieu in which, inspired by polemical critics like Harold Rosenberg and Clement Greenberg, artists engaged in fierce, articulate, and sometimes argumentative intellectual discussions about their work, Pollock was at a considerable disadvantage. Having succumbed to alcoholism, he was more given to aggressive, incoherent rants than to rarefied discourse and was considered something of a wild card and an outsider by his peers. He was regarded as a kind of undeveloped prodigy hailing from the naïve, still wide-open West, perhaps from Wyoming or Montana, not more accurately as what he in fact was, a native son of Southern California.

With his marriage to Lee Krasner in 1945, much changed. Krasner, who was herself not only a formidable artist but also a brilliant and articulate woman, devoted herself to her husband, in whom she saw a genius beginning to emerge. She hastened that emergence by providing for Pollock a way of conceiving of and framing for others what in some way became their joint imaginative project. She became a fierce and relentless polemicist for Pollock's work, thus freeing him from a role he had never been suited to assume. The couple moved to Long Island where Pollock, having sworn off alcohol, safely distant, as though almost a world away, from the temptations and distractions of New York City, produced much of his greatest work.

Pollock, however, eventually found it difficult to deal with his increasing fame. After a legendary photo shoot, destined for the pages of *Life Magazine*, in which he was captured producing one of his famous drip paintings—an experience he found intolerably degrading, as though he had consented to assume the role of a performing monkey—Pollock began to drink again and soon thereafter commenced an affair with a younger woman. Krasner, despairing, unable and unwilling to witness or to abet her husband's self-destructiveness, sued for divorce. Without her, Pollock felt aimless and at sea as he struggled to move on from his drip paintings to some new phase of his work. In the last year of his life, he gave up painting altogether and devoted himself, with little confidence or satisfaction, to sculpture.

The end of this story is well known. Too drunk to drive, Pollock nonetheless, with a new girlfriend many years his junior and a star-struck young friend of hers, got into one of the "Goddamned big cars" of that era, pressed too insistently in the gas, and, taking a corner with reckless speed, drove himself and his passengers straight into a tree. Both Pollock and the hapless friend of his girlfriend died.

Pollock had in some sense always, both to his advantage and to his detriment, been seen as one of Williams' pure products of America. With the departure of Krasner, tragically, there was "no one left to witness and adjust, no one to drive the car."

8.

I should emphasize that the task of consciously developing one's imagination is a high-class or upper middle-class problem, located near the apex of a triangle with which the now-neglected avatar of humanist psychology, Abraham Maslow, once illustrated what he called the hierarchy of needs. Such a problem does not even arise for those located closer to the base of the triangle, where the struggle for survival, or for securing some minimal degree of material security and comfort, in some cases not only for oneself but for one's family, remains paramount, consuming all of one's energies.

Williams had seen enough to recognize that the American myth of upward mobility was in large part just that—a myth, or worse, a kind of cruel sham. It remains so today, with the usual overhyped, anecdotal exceptions of those who have soared from humble (why *humble*?) beginnings to unexpected heights, each of whom becomes visible against the backdrop of the untold numbers who remain invisibly left behind on none-too-solid earth.

I am tempted, in closing, to wax polemical, to say something about how, paradoxically, as our technology increasingly goes into overdrive, many are becoming dazed and half-conscious worshippers of screens that do not reflect us, denizens of a kind of pseudo-present in which we are less and less custodians of the past and guarantors of our future. The already eroded topsoil of American culture is perhaps becoming ever thinner. We are becoming, or have become, quite literally, terminally immature. We have grown no wiser as our technology has ushered in an age of meta-evolution that is driving us, perhaps uncontrollably, who knows where, to the brink of who knows what cliff? Even now, in a kind of metaphor that is no longer merely a metaphor, cars that drive themselves are appearing and will soon become the norm. They will require, of course, no driver, and will render our capacity to witness or adjust obsolete.

5.
FROST'S DOUBLE-EDGED DIRECTIVE

1.

In the late, little-lamented era of the New Criticism, *ambiguity* was a much prized term, referring not only to locally ambiguous tropes but to the structure of certain poems as a whole. It seems to me that there are a subset of poems that are not merely ambiguous but, more radically, are susceptible too, or indeed invite, diametrically opposite or contradictory readings, each of which is equally valid. Robert Frost's "Directive" is a singular instance of such a poem.

"Directive" calls to mind Joseph Jastrow's famous pictorial puzzle that can be read, or more properly seen, either as a duck or a rabbit but cannot be seen simultaneously as both. Likewise, to put the matter at first reductively, "Directive" can be read as either providing consolation or as counseling despair, but fundamentally demands to be read in both ways—insists, in effect, that we pull off the remarkable feat of seeing the duck and the rabbit at the same time.

Even as "Directive" demands a kind of miraculous feat by the reader, the poem itself seems a kind of miracle. It appears in Frost's otherwise undistinguished late book *Steeple Bush*, published in 1945 when Frost was seventy-three. By this time, the force, piquancy, and poignance of his earlier poems was far behind him. He had long since given way to a windy, homespun didacticism that was the pervasive, and dispiriting, default mode of most of what he wrote past the age of fifty. But suddenly, unaccountably, from out of this undistinguished background, as from a sky leached of all color, "Directive," perhaps the greatest of Frost's poems, emerged with the density and force of a meteor.

The poem begins with the powerful, hammering refrain, "Back...Back."

> Back out of all this now too much for us
> Back in a time made simple by the loss
> Of detail, burned, dissolved, and broken off
> Like graveyard marble sculpture in the weather,

Whatever it is that is "now too much for us" leads us to long for a kind of retreat to a simpler time. Such a regressive retreat, however, as Frost reminds us, can only be enabled by loss, a loss that in this case occurs through a kind of violence—as a result of detail being "burned, dissolved, and broken off," three verbs that have something akin to the power of "break, blow, burn" in Donne's "Holy Sonnet" on divine ravishment. The "detail" being broken off is like that of "graveyard marble sculpture in the weather," with the connotations of a graveyard, of course, suggesting man's mortality, a kind of final loss compounded here by the likely dissolution, as well, of the engraved names on gravestones that pitifully memorialize lives that are destined to be entirely forgotten.

It is nature that accomplishes the burning, dissolving, and breaking off, the loss of which the poem speaks, and it is nature, too, that mandates man's mortality. The poem's initial lines seem to promise a movement backward in time that is literally impossible but that suggests a very real longing for a kind of refuge, one which, however, is bound to remain unsatisfied. Any imagined movement backward in time that does not involve mere memory is typically a move toward an idealized space or place, the ultimate prototype of which in the West is the return to Eden, a realm in which mortality no longer holds sway, in which nature itself is transformed in accordance with man's needs and desires. Frost, however, was entirely unsentimental about nature and was as skeptical of notions of a divine, ultimate artificer as he was of any mythological notion of some prior, prelapsarian state, whether of nature or of man.

At a dinner honoring Frost at the Waldorf Astoria in New York on the occasion of his eighty-fifth birthday, the professor and literary critic Lionel Trilling echoed the insights of the poet-critic Randall Jarrell, who in a brilliant essay in *The Kenyon Review* on Frost both identified and emphasized a dark strain in his poetry, a strain evoking a world, including that of nature, that is terrifyingly indifferent to man, that offers him no grand, redemptive possibilities, and few, if any, lasting consolations. Jarrell, in explicating his thesis, referenced "Home Burial," "Desert Places," "Neither Out Far Nor In Deep," "Provide, Provide," and several other poems. The epitome of such poems is perhaps the most sinister of Frost's lyrics, the sonnet "Design," an intricate little *danse macabre,* an instance of nature's casual destruction, somehow all the more terrifying when seen operating at such a small scale. The poem suggests that if there is indeed a design operative in the world, it is more likely the work of a malign demiurge than of a benevolent artificer. Frost, by that point comfortable in his role as the good gray, or white-thatched, national bard, was displeased by Trilling's remarks, but they gave impetus a crucial reevaluation of his poetry.

In "Directive," the nature of all "that is now too much for us," from which we are retreating, remains vague, without detail, is not spelled out. The poem was written during the Second World War, when what Stevens called "the pressure of reality" seemed almost too much to bear. One might also speculate about Frost's biography, about the many tragic losses he had suffered by the time he wrote "Directive." But the poem quite deliberately eschews emphasizing the first person, at least at its outset, and its narrator identifies with the poem's readers by deploying the collective "we." We as readers are made complicit with the poem's narrator/guide, though as later becomes clear, far from being merely one of us, he in fact lords it over us and issues his directives from a kind of impregnable solitude.

Frost either cites or suggests a startling number of biblical references in "Directive." The poem is also Frost's appropriation of the Grail legend, wresting it back from the Eliot of "The Waste Land," from the cosmopolitan to the rural, from foreign soil to native ground. And yet a word of caution at the outset is perhaps in order. The theological citations and echoes in "Directive" serve as fodder for issues of interpretation that are raised by poetry itself. Whether poetry is "spilt religion"—as T. E. Hume, an early proponent of Imagism, wrote famously and disparagingly of the Romantics—or religion is spilt poetry, or both, is with respect to Frost beside the point. Frost, who was wary of professing atheism, subscribed to a kind of deism, and nodded desultorily toward a distant God who countenances natural selection, a subject which *did* interest Frost. Certainly there is very little in Frost's poetry that suggests deep religious feeling of either a conventional or of an unconventional kind. He has nothing of Eliot's orthodox piety; nor of Stevens' desire to replace a vanished God with a compensatory supreme fiction; nor of the occult, hermetic proclivities of Yeats that culminated in "A Vision"; nor even of Pound's hero worship of the poets who comprise his select pantheon of forebears, the poetic equivalent of the elect. Poetry was both Frost's religion and his passion. His chief concern, even when citing matters theological, is poetry itself.

The next three lines of the "Directive" enact, after its initial "Back.../Back..." and its subsequent powerful images of dissolution, yet another harrowing and hammering refrain, this time an equally powerful triple negation:

> There is is a house that is no more a house
> Upon a farm that is no more a farm
> And in a town that is no more a town.

The regressive moment of the poem, as suggested above, is purchased by the "loss" mentioned in the poem's second line. The retreat that it seeks is paradoxically compromised at the outset. It entails an exacerbation of the very sense of loss and alienation that it seems undertaken to avoid. We have not wound up at some comfortingly familiar place, but at a negation of place; we are transported to a ground once, but no longer, inhabited by a house, a farm, a town. Instead of arriving at a consoling somewhere, we arrive at a disturbing nowhere that is characterized only by its having once been a somewhere, a somewhere of which a vestigial road is one of only a few reminders:

> The road there, if you'll let a guide direct you
> Who only has at heart your getting lost,
> May seem as if it should have been a quarry -
> Great monolithic knees the firmer town
> Long since gave up pretense of being covered.
> And there's a story in a book about it:
> Besides the wear of iron wagon wheels
> The ledges show lines ruled southeast-northwest,
> The chisel work of an enormous Glacier
> That braced his feet against the Arctic Pole.
> You must not mind a certain coolness from him
> That seems to haunt this side of Panther Mountain.

The conspicuous appearance of a guide and a road at the beginning of the poem, particularly at the point at which we as readers are beginning to feel lost, calls Dante to mind. One critic, doubtless picking up on this association and noting the theological references in the poem, has pronounced that the road is a kind of *via negativa*, technically called apophatic mysticism, the key feature of which is to prohibit any positive attributes from being predicated of God. The spiritual path of the apophatic mystic is to ruthlessly strip away and negate all of the layers of his experience, both external and internal, until he loses himself in a God with whom he has become one. "Directive" indeed involves a kind of stripping away of multiple levels of what we conjointly tend to acknowledge as a stable reality. But Frost was no mystic, and the narrator/ guide in the poem, as we shall soon discover, is no Virgil. The stripping away of illusions in "Directive" leads to no restitution of Eden, to no beatific vision. Precisely to what it leads, as we shall also see, is a kind of open question.

The biblical echo of Matthew 16:25 in the above-quoted lines, the reference to being found or saved only by being lost, at first seems like the kind of homely, putatively wise homily that Frost increasingly had a fondness for, but this initial impression quickly gives way to a suggestion of something more sly, more ominous. What are we to make of the guide "who only has at heart" our "getting lost?" Once again, though in a different context, we are confronted by loss, in this case by the prospect of getting lost—although surely we are *already* lost. In a poem that skeptically interrogates the Grail legend, and that by its end will again be quoting scripture to subversive effect, the word *lost* here has additional biblical connotations of being fallen, estranged from nature and from ourselves. When read retrospectively, the allusion to Matthew is revealed as an ironic ruse that calls into question rather than confirms the good faith of the narrator.

The "you" whom the narrator now addresses I take to be both the internal auditors and fellow travelers, fictive, phantom presences, whom the narrator is nominally guiding, and we who are readers of the poem. We are akin to, even one with the virtual auditors within the world of the poem, who are entirely dependent on the narrator for any kind of direction, whether literal or spiritual. Increasingly, as the poem progresses, the narrator, the issuer of directives that are commandments in a minor key, comes to seem not so much a guide as a kind of demiurge, a less-than-benign artificer who is subjecting us to a trial by experience that separates the elect reader who correctly interprets the poem from his less hermeneutically sophisticated confreres.

It quickly becomes clear that the guide knowns a terrain that is unfamiliar to us. He, as a kind of semi-omniscient narrator, has been here before, has preceded us, an anteriority upon which much of his authority depends. He is familiar with the abandoned quarry, whose "great monolithic knees," left uncovered, are like those of some enormous, primitive pagan statues—as though the monoliths of Easter Island had been miraculously transported to New England—that bespeak a distant, barely civilized past. He is familiar with the vestiges of tracks once produced by the wear of wagon wheels, and of the rocky ledges deposited by glaciers. The subliminal pun of *ledges* with *ledgers*, in concert with the lines scored in the rock, give the impression of something written and inscribed, like "Directive" itself.

The narrator cryptically pronounces that "there's a story in a book about it." What book? About what, exactly? It appears that the book is one that the narrator clearly knows well, as we, typically, do not. But another possibility cannot be discounted: is the untitled book with its unelaborated story a mere fiction of a book, an empty rhetorical conceit, a book that is not properly a book at all? Given all the theological references in the poem, one can be tempted to identify the book with the Bible, but there is no particular warrant in the poem for such an identification, nor for any other, and so we remain in the dark.

We as readers, after landing in a somewhere that is nowhere, are not granted the kind of pastoral retreat we might have hoped for. Instead, we are constrained to listen to the voice of the guide and to be carried wherever that voice leads us; we are confronted first by the aforementioned great monolithic knees of the quarry, hardly a comforting image, but still within the horizon of human history, as are the traces of iron wagon wheels, which belong to the more recent history of a newly vanished town. These mere traces are in the process of vanishing, and are akin to the wearing away of detail on graveyard marble sculpture.

We next move beyond human time, to an image of vast size and scope, that of a personified glacier who is said to have "braced his feet against the Arctic Pole," whose chisel work indicates that he, too, like whoever carves graveyard monuments, is a kind of sculptor. Frost's personification of the glacier, which seems to be an instance of his whimsical, folksy mode, is, of course, highly ironic. Elsewhere in Frost's poetry, ice is associated with apocalyptic devastation ("Some say the world will end in fire / some say in ice"); Dante's *Inferno,* of course, concludes with Satan frozen head first in a lake of ice. The glacier, the product of an Ice Age both literally and mythically cataclysmic, is precisely that force in the poem that has most distantly preceded the human, that has no place or space for us, and is in no way amenable to us.

Throughout "Directive," Frost plays deliberately with the scale of things in space, which is also related to distance or closeness in time. The more distant in time the grander the scale, the more recent the smaller. Here we are confronted with nature on the largest possible scale, with its tremendous destructive yet shaping force. The great movement of the personified glacier, though unimaginably distant in space and time, has also left significant traces behind, not only in "a certain coolness from him / That seems to haunt this side of Panther Mountain," but also in rocky ledges that are far more stubborn and intractable than the lines that the wagon wheels have carved into their surface. The work of the glacier, its rocky deposits, is responsible for many of the characteristics of the New England landscape and of its land, which, as Frost well knew, is notoriously difficult to farm. Thus the glacier is perhaps in part responsible for houses no longer being houses, farms no longer being farms, towns no longer being towns. Images of petrification, beginning with the eroded graveyard marble sculpture at the outset of "Directive," abound in the poem, always associated with some human activity, often with the attempt to sculpt something lasting out of obdurate material—attempts, like the work of the artist of any kind, including the poet/artificer of "Directive," that are evidence of a drive to leave some lasting record behind, an enterprise that is ultimately bound to fail. Thus images of the stony, the obdurate, which we normally think of as recalcitrant to change, are instead associated with the evanescence of all things, particularly of all things human. The lost, ruined town in "Directive" is a mute testament to the failed human impulse to carve something lasting—in this case, crucially, a human community—out of what are always inadequate, degradable materials.

How do things stand with us here as readers who have wished to move "back out of all this now too much for us," hoping for some consoling place of retreat? We are indeed carried back, but far further back than we might have bargained for, and not to some pastoral retreat but to something like its opposite. Having been told that we must not mind the coolness of Panther Mountain, a legacy of the personified glacier, we are further instructed:

> Nor need you mind the serial ordeal
> Of being watched from forty cellar holes
> As if by eye pairs out of forty firkins.
> As for the woods' excitement over you
> That sends light rustle rushes to their leaves,
> Charge that to upstart inexperience.
> Where were they all not twenty years ago?

> They think too much of having shaded out
> A few old pecker-fretted apple trees.

Once again an almost slightly jaunty tone, an instance of Frost's whimsical and sometimes winsome humor, enters the poem here. The guide has told us that "we must not mind" the coolness left behind by the glacier nor need we mind "being watched." In these lines, the guide/narrator of the poem "Directive" has begun to explicitly issues directives that are here humble versions of the biblical "Thou Shalt Not..." Slipped into the charming, relatively light-hearted depiction of being watched by "eye pairs out of forty firkins" is one of the remarkably suggestive and eloquent turns of phrase that are characteristic of Frost at his best. Even in this most homely of scenes, Frost suggests that we are being subjected to a "serial ordeal." Indeed, the guide in "Directive" is subjecting us, in a narrative carefully staged in space, carefully paced in time, to what, despite its occasional apparently light touches, are in large part—in its reminders of loss, in the blighted and desolate landscape through which it moves—the stations of a highly choreographed ordeal.

As the guide's narrative, and we along with it, draws closer in time to the present, the scale of the scene that he represents, as mentioned above, becomes correspondingly less grand. We begin to move through what was once an orchard, but is now a new stand of trees ("where were they all but twenty years ago?"). The woods are "excited" over us, and immediately transmit that excitement, in the form of "light rustle rushes," to the tops of individual trees. Frost attributes the apparently excited movement of the trees to "upstart inexperience"; they, unlike the displaced trees in the blighted orchard, are unused to the presence of man. Continuing with the conceit of nature as conscious and with the trope of personification, the guide now takes a step further and imputes "thinking" to the trees: "They think too much of having shaded out / a few old pecker-fretted apple trees." In what is another playful phrase, the trees think too much of themselves; they are, as it were, stuck up. Callous upstarts, that have overthrown a previous order. Obeying the not-entirely-benign dictates of natural selection, uncultivated nature deprives what was once a cultivated orchard of light. The ruined, pecker-fretted apples are surely meant to recall the apples of another garden that was likewise eventually ruined.

Frost's penchant for wordplay is fully in apparent in this passage. The leaves' excitement is literally taking place *over* us, who move on the fading road beneath them. The trees are *upstarts*, young rebels, that have only recently *started* to push *upward*. And yet this playfully punning language is being used, again ironically, to describe a desolate scene in which, far from having a kinship with man, nature, again, is relentlessly erasing not only the details, but virtually all traces of the human life that once flourished, or failed to flourish here.

The ascribing of a human consciousness, human intentionality, and implicitly a human voice to so many natural objects in what is a scene of apocalyptic devastation, seems an attempt to repopulate the scene, to restore the human presence or presences that have been lost. The inevitable failure of this attempt intensifies rather than mitigates the sense of all that has been eradicated.

The question "where were they all not twenty years ago?"—which literally refers to the new growth of the upstart trees—also calls to mind the now-vanished human inhabitants of this scene. Where *are* they all? What has become of them? The lines that follow, further narrowing in scope with respect to time and place, recall those inhabitants and their way of life:

> Make yourself up a cheering song of how
> Someone's road home from work this once was,
> Who may be just ahead of you on foot
> Or creaking with a buggy load of grain.

The inhabitants of the town who have who are represented spatially as just "ahead" of us are in fact temporally *behind* us, irretrievably lost to us as we move relatively further from the origin of things. The guide and we know all too well that there is no one just ahead of us traveling on foot or on a wagon creaking with a load of grain. Calling the now-vanished presence of the town's inhabitants to mind serves, again, only to remind us of their absence. The guide's abjuration to himself, and to us, to make up a cheering song that is in fact clearly self-deceptive has, I think, a tone particular to Frost, a tone of ruthless, disabused irony that verges on the bitter, the sardonic. The cheering song, here, is a trope for poetry as a deceptive purveyor of false consolation.

The ensuing lines have a kind of pride of place as the exact midpoint of the poem:

> The height of the adventure is the height
> Of country where two village cultures faded
> Into each other. Both of them are lost.

The "adventure" to which the guide is referring is the regressive quest on which he has been leading us. Its height, or high point, is the site at which we have now arrived, the spot upon which two village cultures have merged, then faded into each other. We have apparently not only been moving backward in time but upward in space. But the high point or height is also a low point or nadir, involving the most central and telling instance of loss and dissolution in the poem. The guide, at this point, withholds from us, gives us no information whatever on how or why these relatively recent cultures have vanished. He might as well be speaking of the rise, followed by a precipitous fall, of two great historical cultures that have left behind no written record sufficient to account for their demise. But again as to why, at their apparent height, these two village cultures have faded, a hint does perhaps occurs later in the poem when Frost speaks of "...the valley streams that when aroused / Will leave their tatters hung on barb and thorn," at which point we think back to Frost's previous mention of "the serial ordeal / Of being watched from forty cellar holes." In a poem in which no detail is a place filler, and which is rife with biblical allusions, it is perhaps not too far fetched to recall the forty days and nights in which Noah and his pairs of animals rode out a flood in Genesis, nor of Moses' forty years of exile in the desert in search of a Promised Land that he never reached, having perished on the verge of entering it. Whether or not the two villages that merged, then faded, were literally destroyed by a flash flood, surely, it seems, its inhabitants have been abruptly and terminally displaced. As for us and the fictive internal auditors in the poem, our wandering in the wasteland "Directive" depicts, like Moses' wandering in the desert, will not result in our reentry into a promised land that is a restitution of a longed-for home.

In the first of the ensuing lines the word "loss" is reiterated from the line that immediately precedes it:

> And if you're lost enough to find yourself
> By now, pull in your ladder road behind you
> And put a sign up CLOSED to all but me,
> Then make yourself at home...

The road on which we have been traveling ends dramatically just past midpoint of the poem, a midpoint that is also a dead end, literally the end of the road. In a bold metaphorical apotheosis, the road becomes a ladder. The image of the ladder, of course, appears frequently in the Bible as a metaphor for that which connects heaven to earth, which would ordinarily, in a more orthodox poem, suggest access to some heavenly realm, but here suggests, on the contrary, a retreat into a kind of solipsistic isolation.

We are now in a position to further reflect on the intentions of the guide who, earlier in the poem, has been represented as only having at heart our "getting lost," with the insinuation, buttressed by scripture, that being lost is a necessary prelude to finding ourselves. Like a rogue parishioner who has elected himself to a church of one, the narrator/guide of "Directive" has advised us to hole ourselves up, like him, in the exclusive fortress of a constricted ego, emphatically CLOSED to all others. Clearly, such an act is unlikely to be in any real way redemptive. As for us, who are advised to replicate this state of imprisoning self-enclosure, is this, again, the result we envisaged when we felt the need, at the outset of the poem, to retreat back and away from from "all that is now too much for us?" If so it is, once again, a retreat purchased at far too great a cost. The typically colloquial phrase "make yourself at home" makes, in this context, a mordant mockery of our longing for home. We are led instead to entrapment in the cell of a self that affords nothing like the consolations of home, and that is surrounded by ruins, specifically by the ruins of what were once themselves homes. The lines immediately following further augment a sense of diminishment, loss, and constriction in space.

> The only field
> Now left's no bigger than a harness gall.
> First there's the children's house of make believe,
> Some shattered dishes underneath a pine.
> The playthings in the playhouse of the children.
> Weep for what little things could make them glad.
> Then for the house that is no more a house
> But only a belilaced cellar hole,
> Now slowly closing like a dent in dough.
> This was no playhouse but a house in earnest.

We behold a children's playhouse, the vestigial remains of a world in miniature, a world in which imagination and the quintessentially human activity of play, of make-believe, have both been given scope. Indeed, we too have been encouraged to practice a kind of make-believe, to sing consoling songs to ourselves, to imagine that a personified nature is in some way responsive to us. We have been encouraged to be as credulous as children. But a world of make-believe cannot last indefinitely. Eventually a harsher reality intrudes. Clearly Frost does not subscribe to any Wordsworthian notion that childhood represents some pure state that is closer to God than that of adult consciousness, nor to the biblical injunction that only by becoming children again will we enter the kingdom of God. Childhood, though close to our own origin, is like the distant, irretrievable past of the natural world in which we are embedded. The children's dishes are "shattered," suggesting some secular equivalent of a fallen and broken world.

As the poem moves from a childhood house of make-believe to our arrival at "a house that is no more a house"—a line that echoes the identical line at the poem's opening—we have come full circle. However, what was there the mere negation of a house here, here is referred to as once having been "a house in earnest," although only traces of it remain. No longer dealing with the childlike world of make-believe and play, and by extension of the imagination, we have returned to the perhaps too earnest adult world of the reality principle, a realm in which we know only too well that all houses are ultimately destined to vanish.

The question of what to make of a diminished thing continues to arise. The scale of the world that we are now observing suggests a nature that has been humanized, that has been carved out by man from unpromising terrain. And yet once again, the world that man has wrested from nature has been destroyed. The fact that its destruction is portrayed here in relatively gentle terms, as the "closing like a dent in dough," a touchingly homely and and domestic simile, does not belie the fact that it is nonetheless destruction, nor that we are looking at a cellar which, even though adorned by lilacs, is still a gaping ruin, presumably one of many such ruins that one comprised a town. The cellar is referred to as a "hole," a hole emblematic, perhaps, of the open, as yet unfilled graves that await us all, that are our destination and our destiny. The poem begins with a reference to a graveyard, a graveyard that is also the end toward which it moves.

After its reference to what was once a house in earnest, the final movement of the poem commences:

> Your destination and your destiny's
> A brook that was the water of the house,
> Cold as a spring as yet so near its source,
> Too lofty and original to rage.
> (We know the valley streams that when aroused
> Will leave their tatters hung on barb and thorn.)

We are led to a brook that once was in service to the human, that once, but no longer, provided water to the house that is no more a house. The brook is smaller that "the valley streams that when aroused / Will leave their tatters hung on barb and thorn." It will not rage or leave things in tatters, but in what sense is this humble brook "lofty?" Merely by virtue of its being on relatively high terrain? Perhaps its very humbleness, paradoxically, makes it lofty, less cheaply histrionic than its raging, potentially apocalyptic sister streams. The brook receives a second honorific title, that of being "original." Perhaps, in drawing close to it, we are finally drawing close to the metaphorical equivalent of the rivers of life in Eden, to our own origins, however humble.

No sooner is such a possibility offered, however, than it is abruptly withdrawn:

> I have kept hidden in the instep arch
> Of an old cedar at the waterside
> A broken drinking goblet like the Grail,
> Under a spell so the wrong ones can't find it,
> So can't get saved, as Saint Mark says they mustn't.
> (I stole the goblet from the children's playhouse)
> Here are your waters and your watering place.
> Drink and be whole again beyond confusion.

Once again, at the poem's close, we have a striking instance of personification, the "instep arch" of the cedar, which is yet another play with both temporal and spatial scale. The personified cedar lives longer than man, who once again seems small, diminished by comparison to the relatively lofty tree. The biblical "cedar," a kind of tree of life close to the waterside, has Edenic connotations, which are here called forth not to be affirmed but to be negated, subverted.

We have, perhaps, just begun to trust our narrator/guide, and yet in the poem's closing lines he is at his most unreliable and disingenuous. Suddenly, he begins to speak in the first person, from the space of the individual ego, the sovereign and isolated "I." We have returned, with the reiterated mention of the children's playhouse, to the childlike scene of make-believe, but here from the perspective of a disenchanted adult, not a child. Assuming the role of a thief, the narrator has stolen a make-believe or metaphorical grail by plundering the presumably innocent precinct of childhood. After hoarding the grail and hiding it from others as though it is his own private property, the narrator puts it under a spell, so "the wrong ones can't find it, / so can't get saved /as Saint Mark says they mustn't." Whether or not the narrator considers himself one of the wrong ones or among the elect, it is clear that neither stealing nor the casting of spells are exercises of which Saint Mark would have approved. What the narrator takes from Mark, the notion that only the few who can correctly comprehend Christ's parables can be saved, reaches its broader, final apotheosis in the the Book of Revelation, where the wrong ones, the vast majority of mankind, are cosigned to hell fire, while only a relatively few elect souls are saved. This brutal final apportionment of souls is perhaps the single most morally disturbing doctrine of Christianity. In this context, the final line of the poem, "Drink and be whole again beyond confusion," is perhaps the most bitterly ironic in the whole poem.

"Directive," with its references to the Christian romance of the Grail legend, can, of course, be seen as recounting of a quest, or rather an anti-quest. By hiding the goblet that is only "like" a grail, not a grail in earnest, and by referring to it as broken, the narrator/guide has ensured that that whatever quest in which we are engaged will fail. What occurs in "Directive" is a kind of ersatz-quest, a quest that is not a quest. True questers tend to move not away but toward something, remaining alert to the trials of the present while at the same time remaining oriented toward the future. "Directive," on the other hand, is an attempted escape, a regressive move backward and away from something to which one wishes to be oblivious. But of course, again, one cannot really move backward in time, not even in memory, which occurs in the present, and inevitably falsifies the past that it purports to represent.

2.

I have mentioned that the reference to the Grail legend puts "Directive" in apposition to Eliot's "The Waste Land." More importantly, "Directive" was written two years after the publication of Eliot's "Four Quartets," which reassuringly suggest that we can return to the innocence, purity, and priority of our origins, only raised to a higher, more conscious power. Toward the end of "Little Gidding," the last of the quartets, Eliot writes:

> We shall not cease from exploration
> And the end of all our exploring
> Will be to arrive where we started
> And know the place for the first time.

Eliot's "Quartets" are nothing if not ultimately consoling. They suggest that through a pious embrace of orthodox Anglicanism not only the individual but England itself can be regenerated. As M. H. Abrams pointed out years ago in his still-seminal book *Natural Supernaturalism*, Eliot, especially the Eliot of "Four Quartets," for all his professed antipathy toward Romanticism was unwittingly, despite himself, a Romantic or Neo-romantic poet. The pattern of circling back, but at a higher, more conscious level, to the innocence of our origins is one of the mythic ur-narratives of Romanticism. One can, in going home again and knowing it for the first time, at the same time glimpse eternity in privileged moments of time. "Four Quartets" conclude with a vision, set in an Edenic rose garden, of the immanence of the divine *within* time, not simply as its revelation at the *end* of it. "All shall be well," Eliot assures us,

> When the tongues of flame are in-folded
> Into the crowned knot of fire
> And the fire and the rose are one.

Eliot's "Quartets," however, can seem *too* programmatic, *too* worked out in advance, in its consolatory project. Each of the quartets has a symmetrical five-part structure, including an interpolated lyric in quatrains, that roughly echoes the others in form and length, whereas "Directive," by contrast, has no stanza breaks and allows for what seem to be digressions, or stream-like meanderings, even as it drives towards its end. As Keats said of Wordsworth, the "Four Quartets" has "designs" on us, which are perhaps too overt, too obvious. The telescoping of symbols in the poem's last lines, the Pentecostal tongues of flame in-folded in a crowned knot of a fire that is no longer merely purgatorial but that merges with the Dantean rose of achieved salvation, seems a peremptory, unconvincing, and willed concatenation of pat, conventional symbols. One is too aware that the poet is playing his final hand in what is a kind of exalted game, an awareness that undermines what is intended to be the metaphysical transparency of the poem's final complex of images. Certainly Frost would have reacted suspiciously to such a poem, and so "Directive" is among other things a dark reworking of the redemptive project of "Four Quartets."

There is something about "Directive" that feels like an old knight's last throwing down of a gauntlet, largely again, in challenge to "Four Quartets," with their dignified equanimity of tone, with their relentless high, or High Church, seriousness, with their too-neat tying of ends to beginnings, of beginnings to ends.

At the same time, Frost is throwing down a gauntlet to those who have failed to recognize his own craftiness and sophistication as a poet. Frost saw himself as a poet who deliberately has designs on us, though he worked hard to keep those designs at least partially hidden. The characteristic vernacular tone of Frost's poetry, which in the case of "Directive" is the tone of the narrator/guide's address to its auditors, often serves to conceal, and thereby to abet, his subversive purposes.

Frost insisted that the basic unit of rhythm and sense in poetry is the sentence, or more precisely the sound of the sentence, and he likewise insisted that the sentence-sounds in poems should should hew as closely as possible to the timbre, pitch, and tenor, to the rising and falling cadences, of common speech. We are subconsciously liable to trust and give credence to a voice that sounds much like our own. Frost's sentences insinuate themselves into our consciousness as though it is we ourselves who are speaking them, or perhaps overhearing them, and thus serve to camouflage, in the case of the naive reader, their often complex purposes. And, of course, Frost's language, with its etymological punning and other forms of word play, is anything but simple. To those few readers whom Frost trusted he emphasized his caginess as a poet, his penchant for serious, sometimes deadly serious, fooling.

With characteristic perversity, Frost insisted to his chosen initiates or disciples that he wanted his poems to be "read wrong," especially by common, uninitiated readers who conferred upon him his status as national bard and the unlikely fame upon which he came to depend, even as he was inwardly troubled—as his poem "Provide, Provide," in which his savage irony is directed against himself, makes clear —by that very dependence. At the same time, Frost wanted to be read "right." Like Christ's parables, Frost's darker poems are designed to separate the wheat from the chaff, those who have the ears to hear from those who do not. A poem like "Directive" is a kind of test of the reader, a "serial ordeal," a trial by experience, that separates the initiate from the non-initiate. Frost as poetic artificer is in fact passing judgment on us. The theological language of "Directive" centers on passages, like that cited from Mark, which suggest the extraordinarily high stakes that can be involved in questions of interpretation. Those of his readers who are canny enough to realize that they are being tested pass the test and are admitted to the ranks of the hermeneutical elect.

I would like to make one final suggestion about the role of the narrator/guide in "Directive." Frost had a particular mistrust for academic critics, professional guides to the meanings of poems, who he thought, with some justice, consistently underestimated—when they did not outright dismiss—his work. Indeed, his poetry continues to this day to receive relatively scant attention from academic critics. And so the guide in "Directive" usurps, preempts the role of the critic while at the same time passing judgment on him or her as surely as he passes judgment on his common readers—and as surely as Christ's parables passed judgment on the interpretive powers of their auditors.

3.

Frost, among major Modernist poets, had a kind of anomalous singularity. He had little in common with Yeats, Stevens, Pound, Eliot, or Williams. Much of this singularity, I suspect, arose from his many years of isolation, both literal, spatial isolation and temperamental isolation from his poetic peers, during which time he wrote most of his finest work. Frost's early poems were the means by which, in the absence of congenial interlocutors, he conducted arguments with himself, arguments that were never fully resolved. Frost greatly admired Keats and professed a darker version of Keats' negative capability. He insisted that, whatever his intention in writing a poem might have been, in the process of writing he almost always deviated from it, as though the poem came to have a mind of its own, to reveal an intention not his own, or hitherto unrecognized as his own. And so Frost, at times the slyest, most manipulative, most controlling of poets, also experienced the writing of poems —particularly of formal poems, with their taxing and exigent demands—as a relinquishment of control, as a means of discovery, of opening up new perspectives that contributed new elements to the poet's ongoing arguments with himself.

Frost famously wrote, in his essay "The Figure the Poem Makes," that poems provide, both for their writers and for their readers a momentary stay against confusion, perhaps the very confusion to which the last line of "Directive" refers. For Frost, confusion had an alarming potential to veer perilously close to something far more threatening, to psychic chaos, a chaos that could lead to a complete disintegration of the ego. Frost lost his son Carol to suicide; his daughter Irma, increasingly prone to bouts of paranoia, was remanded, after her marriage had failed, to what would become a permanent incarceration in a state mental hospital. Well-versed in Darwin and his notion of inherited traits, Frost, who was himself subject to spells of depression, had cause to fear that he too might be vulnerable to the encroachment of madness, a vulnerability enhanced by his sense of his own desert spaces, his own inveterate and at times frightening solitude, a fear later mitigated by his social role as the much-in-demand poet of the common man. The writing of poems could be a way of preserving one's sanity, of exerting a measure of control over overwhelming feelings, of granting them form as a stay against formlessness, chaos, and entropy.

Thus far I have emphasized what might arbitrarily be called the dark reading of "Directive," the work of the poet/artificer who has covert designs on us, who only has at heart our getting lost. In this reading of the poem, its narrator leads us to a kind of bitter self-knowledge or gnosis, situates us in a constricted imaginative world, which we have no choice but to inhabit. And yet, at the same time, far from being merely a clever exercise in cynicism and despair, the poem can also, must also, be read as an expression of pathos, of deep feeling.

The Frost who wrote dark or even despairing poems also, of course, wrote relatively transparent, incandescent, celebratory poems like "A Tuft of Flowers," "Mowing," "Birches," "The Silken Tent," and many others. When Frost writes, toward the end of "Birches," "Earth's the right place for love: / I don't know where it's likely to go better," he is not, I think, being ironic. Love, for Frost, is an intrinsic human attribute or capacity; it requires no metaphysical sanction to legitimize it. Work, too, is a project proper to man and has an intrinsic dignity. Even solitary work, whether the mowing of fields or the writing of poems, can connect man to his fellow man. In the concluding lines of "A Tuft of Flowers," the speaker, while mowing a field, addresses a previous solitary mower of the same field as a "kindred spirit": "Men work together, I told him from the heart / Whether they work together or apart." It is hard to imagine that in writing what is in effect his poetic *summa*, Frost would not wish to do justice to both of the lighter and darker strands of his imagination, while resisting any impulse to provide some neat resolution between them that would only falsify both.

To give a sense of what I am referring to in characterizing "Directive" as a poem of pathos, I will cite two particularly striking lines in the poem. The first, "where were they all not twenty years ago?," literally refers to the upstart trees that have replaced, by depriving them of light, the trees of what used to be an a cultivated orchard. But the line at the same time registers as a powerful lament, an acknowledgement of the fragile human community that perhaps also existed here not twenty years ago. The second is the line "weep for the little things that made them glad," in which the narrator, heretofore immured within the cell of himself, has sudden access to a kind of fellow feeling. But these are merely local instances of a more pervasive phenomenon. Even while registering what I am calling the dark reading of the poem, one cannot help but be moved by it as an intense expression of feeling, evoking, as it does, a number of deep human emotions, of which the drive to return to a simpler time, to something like home, to an innocent place of origins, is one.

In thinking of Frost, an old Freudian term, no longer much in use, *highly defended*, comes to mind. The highly defended individual deploys, often unconsciously, any number of stratagems to prevent others from catching a glimpse of what is being defended against, some vulnerability to which too much feeling is attached. Often, however paradoxically, the highly defended personality longs for his defenses to be breached, for his vulnerability, his deep feeling, to be recognized and acknowledged by others. "Directive" itself is in this sense over-defended. I suspect that Frost feels, and intends for us to feel, the pull of the longing for home, for our origins, or for simply letting others in, that lies behind his defensive gestures in "Directive." "No tears in the writer," Frost wrote, "no tears in the reader." "Directive" is both a poem of logos and of pathos, and both of these claims, those of the head and of the heart, demand acknowledgement. Ultimately, literarily sophisticated, elect readings of "Directive," sensitive to negation, and naive readings, sensitive to affirmation, are both half-right and half-wrong. Only when read both ways simultaneously is the full force of the poem registered.

I am returning, finally, perhaps too belatedly, to my original thesis. "Directive" can, indeed should, be read both as a rebuke to the purveyors of false consolation, while at the same time affording some measure of solace, however temporary, attenuated, and provisional. The human need to create form, order, community, and meaning against an indifferent or hostile natural and cosmic backdrop can seem merely deluded, as though we are all always dwelling in a children's house of make-believe. At the same time, however, the need to create such orders, even if only momentary stays against confusion, can also and equally be seen as valiant, as the expression of a kind of existential bravery, however quixotic. I believe that Frost viewed the human project, both individual and collective, in both of these ways, and that both have equal pride of place in "Directive."

The creation of art, too, and specifically here the writing of poetry, is of course, like the capacity to feel and express love, a quintessentially human project, one that involves the inscription of significant patterns, significant designs, an activity that underwrites the experience of tentative meanings which are imbued with more than usually intense feeling and which, in the words of Wallace Stevens, "help us to live our lives."

And so the poem's unreliable narrator/artificer/demiurge, a trickster, misanthrope, and thief, ultimately does, as though despite himself, lead us to the riverside, to life-giving waters, which, if not at their source, at their point of origin, are at least *near* to it. The poem is as sensitive to human needs as it is skeptical of them. "Directive" demands to be read as valorizing man's fragile and heroic efforts to create a home for himself in an indifferent universe, a reading that, when sensitive to the poem's complexities, need not be seen as merely naive but as necessary to registering its full impact.

Finally, or yet again, the point where all of the contrary vectors of "Directive" seem, in true teleological fashion, to meet, is in its remarkable last line, which is also its last directive: "Drink and be whole again beyond confusion." How one reads this line is indicative of one's response to the poem. Is some kind of consolation truly being offered, or is the line sadly, bitterly, ironic? Or are both, as I am suggesting, somehow the case?

When I first read this line, many, many years ago, as a young man and as a novice poet, its sound struck me in some powerfully inchoate, unaccountable way. It was as though some strange new note had been added to the scale. What I felt and still feel as inexpressibly moving is that this line, like the double-edged sword in the title of this essay, somehow manages to cut, and cut deeply, both ways, is intended both to offer a kind of provisional consolation, while and at the same time, with a *sorrowful irony*, disabusing us of the notion that any final consolation is possible. The holy grail is a mere toy that is broken and will remain broken. We will not again become the children of whom it is said that they alone will enter the kingdom of heaven. Perhaps the new note to which I am referring is that of sorrowful irony itself, a sorrow that acknowledges the force and nobility of the human need to recapture origins even as it registers the impossibility of doing so.

6.
VOICING ORPHEUS

1.

It is said of lawyers that only fools take themselves as their clients. It might with equal justice be said with respect to poets that only fools take themselves or their poetry as their subjects. As I have elsewhere, and repeatedly, emphasized, once a poet is finished with a poem it is definitively out of the poet's hands, and he or she has no claim to special authority with respect to his or her judgments about it. Much has been written about unreliable narrators, a device consciously chosen by many writers of fiction and by some poets. With respect to his or her own work, a poet is likely to be a more than usually unreliable *reader*. In the ensuing discussion of the genesis and gist of my long narrative poem "Talking Head," written in the voice of Orpheus, that follows, I hope to avoid the sin of self-exegesis by focusing as much on the myth of Orpheus itself as on my poetic recasting of it.

The path that eventually led to the writing of "Talking Head" commenced when, after having suffered a bout of depression, I was prescribed an anti-depressant that catapulted me, happily, into a hypomanic state. As this jolt of dopamine in the form of a pill kicked in, I felt inspired to reread Shakespeare's plays, particularly his tragedies, with renewed attention, discipline, and focus. Reading Shakespeare and works on tragedy in general also inspired me to read the great Greek tragedians both more widely and intensively than I had before, a project that included reading translations of all of Euripides' extant tragedies, among which *The Bacchae* held a peculiar fascination for me.

Before proceeding further, I will simply stress the role that apparently eccentric and haphazard yet occultly purposeful reading has played in my life as a poet. During the course of such reading, the left hand, the straightforward process of reading itself, does not yet know what the right hand, the imagination's preconscious mulling over of such reading, is latently doing, and later, at some unexpected time, patently *will* do. I have mentioned elsewhere that for great scientists, it is often only after pondering seemingly intractable problems for years that revelatory insights finally flash upon the conscious mind. For the poet, if he is lucky, intensive reading, in concert with his or her life experience, plays such a role. The imagination needs materials noiselessly and patiently, like Whitman's spider, with which to work, a work of synthesis that takes place just beyond or before the horizon of the conscious mind. In the act of writing a successful poem, this synthesis, as it were, crosses a preconscious threshold and finally presents itself, in the form of a revelatory insight into the work that is to be manifested, to the conscious mind.

Rereading Greek tragedy led me to explore, for the first time with any enthusiasm, the world of Greek mythology and to take, finally, a more extended and intensive look at classical literature—alas, in translation—than I had previously assayed. Greek mythology had earlier seemed to me superficial in its tracking of the multifarious adventures of a vast array of all-too-capricious gods, goddesses, and demigods. Greek and Latin literature, which I imagined to be too mimetic for my taste, I had, quite parochially, relatively neglected in favor of more biblically grounded writers, although I could not fail to register the fact that almost all great Western literature from Dante's time onward has incorporated figures from classical myth and literature as well. Nevertheless, for a long time I remained firmly in what I considered or imagined to be the biblical camp. I preferred the suggestive lacunae or gaps in biblical narrative and its successors to the skillful filling in of the foreground details of the phenomenal and human world characteristic of more mimetic and classically-based works. And yet here I was, finally, in my early fifties, suddenly becoming engrossed in Greek literature, religion, and mythology.

One work more than any other, Walter Otto's extraordinary, visionary book, *Dionysus: Myth and Cult*, sparked my newfound enthusiasm for classical mythology. The first and briefer portion of the book is a fairly standard attempt at conjecture, through research into the material then available, as to the nature of the cult, or rather of the various related cults, of Dionysus. It is the kind of necessary scholarly work that is routinely superseded when subsequent research uncovers new material.

The second, longer portion of the book is something else altogether. It is as though through some visionary leap of the imagination Otto has placed himself behind the mask of the deity, an empty mask, the height of a man, that is one of the most common forms in which Dionysus appears, while at the same time allowing himself, in effect, to become one of the god's votaries. Dionysus in one of his aspects is the preeminent god of the epiphanic; he suddenly, inexplicably *appears*. Through a feat of the sympathetic imagination, Otto manages not only to take into account the loosely related, multifarious forms in which the god manifests himself, but also to recount the various tales of Dionysus as instances of a single, integral phenomenon, each reinforcing and adding to the power of the others. I felt while reading Otto as though I, too, was falling under the spell of this strange and inexhaustibly rich deity.

Dionysus, androgynous youth hailing from the mysterious East, disrupter of social norms; inspirer, in his *maenads*, his ecstatic female devotees, of a mania bordering on psychosis, of a power so great that it impels them to rend wild beasts with their bare hands; Dionysus, who himself appears in the form of wild animals, who is torn apart only to be repeatedly and miraculously reborn; Dionysus, god of wine, under whose influence nature herself, like his maenads, spins into a kind of hopped-up overdrive, yielding not only grapes but copious jets of milk with the tap of a *thyrsus*, a phallic stick or staff that itself oozes a seminal manna; Dionysus, the ultimate shapeshifter, who appears in the form of a bear or basilisk in the hold of a ship in which tendrils of vines suddenly sprout everywhere, and who slaughters its sailors as though in sport, wading exultantly in their blood; Dionysus, everywhere and yet nowhere, who assumes many shapes, many guises, but who himself has no fixed identity; who appears, again as an imposing mask the height of a man, a mask worn by no one and concealing nothing, a nothing that is not only the absence of any particular presence but is nothingness itself, a vacancy that nonetheless projects a kind of profoundly unsettling power and force.

Finally, to discuss last things first, as befits this strange, equivocal deity, there are two accounts of Dionysus' birth which taken together suggest much about his nature. According to the first story, Semele, a mortal girl, is impregnated by Zeus but fails to live long enough to give birth to the child. To save the fetus, Zeus sews him inside his own thigh, which becomes a kind of womb, and after a period of gestation gives birth to him. Thus, Dionysus is a male born from a makeshift womb-like enclosure within another male, a myth that entails a bizarre scrambling of the male and the female. This tale is oddly reminiscent of that of the birth by parthenogenesis of Athena, who was born fully formed from the head of Zeus, and who thus, likewise, had a kind of male mother. From this myth sprung too, the myth of Dionysus as the twice-born Zagreus—one of the many cult names of the deity—as well as a cult of worship of Dionysus in the form of an infant.

According to the second story, Hera was jealous of the progeny of Zeus and Semele and persuaded the Titans, a prior, overthrown, chthonic race of gods, to attack the infant Dionysus. Not only did the Titans dismember him, but they also devoured him—all but his heart, which Athena rescued. From this organ the rest of the god was resurrected in the form of a horned serpent. Here the often-repeated motif of Dionysus' dismemberment appears. Here, too, Dionysus is intimately related to the Titans, a prior, atavistic, uncivilized race of gods, as well as to mere mortals, who were said to have been fashioned from the Titans' ashes. Among Dionysus' many animal incarnations, corresponding to his birth as a horned serpent, are both the bull and the serpent or basilisk.

Dionysus is associated with the primal pull of the sea and with the chthonic depths of the earth ruled by Hades. He is associated as well with the mysteries of Eleusis, which reenact the rescue of Penelope by Demeter, a kind of *magna mater*, from the underworld. He also embodies the atavistic, the regressive, the pull of the Freudian moil of the unconscious. Such regressive forces, according to Freud, when their appeal is recognized and assimilated, can be harnessed in the service of the ego. When they are spurned or unrecognized, however, they can lead to its psychotic disintegration. Constantly dying and being reborn, Dionysus is associated with the destruction that gives way to fresh creation, with both Thanatos and with Eros, with the teeming, ungovernable life force that creates, animates, and destroys all things.

My encounter with Dionysus, facilitated by Otto, provided a portal through which to view the other Olympian Gods who, no longer appearing to me as mere stock figures, seemed to exist in a rich dialectical tension with Dionysus himself. Several of the Olympians, among them Dionysus' nemesis Apollo and his similarly shape-shifting spiritual confrere Hermès, themselves became objects of a subsidiary fascination for me.

Finally, while engaged in the process of reading both Shakespeare and the great Greek tragedians, I reviewed, somewhat haphazardly, the attempts of Western philosophers—one of whose traditional domains, of course, is that of the aesthetic— to grapple with the nature of the tragic. I found the book *On Tragedy* by Walter Kauffmann, a scholar best known as an insightful exegete of Nietzsche, to be particularly compelling. In the course of a long review of the attempts of Western philosophers from Aristotle to Hegel to delineate tragedy's essential and universal traits, he highlights their failure to do so, indicating that the diverse forms, the recalcitrant details, of actual tragedies contradict all such categorical assertions, outstrip any limitations engendered by the attempt to impose universal criteria.

Here I should mention that I, of course, reread Nietzsche's *The Birth of Tragedy*. Though his attempts to account for the genesis of tragedy, like Otto's attempts to trace the origins and salient features of the cult of Dionysus, have since been largely discredited by scholars, the visionary force and the seminal importance of Nietzsche's account of the tensions between the Apollonian and the Dionysian remains pertinent and seems intuitively to speak of a dynamic that includes but is not limited to the domain of tragedy itself as a literary genre. It seems precisely Nietzsche's tendency to think intuitively, to approach tragedy not merely like a scientist attempting to isolate its morphological traits, that lead to his still-vital insights.

During the intensive course of reading I have described above, it was as though I had been foraging, collecting twigs and branches, dry tinder, which I was building into a kind of pyramid or pyre that would require only a spark or the striking of a match to give rise to a bonfire. That spark appeared for me in the seemingly unprepossessing form of an old but well-respected, scholarly work on the myth of Orpheus, *Orpheus and Greek Religion,* by W. K. C. Guthrie. Before encountering this book, I had been aware of only a few of the best-known episodes of Orpheus' myth. Doubtless many, as had been the case with me, remain unaware of aspects of the myth which, as we shall see, have been for thoroughly understandable reasons elided or repressed.

We know that Orpheus, in his youth, is both the ur-poet and the ur-musician. He has been granted by Apollo, who is a master of the lyre, the power to himself become a master of that instrument. His enchanting lays have the charm to tame even the wildest of beasts. Even tall trees bend to hear his song. Orpheus almost seems a Greek precursor of Saint Francis. His civilizing effect on nature seems exactly the opposite of that of Dionysus.

At some point Orpheus marries Eurydice, who is summarily snatched into hell, much as Persephone had been abducted by Hades into the underworld. Orpheus makes a courageous descent in order to negotiate for her release, apparently successfully, but as he and Eurydice rise toward the surface of the earth, Orpheus, prompted by an inexplicable impulse, violates the one precondition mandated by Hades—that he not turn back to look at his bride during their ascent to the earth's surface. As a result, Eurydice lapses permanently back into Hades, unlike Persephone, who is granted a reprieve every spring, and Orpheus is tragically fated to remain alone.

As it turns out, however, according to Guthrie, Orpheus' descent into the underworld and failed attempt to rescue Eurydice is a late interpolation into the myth, attempting to suggest that it is because Orpheus is in perpetual mourning for his one true love that he shows so little interest in women. This in effect cleans up any suggestion that Orpheus had *never* been interested in women, had been if not gay, then whatever at the time of the myth's origination had been the equivalent of being gay. In later retellings of the myth, subtle hints or intimations of a gay Orpheus recur until finally, in Ovid, the repressed returns in the form of an Orpheus who is fully and definitively gay. Thus the most sophisticated, urbane interpretation of the myth is perhaps the most in tune with its origins.

What of Orpheus' life subsequent to or apart from his failed rescue of Eurydice? Reading this portion of the myth, it is perfectly clear why it has been repressed. Orpheus' subsequent career is, quite simply, *horrifying*. After his relatively beatific phase as a charmed and youthful enchanter of nature, he is later set upon by a band of stately matrons who, by some accounts resenting his lack of interest in women, tear him limb from limb. Orpheus thus suffers the rending, the *sparagmos* undergone so often by Dionysus, although Orpheus, unlike Dionysus, cannot be reborn—if only because he can never die. Orpheus' severed head, still conscious, is unceremoniously tossed into the river Hebron. He undergoes a long and arduous night sea journey, a kind of cruel parody of a crucial phase in the archetypal hero's quest, a trial through which a differentiated self is typically victoriously wrested from chaos and darkness while at the same time assimilating and transfiguring both. Orpheus, on the other hand, in contradistinction to the many heroic figures in Greek mythology, is a kind of failed hero or anti-hero who suffers endlessly, passively, but cannot act.

After its harrowing sojourn at sea, Orpheus' severed head fetches up on the isle on Lesbos—to the astonishment of a band of kindly maidens who are priestesses associated with a prominent shrine to Apollo that graces the island. Orpheus' head is planted, as it were, in a gouged-out pit in this shrine, where it becomes a renowned oracle to Apollo—until, that is, Apollo decides to deprive this most eloquent of men even of the power of speech.

Without the interpolated story of Eurydice, we have a straightforward tale of a man who began his career as a charmed and all-charming ur-musician and ur-poet whose influence is profoundly civilizing, but who later in life suffers a horrifying fate that drives him into a state close to insanity. Apparently we have here an early instance of what later would become a kind of commonplace expressed by Wordsworth's maxim: "We Poets in our youth begin in gladness / But thereof come in the end despondency and madness."

Viewing the Orpheus myth in this, its aboriginal form, it is in many ways a curious production. With respect to the savage attack upon Orpheus, it seems, again, at first blush, to have been entirely motivated by his lack of interest in women. Freed of the explanatory trappings of the myth of Eurydice, Orpheus' misogyny or mere lack of interest in women as well as his questionable sexuality stand out in clearer relief. But do these attributes alone merit such an attack? It seems possible, even likely, that someone has encouraged the matrons to undertake their brutal mission. But who?

The two possible culprits are Apollo and Dionysus. Scholars have noted that Orpheus has links to both deities. Apollo himself was Orpheus' father, the muse Calliope his mother. Thus, like so many figures in a Greek myth, Orpheus is a kind of demigod, half human, half divine. Apollo also has bequeathed the lyre and its civilizing influence to Orpheus. But perhaps, as is suggested in the myth, Orpheus has learned to play the lyre all too well, and a jealous Apollo has mandated his demise and has arranged, too, for his demeaning role as an oracle—a role more akin to that of a brutally indentured servant than to that of a son. Eventually, however, Apollo seems to tire of Orpheus' oracular voice just as he had tired of or felt threatened by his music, and so he strips Orpheus of his power of coherent speech.

Orpheus' connection to Dionysus is just as strong. Quite simply, he shares Dionysus' fate. He, too, suffers a savage rending, in his case by a band of matrons whose role is akin to that of Dionysus' maenads. Dionysus, moreover, often appears as a youth whose sexual identity, like that of Orpheus, is ambiguous. But what reason would Dionysus have to mandate Orpheus' tragic fate? One answer is that unlike Apollo, Dionysus, incarnation of the excessive, operates outside of the sphere of reason. He is capable of apparently unmotivated, gratuitous actions that are appallingly, brutally cruel, as is made clear in Euripides' *The Bacchae*. But, of course, Dionysus, a god of ecstasy, is also at odds with all things Apollonian, including the harmonious, civilizing music of Orpheus' lyre. Dionysus' musical accompaniment, announcing his unpredictable appearances, consists of shrill pipes and percussive instruments, which together produce a fearsome clamor.

Thus, Orpheus has definite links to, as well as significant differences from, both Apollo and Dionysus. His myth is regarded by a number of scholars as an attempt to mediate between the two gods, who are in significant ways polar opposites. Alas, in this process of mediation, Orpheus is caught and then literally torn between them. He is something like what is now called a contested site. He becomes the embodiment of polar forces, forces that prove impossible for him to reconcile.

My original question about which god, if either, mandated Orpheus' demise, is ultimately impossible to answer. It is entirely possible that the matrons were acting alone. In my poem "Talking Head," Orpheus suggests a third possibility. Perhaps Apollo and Dionysus have been working in concert. Perhaps Orpheus has successfully effectuated a rapprochement or truce, even if only a temporary one, between the two, which results in his becoming a sacrificial victim. Apparently polar opposites are, of course, often in a reciprocal relationship, operating together as a kind of dyad. Their very opposition is belied by an occult accord. Certainly Apollo is not merely a rational figure, a force all radiance, clarity, and light, but is also, like Dionysus, a being capable of capricious acts, many of them sexual, some of them homosexual. Apollo is associated not only with the sky but also with the chthonic, with the buried shrines of his fatefully riddling oracles whose speech is irrational, or perhaps rather para-rational.

2.

It is no wonder that the myth of Orpheus provided the spark that became "Talking Head," my minor poetic conflagration. Quite simply, Orpheus was both gay and caught between irreconcilable forces. I, too, am gay, a predisposition with which, after considerable turmoil, I was just becoming comfortable when I encountered an Indian guru, an experience whose power radically upended my life, leading to over ten years living a highly disciplined and regimented life as a celibate renunciate in his ashrams in India and in upstate New York. As a result of my guru's condemnation of homosexuality, conflicts about my sexuality resurfaced. Additionally, my vocation as an author began to seem at odds with my newfound vocation as a spiritual seeker. I began to feel that my work as a poet, and specifically and self-consciously as a literary, Western poet whose poems were seldom straightforward celebrations of the divine, was a costly distraction, a manifestation of ego that ought to have been extirpated and renounced. These conflicts seemed to be irreconcilable. They led, along with an extensive early history of trauma on my part and a genetic predisposition to mental illness, to the recurrence of episodes of depression during which, at their most extreme, I experienced a kind of horrifying evacuation of the ego, a disintegration of any coherent sense of self. The more I learned about Orpheus, the more it must have subliminally dawned on me that his fictional state, as a locus of impossible-to-resolve conflicts, and my actual states had much in common.

For most of my career as a poet, I had attempted, like Walt Whitman or Wallace Stevens, to say "yes" to life. Kashmir Shivaism, the Indian metaphysical system that most appealed to me, is as fundamentally optimistic as some forms of Buddhism are fundamentally skeptical. In its radical monism, it sees all things as saturated in the bliss, joy, and freedom of Supreme Consciousness. My own poetry tended to follow a common Romantic or Neo-romantic pattern, moving from a position of simple, blissful unity to one of pain, exile, and estrangement, and finally to a more complex unity, a return to a joy raised to a higher power. The ending of such poems tended, of course, to be redemptive.

Though I continued, for a while, to coerce my poems to conclude with the final twist of an upwardly mobile spiral, it became all too clear to me that my life, which continued to be riddled by intractable conflicts and by a series of disruptive episodes of depression, was unlikely to end in a state of complex unity or joy.

And so it was that one afternoon I sat down, with no premeditation or forethought, to write a poem in the voice of Orpheus. Initially I had only a kind of synoptic intuition with respect to the task at hand. I had no idea how long my emergent poem would be or where Orpheus' voice would lead me. But as mentioned previously, I was once again in a blessedly hypomanic state. The synapses in my brain were firing with a happy alacrity and abandon.

In one of his letters, Keats writes that "if poetry comes not as naturally as the leaves to the tree, it had better not come at all." This had not always, or even usually, been my experience as a poet. In writing "Talking Head," however, for the first and only time in my poetic career, I felt almost as though I were being possessed by a voice both my own and not my own, as if I were channeling the voice of Orpheus, acting more as the poem's amanuensis and scribe than its creative origin. This experience was more uncanny, less organically benign, than Keats' axiom would suggest.

When I sat down to write the poem, I had no preconceived notion either of its contents or of its formal properties. What emerged was written in a kind of flexible variant of blank verse, a five-beat line that instead of having ten syllables, as in iambic pentameter, had, with rare exceptions, anywhere between one to three extra unstressed syllables per line. Maintaining this flexible line took no conscious effort on my part. It was simply something I was hearing and writing down. Like an actor who remains in character, I, or the poem I was now writing, retained this characteristic rhythm as well as the characteristic pitch and tone of a voice that had strangely colonized my own. At some point I recognized that the form of "Talking Head" represented an advance over my poem "The Road to Damascus," which was written in stricter blank verse.

"Talking Head" took about three months to write and another month to revise, during which time I reverted to a kind of monastic regimen. I wrote for about six hours a day every day, almost without exception. I began early each afternoon and wrote until early evening. At a certain point I became aware that I was writing what would eventually turn out to be a long poem. The more I wrote the longer, it seemed to me, the finished poem would ultimately become. This created a kind of tension. Of course, one never knows, in the process of writing a poem of any length, if one will be able to pull it off. But with this poem in particular, the stakes kept being raised. The possibility that I might not ultimately successfully complete the poem, after such a promising start, and after the expenditure of so much time and energy, lurked continuously and somewhat disturbingly at the back of my mind.

Nonetheless I managed to soldier on. A number of my lyric poems, particularity those of mid-length, contain rudimentary, in some cases very rudimentary narratives: "I set forth, then come back; I recall having been in this place, now I have returned; I depart and keep on going." And so on. Now I was writing a far longer narrative poem, and in fact quite a complex one, with a number of interpolated passages, brief detours, stories within the larger story. The poem unfolded without my once veering off course—certainly never in a major way but likewise, to the best of my recollection, not even in a minor way. From whence had this ability to write a long, complex narrative poem in flexible blank verse arisen? It is a question for which I have no answer, except from the impossible to verify and too presumptuous notion that some kind of poetic equivalent of grace was operative.

Yet another departure from previous precedent was taking place. Aside from the occasional echoing or borrowing of passages from the work of previous poets, a practice more than usually rare for me because of my quite shockingly un-retentive mind, I had never written poetry that was in any conspicuous way allusive. Now, however, I was writing a poem that was quite densely allusive, in large measure but not entirely due to the fact of its multiple references to Greek myth.

Indeed, I began to worry that the poem was *too* allusive. From those few intrepid friends I asked to attempt to read the whole thing, I tried to extract a promise that they not Google one arcane reference after another, thereby disrupting their experience of the flow of the poem. I averred to them what I believe to be true, that the poem is every bit as comprehensible or incomprehensible whether or not one bothers to pin down all of the fleeing references thrown up by it like the spindrift of an ongoing wave. I confess that I have always tended to feel annoyed by excessively allusive poems. It has become trite to say "be careful what you wish for." It is perhaps not quite as trite to say be careful of what you condemn or disdain.

3.

"Talking Head" begins with quite a long peroration, and specifically with Orpheus' contemptuous, disdainful, offhand dismissal as mere fiction of the tale of his marriage and of his escapade in the underworld. He denounces, too, with equal disdain, and with his authority as ur-poet, the wearisomely repetitive poetic representations of that myth and the inferior, derivative poets who have produced them.

Orpheus' peroration then proceeds with extended musings on Dionysus, a figure who, as it turns out, is with good reason a subject of fascination for him. Dionysus is portrayed as part-androgynous rock star, fated like Adonis or Attis never to grow up, a version of Jung's archetypal *puer aeternus*, and part-fascist autocrat and orator, but in either case a charismatic figure whose music or words whip audiences into a frenzy that almost causes the stadiums in which he appears to buckle on the verge of catastrophic collapse.

But the greater portion of this peroration is a recounting of the events in Euripides' *The Bacchae*, perhaps the cruelest of all Greek tragedies. *The Bacchae* had long haunted my imagination and had inspired a profound fascination in me. Indeed, I had once again read and reread it in the period of intensive reading that had led up to the creation of "Talking Head."

The Bacchae begins with the sudden, mysterious appearance of Dionysus, an androgynous youth who has wandered into Thebes from Thrace, from the mysterious East. He soon encounters Pentheus, the inexperienced and thoroughly unimaginative new king who has just taken over the throne of Thebes upon the retirement of his aged father, Cadmus.

Dionysus imperiously makes it clear that things will now have to change quite dramatically in Thebes and that Pentheus has only one viable option, which is to get with the new program. Pentheus indignantly and predictably asserts his authority and attempts to set the newcomer straight, slapping him into prison, which Dionysus, ever the escape artist, summarily and magically reduces to rubble. Indeed, Dionysus is inimical to civic structures, analogous to and identified with the reified structures of thought and the hidebound rules and hierarchies governing the polis, which he causes not merely to buckle, like the stadiums on his aforementioned tour, a motif that I have interpolated into his myth, but to reduce, in an instant, to rubble.

Come nightfall, Dionysus' spell transforms all of the women in Thebes into *maenads*, devotees of Dionysus who are rapt out of themselves into what appears to be a state of manic psychosis. Repairing to Dionysus' mountain haunts, they are granted a kind of supernatural strength, among whose manifestations is their aforementioned ability to gleefully rip wild animals limb from limb.

Meanwhile, himself falling under Dionysus' spell, Pentheus recants, too late. Massively deluded, he is determined to spy on the nocturnal rites of the *maenads* by perching high atop a tree. Immediately spotted, he is quite literally brought low, whereupon he, too, is predictably torn apart.

In the play's final scene, Agave, wife of Cadmus and mother of Pentheus, strides into the courtyard of Thebes, vaunting a trophy which, still under the spell of Dionysus, she imagines to be the severed head of a lion. When Dionysus' spell suddenly wears off, Agave becomes aware that she is in fact holding the bloody head of Pentheus, her own son, whom she has unwittingly slain. Dionysus, as it turns out, is a master, like Artaud, of the theater of cruelty—which is also a sublimely terrifying theater of the absurd.

Based on the long peroration just recounted, most of my now merely virtual readers would initially suspect, I would imagine, that they are reading a poem about Dionysus, not Orpheus. Why this initial emphasis on Dionysus, and on *The Bacchae* in particular? The events unfolded in *The Bacchae*, and particularly the brutal rending of Pentheus, clearly rhyme with Orpheus' own tragic fate. Though no Pentheus, though a far more compelling and imaginative figure, Orpheus, too, as we shall see, is finally undone by his encounter with Dionysus.

As the poem progressed, I continued to take license with the myth of Orpheus as recounted by Guthrie. In the passage subsequent to Orpheus' peroration, he is refashioned by me into my own image as a kind of celibate gay priest. It would be difficult to imagine that one who is *not* gay could have composed the lines that follow, in which Orpheus' music has its way with a band of young soldiers who are visiting his grove. The passage also provides a depiction of the Apollonian joys of Orpheus' prelapsarian state, pouring out songs that are the soul of harmony itself.

> I seemed to move within a column of light
> Whose radiance spread about me everywhere.
> My senses, quick, engrossed their several objects
> Not serially, yet distinctly--O all at once
> They vanished, reappeared in that golden shaft
> Expanding, contracting, humming with such speed
> It seemed to annul all sense of time itself
> And so not to move at all, still standing fast
> Like Zeno's arrow, staying while it flew.
> And yet my song's circumference grew wider;
> Tall sentinel trees bent toward it, and wild beasts,
> Quitting their lairs, grew tame within my sight,
> Breathed softy as I stroked my lyre's strings...
>
> I hymned a living sum, a breathing cosmos,
> The whole in each part, each part in the whole
> Addressed to every other in just proportion,

In numbers that my instinctive octave sounded
And sounding, did its own part to uphold.
The stars and planets spinning in their courses,
Each root, trunk, branch, leaf, and winding vein
That flourished beneath the slow arc of the sun,
The rainbow parsing its colors in bright mist,
Constraining banks permitting streams to flow,
All spoke to my eyes a proximate symmetry;
O, only by being bounded were things free
To open outward toward light's unscored sea
Forever unreachable, lost to my command.
I preferred the vocation, sweet, enjoined on me -
To be just where I was, and not to wander
In thought or act from work that came to hand:
To care for, cure my plots of native land
And find, in cloistered clearings, the green fields
Of Elysium, redeemed from distant shores.

Meanwhile, my vision frequented its stores;
A seer perhaps too enamored of sight itself,
Of the play of dappled shade on indolent limbs.
I cherished not only pristine things, self-sealed,
Forever turning into themselves, rapt spheres,
But the charged, immaculate spaces between them
Like the silence between words, its reticence,
The vibrant precondition of utterance
Or of its meanings, multiple yet coherent
Though intangible as a temple's atmosphere.
I sought an art, a being, composed, intact.
I never longed to pierce, or to be pierced,
(Whether by Eros or by some warrior's arrow)
To strike beyond surfaces to the pith within,
Or to be stricken, like some wounded deer,
Or if I yearned to, was balked by an urgent fear
Somehow instilled in me from my first years.

No mere poet, after all, but a latent priest
Clairvoyant in the simplest of senses,
My vision clear, my body modest, chaste,
I only wanted to gaze, no, never to taste.
And that is why my boys were drawn to me

Or to my songs (I almost thought them the same).
They knew that I would seek, ask nothing of them,
Unlike their parents, lovers, girlfriends, wives,
And so they submitted to my words' designs
And lay about me, innocent, undefended,
Not thinking, for a time, of martial feats,
Of training in their unconquerable phalanx
Which melded all, incorporate, in one body,
A soldered file of soldiers, arm in arm,
A single faultless wall of brazen armor
Deployed to repel the brashest of attacks,
To shield their polis from all threat of harm
(The antitheses of Maenads' swarming packs,
Each feeling herself the sole spouse of her God,
Each reveling, proud, in all the others lacked).

But now, lost in my songs' untended moment,
The willing captives of its yielding spell,
They laid their shining shields upon the grass,
Reclined, half-shut their softly lidded eyes.
Why, they seemed almost, almost feminine
And I, a mere poet, was their trusted captain,
Confederate in the arts of peace, not war.
I gazed on their rapt features like a lover
Who wakens first, and finds the face beside him
More lovely still in sleep's unvexed repose,
And felt the aching tenderness of a mother,
A vigilance more poignant than any dream.
Still cradling my lyre, I felt its subtle humming
Along my nerves, converging on my heart
From which, redoubled, then sent forth again,
It found its way into my burgeoning song;
Its words, though uttered singly, were blended
Like drops of water vanishing in a stream.
Perhaps I was not so different from my boys;
Well, I of the lyre, they of the heavy bow–
We both were masters of the tense, plucked string.

Orpheus' music is ordered, harmonious, Apollonian, and his world seems
bathed in a kind of contemplative glow. His music is meditative rather than ecstatic.
It induces something akin to a profoundly mystical state, a charmed trance, a blissful

quietism in which, in Wordsworth's words, we are "laid asleep in body, and become a living soul," a quietism that is inimical to the unruly ecstasies of Dionysus.

As I mentioned earlier, there is ample precedent in Guthrie's ur-myth, and in later extrapolations of it, for regarding Orpheus as sexually ambiguous or gay. Nowhere, however, is there a suggestion that Orpheus is celibate, and so my designation of Orpheus as such is one of my many emendations to, or riffs on, Guthrie's interpretation. This renunciation, in the case of Orpheus, is as much that of the artist as of the priest, enabling a kind of rapt contemplation on beauty and on the aesthetic expression of it. Orpheus' embrace of the contemplative and the beautiful is typical of a kind of mystical path that is inimical to Dionysus' ecstasies, whose aesthetic analogue is not beauty but a kind of daemonic sublimity.

Orpheus' lyre is a preeminently civilizing force. His native precincts are peaceful groves traversed by burbling streams animated by benign spirits. His world seems to epitomize the golden mean, to have no place for extremes of any kind. It is that of a tamed and civilized nature that is closely connected to and an extension of the Greek city state or polis, a zone that is associated with the genre of the pastoral. Indeed, the cultivated ground just outside the city was a locus in which, as in the passage quoted above, youths underwent military training, were initiated into their roles as adult citizens of the polis. As *The Bacchae* suggests, the Dionysian is inimical to the organized life, to the hierarchical structure of the polis, which it continually threatens to subvert.

Orpheus quite naturally feels pride in his civilizing power. Speaking in retrospect, after his ruin, Orpheus' poses a crucial rhetorical question: "I had my pride / should I have let it go?" In a long passage following this question, Orpheus first expresses contempt for occult practices such as divination and the consulting of oracles, and for sacrificial rites themselves, as repellent, and yet, in a kind of savage irony, perhaps because of that disdain, he himself becomes both a sacrificial victim and an unwilling oracle. He goes on to excoriate anything that approaches the ecstatic strain of mysticism, and particularly the admixture of the ecstatic and the chthonic typical of the rites of Dionysus. Several accounts of descent into and ascent from Hades in Greek myth, most prominently the myth of Persephone, suggest a kind of occult alliance between Dionysus and Hades. No less an authority than Heraclitus is cited to this effect in "Talking Head" in lines that juxtapose and join two of his aphorisms:

> *Dionysus and Hades are one and the same,*
> Heraclitus, the lord of paradox, proclaimed,
> Who knew that *the way up is the way down.*

The way up and the way down, heights and depths, are one for Dionysus, whose vision subverts hierarchical structures of all kinds.

Orpheus' contempt for Hades and its supposed Lord, as well as his view of his own supposed adventures in the underworld as contemptible fictions, leads him to spurn as well the ecstatic mysteries of Eleusis, whose participants re-enacted a primordial myth entailing a sojourn in the underworld and a blissfully liberating ascent from it, culminating with a visionary state induced by the ingestion of an hallucinogenic manna. As a result of its power, participants in the rites—which, remarkably, recognized none of the hierarchical structures of the Greek polis and were open to all strata of society, including the enslaved—experienced a communal, spiritual rebirth. With a kind of aristocratic disdain, Orpheus professes no need for such a rebirth. Ultimately, however, his rejection of the depths of the chthonic and of its unbridled life force leads to his being interred in those depths, being buried alive, as a severed head, in his terminal, antipodal outpost in Lesbos.

Orpheus' rejection of the Eleusinian rites of Demeter is one of many instances of his contempt for or indifference to the power of the feminine, not only in its external manifestations but also within himself. This rejection ultimately leads to his evisceration by that power, and finally to the grotesquely parodic reverence in which his severed head is held by the maidens who eventually rescue it when it fetches up on Lesbos.

Orpheus rejects not only the story of his descent into Hades but what Guthrie regards as yet another another late interpolation into Orpheus' ur-myth, his supposed participation, as a passenger on the Argo, in Jason's quest for the Golden Fleece. Indeed, Orpheus has a particular antipathy toward what he calls "the sea's livid flux," its atavistic shape-shifting formlessness. As it happens, Dionysus is not only associated with earthy depths, as a confrère of Hades, but also in particular with the sea, from which he is seen as having originally emerged and manifested himself, an aboriginal event celebrated by raucous rites for which, again, Orpheus expresses a particular contempt.

> His act all hollow percussion, driving beat,
> It was he who started underground, made it big,
> Emerged as from some source enticingly foreign,
> Tossed on our white sands as by the sea,
> A metaphor his crazed fans took literally–
> Thus that lurid, odd, biennial argosy,
> Their idol wheeled, shore to city, in a ship,
> A painted prop, too fragile for any wave,
> While they raved loud around him, a procession
> Graced, too, by loutish goatboys wielding dildos,
> Chanting his lewd dithyrambs, his punk anthems,
> His solemn rite turned plain obscenity;
> The advent of their hero–precious captive!–

Roused a mock greeting fit for a pilfered slave
Who slipped away, and headed for the hills,
Their capsized hearts left seized yet dispossessed,
By his daft abandon ravaged and enthralled.

Just as Orpheus' rejection of the chthonic power of the depths of the earth leads to his terminal internment in that earth, so his disdain for the sea and for its primeval life-giving powers leads to his ultimate subjection to the seemingly random, entropic, undifferentiated flux of that sea and to the loss of any meaningful identity. Additionally, Orpheus, as a celibate and a renunciant, rejects the primal force of Eros, one of whose expressions is the unbridled yet generative force of sexuality itself.

Orpheus' haunts, his beloved groves, are, as it were, close to sea level, whereas Dionysus, as we have seen, is connected to depths, whether subterranean depths or the depths of the sea, and with the mountain heights in which his ecstatic rites take place. Dionysus, bipolar god of extremities, is associated with realms that are foreign to the golden mean of Orpheus' harmonious pastoral world.

In another swerve from the ur-myth recounted by Guthrie, I recount in "Talking Head" a grim transitional time between Orpheus' happier life and his ultimate destruction. This interlude is inaugurated by Apollo's command that Orpheus mollify his rival Dionysus by eschewing his role as an Apollonian rhapsode. Instead, he is told to transform his music into something more percussive, wild, dithyrambic. This new charge requires that Orpheus depart from the tame, sylvan, civilized Apollonian groves that have heretofore been his home and go into a postlapsarian exile. He is now forced to rove and survive in the mountains that are Dionysus' haunts, which nothing in his background has prepared him to negotiate. His life becomes a grim and and demeaning struggle for survival.

Orpheus has no more affinity with mountainous heights than with the depths of Hades. Orpheus' period of mountain exile finally results in a devastating epiphany in which Dionysus appears to him in all of his terror and glory. This epiphany both seals and accelerates Orpheus' tragic fate. I should briefly note that Orpheus, like any good religious ascetic, has become, during his sojourn in the mountains, a cave dweller, and it is while in this cave that Orpheus first becomes aware of Dionysus as a shade cast inward on its floor. The allusion to Plato's parable of the cave is entirely intended. In the immediately subsequent passage, Orpheus turns around and confronts Dionysus not as a shadow or, as it were, in a glass darkly, but face to face:

His mask uprose, fresh-dripping from the sea,
All head, no body, that head the height of a man,
And faced me, as others, fully frontally,
His face with a gentle smile like a Bodhisattva's
That seemed to cancel all desire and fear.

But O, that smile was nothing if not deceptive,
More like the Mona Lisa's, Madonna or vampire;
Sweet monster, posed before a rocky wasteland,
Her lips, forever sealed, conceal a rictus,
A laugh whose echoes, dumb, remain congealed.
How glibly the God accosted me: I am here,
As he conjured up his visage, ex nihilo,
Challenging me to meet his steadfast gaze
As the roar of raw chaos itself assailed my ears.
...
His mask turned inside out, turned outside in,
Was both yet neither, other to no other,
Created a space not space, a warped lacuna
Where here was always elsewhere, elsewhere here;
To gaze at him was to be displaced, unplaced,
To banish oneself completely, unless one hid,
Retreated behind his mask, saw through his eyes,
Beholding the absence where one used to be;
Strange ecstasy! Not even my shadow lay
Before me, although it was far from noon,
So wholly was I consumed by his disguise.

Like a lunatic swapping places with a cipher,
I reverted to my own form, his mask vacated.
I shuddered awake, as into a further dream
Until, beside myself with joy or terror,
I once again confronted his grinning façade.
His features seemed mere copies of themselves,
The copies of a copy, themselves a copy
Of which no lost original could be found;
Reveal to me your face before you were born
He seemed to taunt, a cruel simulacrum
Delighted to laugh at my too earnest state.
Neither kindly master nor fierce nemesis,
He vaporized as soon as I would oppose him
And left me, lost, with nothing to retard
My headlong fall through an abyss that opened
(Within me or without – I could not tell)
Until, in the splitting of an orphaned moment
I caught sight of his blank, unmoving eyes;
And then I was not plummeting, merely standing,

Still as a statue, balked and paralyzed,
That as by some undue miracle comes to life,
Breathes, moves, exulting in the morning air,
And feels the living sunlight gild his limbs,
A slight breeze rise and fall in his flowing hair.

At last, beside me like a lost twin brother,
I glimpsed D's human form for the first time:
O beautiful past beauty!—man, woman, God,
Converging, found the zenith of their spring,
Sap rising, in his lithe and tender limbs,
All golden light, and glistening as with dew;
He smiled at me, moist eyes blue as the sky,
And in that moment, lost to all I once knew,
I felt myself his consort. Dancing for me,
For me alone, his sole, his chosen peer,
He deployed himself before my enchanted eyes
In gestures free and playful, hieratic and grave,
Indulgence fused with awesome majesty,
Until I was ready to tender myself his slave,
Almost, almost... A doubt shaded my mind:
Was this, his revelation, his cruelest disguise,
Bright unconcealment his preeminent ploy?

Quicker than thought his features reified;
A mask upreared, not smiling as before,
Its broad mouth twisted into a ludic leer,
From which a tongue, rude, lecherous, protruded,
The face of Gorgo, love transformed to fear,
The sneer of a sniggering, petulant, ancient child,
Polymorphously self-pleasuring, obscene,
Thick snakes coiling, uncoiling in her hair,
Tusks sprouting from her forehead to impale
Some crude impostor not yet turned to stone
By her petrifying need to seize, possess.

The mask was lifted. In its place a skull
Flashed fast before me, the last shreds of skin
Unpeeling from its shut, marmoreal jaws,
The concavities of its temples a searing white,
The all-color color of nothingness. I peered
Through hollow sockets that once harbored eyes

> At the wide and disarticulating sky
> Supersaturated, stained one immaculate hue,
> Engulfing and absorbing my stupefied stare
> Until a strange vision rolled within my mind;

Until the writing of "Talking Head," my poetry, as previously mentioned, had not yet dealt with or acknowledged the disturbing reaches, the dark extremities of my own experience. These experiences tended to involve what psychiatrists, with a typically charming locution, call decompensation, which is a kind of sudden disintegration of the ego, a terrifying and disruptive evacuation of the self in which one experiences a void, lacuna, or abyss in the place where the ego used to be. In some sense, decompensation, a kind of psychosis, is the complementary obverse of self-loss in mystical experience; is the daemonic, dark double, the other side, of mystical ecstasy. In this, decompensation resembles Dionysian ecstasy, in which the god subjects his devotees to a manic state that leads to a type of psychosis. Manic states at their most extreme *do* often, of course, lead to psychosis that often often involves a kind of superhuman strength on the part of those, like the maenads, afflicted with it.

In the passage that follows the one just cited, Dionysus, who seems able at will to infiltrate Orpheus' mind, to project on its inner screen a kind of cinema of derangement, subjects Orpheus to a "strange vision," which takes the form of an hallucination of the Ganges. This vision manifests in two parts, the first of which presents a conventionally pious tableau of Indian Brahminical spirituality, of devotees reverently and contemplatively immersing themselves in sacred waters, an act which is aligned with Vedic orthodoxy. The second, however, portrays the world and practices of the Kapalikas, a Shaivite sect representative of the transgressive, antinomia strain of tantric spirituality in which adepts, performing prohibited, repulsive, nocturnal rites amid the smoke and stench of cremation grounds, seek to overcome not only attraction to the seductive things of this world but an equally involuntary aversion toward that which inspires revulsion and disgust.

If this insertion of a vision of India into a poem about a Greek demigod seems odd, I should briefly note that when Alexander reached India and visited shrines dedicated to Lord Shiva, he regarded, in a remarkable feat of the syncretic imagination, Lord Shiva and Dionysus as essentially one, as a result of which Shiva temples and the worship conducted in them were left undisturbed. Indeed, the great French polymath Alain Danielou and others have noted the quite remarkable homologies between the world views, mythic underpinnings, and rites and practices of the cults of Dionysus and Shiva, suggesting that they emerged from a common matrix. Both cults are seen by established religions as foreign, as conductors of a promiscuous, unpredictable, chthonic life force that is akin to that of nature itself. Their presiding deities are regarded as dangerous interlopers, as threats from without to established polities and their social orders and hierarchies, including their pantheons of gods of the sky.

That which apparently irrupts from without, which seems foreign to the rational mind, when not acknowledged and respected, has the insidious power to subvert both polities and individuals as though from within. Though traces of this strain of spirituality can be found in the West, it has mostly been repressed.

After the devastating epiphany just recounted, in which Orpheus is indeed subverted from within, the subsequent events of his sad career are ineluctably set in motion. Orpheus decides to flout Apollo's interdict, his demand that Orpheus not return to the sylvan lakes that were once his home. Alas, however, Orpheus' brief return to the site of his youthful happiness serves only to underscore all that he has lost. Nature and creatures both tame and wild are now indifferent to him, and the young soldiers who were once entranced by his poems have vanished. Orpheus is now radically alone. Meanwhile, the strangely stately matrons who are soon to accost him lie in wait, then perform their savage duty.

And so Orpheus' ghastly posthumous or not-quite-posthumous career as a severed head begins. Orpheus' bodiless head and the numerous allusions to decapitations in the poem seem to me a metaphor for subsequent tendencies in Western societies in which too often the head, the intellect, is severed from the body, the intellect from the heart, a severance which is analogous to Orpheus' rejection of the feminine. I recall in this context what I had quite consciously conceived of many years prior as the proper role of the poet or at least of my poetry. Poetry had seemed to me—with its unique combination of discursive and non-discursive elements, with its wedding, as it were, of words and music, including the music of the breath and the heartbeat—to be singularly well-suited to effectuate a marriage of the head and the heart.

And yet here in my perhaps most ambitious poem, I was writing of their final sundering. This severance, along with the many other psychic, spiritual, and political fault lines traced in "Talking Head," results in a kind of madness, a madness given voice to by Orpheus in a wild soliloquy in which he first likens his fate to that of Coleridge's "Ancient Mariner," with the crucial difference that he will be granted no respite, not even that of death itself:

> O, nightmarish *life-in-death* and *death-in-life*
> Of which one later singer had heart to tell
> Who became the mute Orpheus of his inner hell,
> Though he at least was granted the grace to die,
> His obsessive perseverations thereby stilled,
> Distilled into the notes some remember him by,
> You grant me no respite. I cannot wake and die
> But eddy on like the Hebron in which my top
> Was tossed like refuse by some bloodied hand.

In the immediately following stanza, Orpheus' shattered ego attempts to wrest some degree of control, if only delusory, from chaos by issuing a kind of mad commandment, a fiat that in fact pointlessly ratifies a state of psychic disintegration that is a fait accompli mandated not only by his internal conflicts but by external forces beyond his control—the lawless forces that when spurned lead to misrule rather than to rule, and that propel him he knows not whither.

> I commanded myself: let *I* now stand for *head*,
> Shorthand for the part still left of me, its pith
> More corporeal, more real, than my abstract *self*,
> A concept depleted of all its inherited wealth.
> *So henceforth shall it be.* Thus I decreed it
> Who had no further power to set the terms,
> The rules for the misrule by which I was led,
> Misled, launched on my false pilgrimage
> Toward nowhere I had the knowledge to predict;
> By rights my syntax, too, might have been mangled,
> Though I was left, small solace, the gift of speech
> Yet granted no audience for my protestations—
> Which, had it assembled, would have spurned them
> As if each tender ear were plugged with wax.

By the end of the poem, of course, Orpheus is stripped by Apollo even of the power of speech.

Finally, I do not mean to suggest, in any of the above, that I favor the Dionysian and its ecstatic, often unruly elements over the contemplative, orderly, harmonious realm of the Apollonian. Rather, as with all apparently polar opposites, they are in some sense complementary, as the possible hidden accord between Apollo and Dionysus in the poem suggests. The relationship between the two gods, like that of Vishnu and Shiva, is susceptible to a kind of partial alignment that recognizes the necessity of both.

There is nothing essentially wrong with Orpheus' youthful Apollonian vision. He mistakes its "breathing cosmos," which is in fact a kind of pastoral microcosm, for the wider world of the cosmos itself, and so is unable to incorporate within himself, and come into alignment with, the Dionysian as well.

The possibility of alignment between Apollo and Dionysus as deities, and between the intra-psychic forces that correspond to then, entails also the possibility of a radical and catastrophic disruption of that alignment, a disruption manifest not only within the individual psyche but also within society. Such societal dislocations may reveal themselves in individuals, but they are often beyond any given individual's capacity to remedy or allay.

4.

Having, as it were, earned my spurs by writing, in "Talking Head," a complex narrative, I want to suggest some of the implications of the poem with regard to narrative itself. I would begin by observing that in leading our lives, all of us, some more successfully then others, are constructing narratives. We do not typically experience the events of our lives as entirely or merely random, haphazard, or contingent. Rather, we *lead* our lives, attempt to shape them, in a way that satisfies a quintessentially human hunger for meaning, a hunger that is satisfied in any number of possible ways. In the living of our lives, we are at the same time engaged in the process of making sense of them, or of ensuring that they make sense.

At times, however, for some of us, events irrupt that are so unexpected, so anomalous, so radically painful and new, that they threaten not only to disrupt but to entirely scuttle the narratives we have so painstakingly and for so long been constructing. At this point some sort of recuperation in the form of a new narrative or a drastic emendation of the old is required, one in which radically anomalous events are eventually assimilated into some new structure and are thereby, once again, granted a semblance of meaning. But there are cases, of course, in which such anomalous events are so radically, horrifyingly disruptive that no recuperation takes place.

From a historical, not merely a personal perspective, one might ask, for example, as many poets and historians have asked, if the Holocaust can be recuperated, become part of a new narrative in which its horrors become meaningful. The answer is that for many who lived through the Holocaust, such a recuperation is not possible. On a larger, more historical scale, there is a question as to whether, even were it possible, an event like the Holocaust *should* be recuperated, and thus in a sense domesticated. For many, including the great post-war Jewish poet Paul Celan, who was enslaved in a forced labor camp from which he eventually escaped, and both of whose parents died in concentration camps, such a recuperation seemed falsifying. Celan's poems read like the shattered remnants of some terrible explosion. I discuss him in the context of Lurianic Kabbalah in the last essay in this book.

With respect to Orpheus' fate in "Talking Head," he is confronted with just such anomalous events. In his case, the radical disruption of his life becomes so extreme that that there is *no* possibility that the fate he has suffered can become assimilated to a new structure of meaning—a realization which, when registered, leads to a terrible and irrevocable despair. The self, or the remnants of the self, are torn, traduced, undone, marked only by the violent traces of a terminally disruptive event.

There is a brief passage in "Talking Head" in which Orpheus attempts to describe or evoke the nature of such an experience.

The mind is its own place? Well, not entirely.
I'd become, as sophists say, *the contested site*
Of irreconcilable forces that now controlled me,
Converging from without, emergent within,
The self, self-scandalized, traduced, undone,
A gutted field, a text ripped, shredded, burned;
The strings of a lyre vandalized and slashed;
Half-finished figures cut from a shattered loom,
Meaning shorn of context, orphaned, misplaced,
Its butchered fabric dangling severed threads;
Disembodied echoes sealed in an empty room;
An effigy formed of straw stuffed in a tomb;
Bare substance, uncreated, poor, forked thing
From which—as something else--I was reborn,
Divorced from the plighted life I dreamed I led,
Blank legend that my name no longer named,
As insubstantial, lost, as the absent wind
That still refused to rustle through my glades.

The words "text" and "textile" have, of course, the same root. The narratives of
our lives, when they generate satisfying meanings, are like a textile woven from many
strands, which ultimately create, as in a tapestry, a coherent picture. But when too-
disruptive events occur, it is as though these threads are brutally severed, shorn. In
the brief passage alluded to above, Orpheus deploys this as well as other metaphors
to evoke the nature of his irredeemable state.

Finally, as my writing of "Talking Head" thankfully drew toward a close, it
seemed to me that the very end of Orpheus' story—his installation, like a kind of
potted plant, in a temple to Apollo, wherein he becomes an unwilling oracle—was
perhaps so grotesque, so over the top, as to seem almost a kind of parody of tragedy
rather than genuinely tragic.

It occurred to me, as I began to write this last passage of the poem, that mordant
humor was required. I instinctively turned to Samuel Beckett, a figure whom Harold
Bloom, with his sometimes uncanny insight, calls "the saintly Beckett." To find the
tone I was after, I decided to reread *Endgame*. I was about halfway into this reading
when a friend called and said that he had an extra ticket that night to what turned
out to be a superb production of *Endgame* starring John Turturro, who declaimed
his lines, brilliantly, with a kind of Shakespearean orotundity at once grandiose,
funny, and touching. Here was the voice I was looking for.

I have decided to let Orpheus have his voice again here, to draw to the end of
this piece by citing the conclusion of "Talking Head." Here, Orpheus expresses, as in
the beginning of the poem, his weary objection to all the sentimental poems that

have been written about him, as well as his disgust that his name has been associated with so-called Orphic cults, often allied with those of Dionysus, for which he feels a literally undying contempt.

> *So many words have been forced into my mouth*:
> Elegies, lyrics, soliloquies, sonnets enthralled
> By noble panegyrics, proud poets' skilled
> Self-flattery tricked out in my borrowed guise,
> Their heads bay-crowned, my cruel fate falsified,
> My ruptured flesh, my seasonless inner hell,
> Atrocity's garbled shame, its torturous syntax,
> Smoothed out in rolling numbers, tolling rhymes,
> All forcing me to bear glib hymns of praise:
> *O Orpheus, O tall tree in the ear!*—from which,
> Bent low, dismasted, unmanned, cut down
> I, too, like luckless Pentheus, was uncrowned.
>
> Enough! Enough sublime, stentorian lines;
> It is time, past time: I refuse to ventriloquize,
> Charge all to heed the ultimate reprimand
> That brave Apollo poured in my stopped ears:
> Even now can you not curb your wagging tongue?
>
> For God's sake, turn away, let me be silent;
> I suffer blank, unspeakable, tractless days,
> Each pinned to the ruined pediment of no future
> As pain sifts through my brain as through a sieve—
> O, sleepless nightmare, truth wracked past belief!
>
> Quit me, now, be *quiet*—and dream that you live.

In simply letting Orpheus have his voice here, I am attempting to circle back to the proposition, or the proposition in the form of a warning both to myself and to the reader, with which I began this essay—that once a poem is out of a poet's hands it is no longer his or her own; that the poet has no special authority over it and that moreover is likely to be a particularly unreliable exegete of it. He or she may well be blind to aspects of it that might seem obvious to any competent reader, who moreover is likely to tease out any number of implications that might come as happy revelations to the poem's author. And so the voice of Orpheus in "Talking Head" is not mine, is not that of a ventriloquist's dummy, but is his own. The poem's future auditors, if it is to have any, alone will reanimate that voice while translating it into new dimensions that are beyond my ken.

Any poem of lasting worth has a surplus dimension, or dimensions, that is/are neither exhausted nor exhaustible, including not only its subtle architectonics of sound and sense but also something that elides sense, that evades any identifiable meaning or complex of meanings, altogether. All interpretations are reductive. The best, however, are like trails that lead the reader past cultivated land and into a kind of wilderness, both inviting and forbidding, which it is then up to him or her to attempt to navigate. This is mysterious terrain, which can be traversed in any number of ways, some that open out into surprising perspectives while seeming to block or foreclose others.

In closing, I would like to say a few words, hopefully not too egregiously narcissistic, about the nature of the finished product. First, of course, "Talking Head" is a narrative poem, but it is also a poem in which, line by line, I strive to achieve the density and intensity of lyric, to "load every rift with ore," to unleash a full panoply of rhetorical sound effects—alliteration, assonance, medial rhymes, irregular end rhymes, and so on—as well as a wide range of tropes that likewise arise in dense clusters. Finally, I give myself license, as I had so many years ago in writing *The Fall of Miss Alaska*, to indulge in frequent word play, including egregious punning. I hope it does not appear that any of these effects are indulged in for their own sake. I hope, and believe, that their density and intensity help to suggest the extremity of the experiences undergone by the poem's protagonist.

Finally, it seems to me that "Talking Head" is generically indeterminate, or perhaps generically polymorphous. It is not merely a narrative poem, or a narrative poem with the density of lyric, but more fundamentally, I think, a tragedy, or a tragic soliloquy. I have even wondered whether with the right actor, or with the right director, it might be performed as such. Once again, Beckett comes to mind. It occurs to me, if I remember correctly, that one of his last plays was performed by an actor behind a scrim in which there was a small cutout from which only his heavily made up face protruded. Once again, almost literally, a *talking head*.

It may be supremely presumptuous to propose that "Talking Head" can perhaps be read as a prophetic anatomizing of at least part of a state or states of affairs, of what "is the case" culturally, socially, and metaphysically, in the Western world in which I and the poem are situated. What "is the case," contra Wittgenstein, or more properly his reductive progeny, cannot be captured by any speech, act, or syllogism, is proof against all proofs. "Talking Head," though personal, though voicing my own malaise, is I hope more than merely personal. Many of its implications, I likewise hope, outstrip my own all too-limited awareness.

7.

MY LATE LAST LOVE

A Brief Panegyric

1.

I cannot forbear confessing or professing here the last of my poetic loves, Catullus. Scholars agree that he was born around 80 BC in Verona, a provincial outpost far from Rome, a verdant region where his prosperous family thrived. Catullus is generally thought to have left Verona as a youth. He returned only once, at the time of his brother's death, memorialized in one of his most touching poems. He died around 55 BC, in his early thirties.

Catullus' 116 or so extant poems are generally divided into three groups: the so-called polymetrics, written in an almost dizzying array of different meters, which include the first 64 of Catullus' poems that have come down to us; eight longer narrative poems; and finally, a group of epigrams in elegiac couplets. Though I will go on to note that many of Catullus' works have an immediacy of impact that feels almost contemporary, one characteristic is inevitably lost in translation, which is that Catullus' poems display an almost unparalleled mastery of prosody.

Catullus' best known poems are his polymetrics, a number of which praise or disparage his sometime mistress Lesbia, a figure who is in no way an idealized lady. On the contrary, she is a vividly carnal antithesis of Dante's Beatrice or Petrarch's Laura. These poems inaugurated the genre of the Latin love elegy, which found a more decorous expression in Propertius and Horace. But they have more in common with Ovid's *Metamorphoses*, with its serial copulations and depictions of transformations that are as miraculous as those wrought by the powers of a tantric adept, and with his *Ars Amatoria,* full of wonderfully worldly and at times cynical advice poetically tricked out. With Ovid, the love elegy makes a triumphant, sophisticated return to the profane. Catullus and Ovid, despite the latter's nod to Pythagoras at the end of the *Metamorphoses*, are as far from being mystical, or purveyors of mystification, as one could imagine.

Catullus' poems in elegiac couplets are characterized by their unremitting tone of invective. Almost all are addressed to his contemporaries. A number of them indulge in a kind of gleefully over-the-top scatological language, threatening (all in good fun, if not entirely in good fun) various acts of sexual violence against their addressees. Here, as is often the case, such acts—in this case, of course, rhetorical acts—have more to do with power than with sex. Catullus is defending himself and his poems against charges of softness and decadence while asserting his masculinity in a tone that is anything but soft.

Those within Catullus' cenacle, like those of any brilliant in-group of whatever epoch, make a exuberant mockery of those outside it, particularly of those vain, bad poets and corrupt politicians, who are their nominal social superiors, possessors of the capital of influence and power that they, too, covet, but who are in every other way their intellectual and artistic inferiors. Above all, Catullus and his peers were entirely willing participants in the unruly spectacle of the secular life of their epoch. They neither floated above nor sank below it.

Several of Catullus' most charming poems in polymetrics were written to and and about his poetic peers. Among these my favorite is Catullus 50:

> Yesterday, Calvus, idle day
> we played with my writing tablets,
> harmonising in being delightful:
> scribbling verses, each of us
> playing with metres, this and that,
> reciting together, through laughter and wine.
> And I left there fired with your charm,
> Calvus, and with your wit,
> so that, restless, I couldn't enjoy food,
> or close my eyes quietly in sleep,
> but tossed the whole bed about wildly
> in passion, longing to see the light,
> so I might speak to you, and be with you.
> But afterwards I lay there wearied
> with effort, half-dead in the bed,
> I made this poem for you, pleasantly,
> from which you might gather my pain.
> Now beware of being rash, don't reject
> my prayers I beg, my darling,
> lest Nemesis demand your punishment. She's
> a powerful goddess. Beware of annoying her.

The homoerotic tone of this poem is not atypical. Catullus had male lovers—chief among them Juventus, a comely youth—as well as, more frequently, female ones.

The poems of Catullus and his cenacle are entirely of their own moment, a moment that like any moment quickly passed. They seem to me in some way akin to the poems of Frank O'Hara, likewise part of a small cenacle, a circle of poets and painters, many of whom hailed from the proverbial sticks, who were born into circumstances considerably less advantaged than Catullus, who then made their way in the contemporary Rome of New York. O'Hara, who became a curator of the Museum of Modern Art, and who was as sophisticated and erudite as any Alexandrian, bragged of his sexual conquests but had the tact, like his peers, not to show off his erudition. He wrote a number of brief, sometimes epigrammatic, often witty poems that were dashed off with brilliant elan, often during lunch breaks. Though they frequently reference the political, poetic, musical, and cinematic news of the day, they never feel dated. O'Hara, like Catullus, died young, run over by a dune buggy on Fire Island.

Catullus' poems, like O'Hara's, do not feel dated. Indeed, they feel oddly modern and contemporary, and seem to address us with a peculiar immediacy, directness, and force. The trite would-be mystics of our own day prattle about living in the moment. Surely Catullus, like O'Hara, lived in the moment, in the pulsation of an artery, every bit as much did the Blake who in his *Marriage of Heaven and Hell* proclaimed "damn braces, bless relaxes," who was of the devil's party as well as of the angel's, and who, had he read Catullus, would surely have found in him a kindred spirit.

Catullus' poetry can seem, on the one hand, tantric, antinomian, heterodox, and decadent, and on the other as mainstream, in its own way orthodox, conventional, worldly, and in no essential way decadent—which is to say that Catullus is essentially elusive, is neither merely obscene nor merely refined, neither left-handed nor right-handed nor ambidextrous. In the same way, Catullus is neither a hoarder of spiritual capital nor a squanderer of it. His poetry breaks down the distinction between the drearily, self-consciously spiritual and whatever has been or might be taken as the opposite.

2.

The eight narrative poems of Catullus are less well-known than his brief lyrics. The briefest, most lurid, most outré of these poems, Catullus 63, depicts the rites of the cult of Cybele, which originated, like the cult of Dionysus, in Asia Minor. Her male devotees, the *corybantes*, dressed in the plumed and crested garb of warriors, took part in ecstatic dances to the pounding beat of drums, the percussive din most favored by Dionysus. Indeed, the cult of Cybele seems akin to that of Dionysus, but with the gender roles reversed, Cybele's corybantes being a male version of Dionysus' maenads. Those initiated into Cybele's priesthood were required to be castrated. Catullus, himself something of a foreigner, perhaps felt an affinity for these foreign and enticingly mysterious cults. Both in Catullus 63 and at the end of Catullus 64, he conveys something of their disruptive, ecstatic charge.

Catullus 65 and 68b are entirely different in tone. They are moving accounts of Catullus' return to Verona upon the death of his brother, and are the most personal and transparently moving of his narrative poems.

Catullus 64, his epyllion or brief epic, will be my primary focus here. The epyllion, of which Catullus 64 is one of only two extant examples, was thought to have originated in Alexandria during the Hellenistic period, which, like Medieval Spain and Renaissance Italy, was a remarkable center of learning, the site of a confluence of many different philosophical and literary traditions. Philo of Alexandria, a Hellenistic Jew, was its leading philosopher. Callimachus, foremost among the Alexandrian school of poets whose highly cultured and cultivated work tended to be erudite, witty, allusive, ironic, and epigrammatic, was credited as the originator of the epyllion. Though most of his works were lost, he was nonetheless particularly venerated by Catullus and his circle, who adopted his allusive, witty, and epigrammatic style, and who were condemned by their political and literary detractors as decadent for their adoption of foreign forms—a label which they were as happy to embrace as to reject.

Catullus 64 displays his mastery of prosody. It is written, in imitation of Greek epic poetry, in dactylic hexameter, a long line of six feet or metrical units. It deals with mythic material, in no way uncritically, yet at the same time registers something of its seductive power. I find the poem endlessly fascinating for its ring structure, into which I cannot delve here without too involved a discussion; for its scintillating wit; for its extravagant and deliberately over-the-top use of metaphor; for its deliberate scrambling of time frames; for its allusiveness; and finally, again, most of all, for its strange, seductive, ultimately moving power.

The poem begins with a brief account of the mythic marriage of Peleus and Thetis, after which the wedding guests turn their attention to a glorious tapestry that details episodes in the relationship of Theseus and Ariadne. The poem is not only an epyllion but an instance of *ekphrasis*, a genre, as popular now as ever, that depicts and expatiates on works of plastic or visual art and which, in Catullus' case, emphasizes the artfulness of his poetic enterprise.

The poem concerns itself principally with the plight of Ariadne, the daughter of Minos, king of Crete, whose native religion is thought, though archeological evidence is scant, to have centered, like the cult of Cybele, on a female goddess venerated by a youth, possibly her son. Crete was considered foreign and potentially hostile by the Greek city-states and was an active foe of Athens in particular. Theseus' slaying of the Minotaur and abduction of Ariadne could thus be seen from the

Athenian perspective as a civilizing mission, a symbolic vanquishing of a foreign culture.

According to a prominent version of the myth, Ariadne, having served her appointed role in devising the means by which Theseus slays the Minotaur and exits the labyrinth created by Daedelus, thus betraying her own culture, is in turn betrayed, abandoned by Theseus during his return to Athens. She is left behind on the island of Naxos, whereupon she is rescued by Dionysus, becoming one of his many brides. In Euripides' *The Bacchae,* Dionysus is a dangerous subverter and foe of Thebes and by extension the Greek city-states in general. The marriage of Ariadne and Dionysus, both associated with cultures foreign to and in enmity with Mycenaean city-states, is thus symbolically appropriate. And yet one wonders how Ariadne, the product of a sophisticated urban culture, will function in the more chthonic realm of Dionysus that she has entered. Or rather, one does *not* wonder: she will clearly be betrayed by Dionysus, the ultimate shapeshifter, as well.

Catullus 64 is entirely sympathetic to Ariadne and depicts the supposedly civilizing Theseus as an antihero, as a heartless betrayer and cad. The poem, for all of its wit and sophistication, is also remarkably moving in a way that, as it were, sneaks up on the reader. Ariadne has no viable place in the world. She has spurned, irrevocably left behind, her own homeland and culture. Theseus has spurned her, and so she will not be adopted, as she had hoped, by a foreign culture that she has sacrificed much to aid. Finally, again, as the former princess of a highly evolved culture, she will have no viable place in the outlandish world of Dionysus. Her plight speaks to that of any individual who feels some connection with multiple cultures but finds no real place in any, and who thus feels marginalized, existing as though between worlds. The poem addresses the potentially tragic consequences of such a plight, which was in some ways analogous to that of Catullus himself. Self-exiled from his beloved provincial homeland, Verona, nominally an aristocrat but not a noble, Catullus, like his confreres, struggled but ultimately failed to attain any privileged status, any real political or social toehold in Rome. Like the expiring gods of many mystery religions, Catullus died young, leaving scarcely a trace of his existence behind.

Catullus 64 is moving in yet another way. It is rare in any epoch, though Euripides' tragedies are an exception, to find a male poet who so thoroughly identifies with a female protagonist—and this despite the masculine posturing of his briefer, more epigrammatic poems. In sum, Catullus 64, for all of its brilliance, sophistication, and wit, also feels deeply personal, and has real emotional force.

Finally, despite its emotional impact, and unlike Catullus' many briefer poems, which have a strikingly contemporary feel, Catullus 64 feels enticingly foreign. Catullus' work, taken as a whole, is impossible to definitively characterize or pin down.

I will cite two brief excerpts from Catullus 64 below. The first, which seems almost Pre-Raphaelite in its languorous sensuality, portrays Ariadne, half mad and partially, then fully, disrobed, wading out into the waters of Naxos as Theseus departs without her. Both the poem and this excerpt have, however, an authentic force far greater than what one finds in the derivative, decadent confections of the Pre-Raphaelites. The second excerpt depicts the putatively providential arrival of Dionysus' *maenads*, heralding the approach of the god whom she is destined, for better, or mostly for worse, to marry—and to share with countless others, thus finding herself doomed to suffer a series of further betrayals.

The first excerpt is my own version, worked up from prior literal translations. The second is from *The Complete Poetry of Catullus* by David Mulroy, published by the University of Wisconsin Press.

Staring forth from amid wave after breaking wave
resounding on the forlorn shore of Naxos,
bearing a host of wild furies within her heart,
Ariadne, helpless, beholds Theseus' swift fleet departing,
Her spirit scarcely believing what her own eyes see.
As though one awakening from some deceptive dream
She sees herself miserable, deserted on the empty beach,
As her heedless young spouse strikes the shallows with oars,
His promises annulled, abandoned to stormy winds.
The bereft Minoan, draped with seaweed, stares
With sorrowful eyes toward the far horizon.
As frozen and motionless as a statue of Bacchus
She raves as great waves of rage assault her heart,
As her delicate headdress slips from her head,
As her finely woven bodice falls from her pale breasts,
As all else deserts her body, left naked and alone there
As salt waves lap as though in sport at her feet.
Not with some filament of thread but with her whole heart,
With her whole spirit, with her whole mind, although lost
She clung to you, Theseus, as you betrayed her...

Just after these lines is the beginning of what is a long litany of powerful protestations and imprecations, voiced by Ariadne herself, as sternly as Cassandra, her words competing with the sounds of the winds and the waves, retelling the whole of history of her relationship with Theseus from the point of view of its suddenly tragic end. Finally...

From another direction, however, Iacchus was flying
To your side, Ariadne, ablaze with desire for you.
Sileni from Nysa and capering satyrs were there,
Delirious Thyades frantically thronged the divinity,
tossing their heads and chanting the Bacchic "Euhoe!"
some of them brandishing wands with leafy points,
some of them tossing the limbs of a slaughtered bull,
some of them wreathing their heads with coiling snakes,
some of them tending to mysteries hidden in baskets,
mysteries skeptics vainly desire to penetrate;
others were beating drums with lifted hands,
eliciting shrill responses from polished bronze;
many raised a raucous blare with horns;
barbarian flutes were raising their tremulous song.

These passages, taken together, betray both, in the first instance, an almost voyeuristic sensuality, and in the second, a clangorous vigor, both of which were aspects of Catullus' protean and many-sided poetic repertoire. One can only imagine how terrified the formerly privileged, domesticated, and highly cultured Ariadne would have been by the shrill, percussive din typically associated with the uncivilized advent of Dionysus and his riotous horde of daemonic, possessed devotees.

3.

Alas, I encountered Catullus, the last of my great poetic loves, to whom I have offered here a too brief panegyric, too late. But not too late for him to influence one of the last of my poems, "Elegy in Broken Stanzas," my own attempt—considerably, alas, more decorous than those of Catullus—at writing in the genre of the love elegy.

While an undergraduate at Harvard, I was a member of a relatively small circle or cenacle of poets, a congenial group that migrated from one poetry workshop to another. I remember that what was for me the last of these was held not in a classroom but in the apartment of the young poet who was our teacher. Wine was supplied in abundance. Our final assignment was to write parodies of each other's work. Much hilarity of a type not dissimilar to the spirit of Catullus' 50 ensued.

I had a crush on one particularly attractive member of our little group. He and I, as much as is possible in America, shared an aristocratic provenance that both of us were at pains to conceal, partly to avoid being stereotyped, but partly because the power of that provenance was already on the wane. I was also gay. And so in my own way, despite my nominally privileged status, I felt marginal, in some way connected to several worlds, though fully at home in none of them. My childhood dream of being a politician was dashed when I realized, at the age of twelve, that my gay proclivities would not comport with such a career. The writing of self-consciously literary poetry then emerged as an attractive but in no way mainstream alternative avenue for my ambition.

Several weeks after my last poetry workshop as an undergraduate, my paragon and I, along with several others of our cenacle, were invited by one of our group to spend a weekend at her family's house on a bluff overlooking Cape Cod. There, at night on the beach, I almost had a sexual encounter with my charismatic friend but failed, typically, to seize a moment that, like Prufrock's, was "coming to its crisis."

Many years later, at the end of my poetic career, I found myself memorializing an event, apparently trivial and yet revealing much, that occurred near its outset. I had by then landed in what is euphemistically called an assisted-living facility. My state had devolved into a space of fear and terror in which freedom has no place. I found myself as it were discarded, like Ariadne, alone, deserted, abandoned as though on a beach from which some ship, having purloined all that I valued, had set sail, but from which I had no hope of being rescued, not even by the most feckless and disreputable of gods.

But this is another story, one of interest only to me. Assuming that the failure to successfully imitate can also be a sincere form of flattery, I will make the strategic blunder of citing the last lines of my own belated love elegy here, in a context in which it can only pale by comparison. My poem begins with "gladness," with a depiction of the aforementioned cenacle, with the excitements and hopes of my late, lamented youth, but in the lines that I cite, it is clear that their erstwhile narrator, having assumed the retrospective position of old age, has descended, if not into madness, then certainly into a kind of terminal sadness. The author of this poem, who ultimately finds himself alone and deserted on a beach, would clearly identify more with Ariadne than with Theseus.

FROM: ELEGY IN BROKEN STANZAS

...I was an aristocratic boy,
*   you were an aristocratic boy;*
We strove, each in his way, for a nobility of spirit,
A standard I, at least, never quite attained.

Eventually our little group dispersed,
                an inevitable diaspora.
Some, I heard, kept in touch, even organized
A few raucous, high-spirited reunions;

Most, of course, abandoning poetry,
      became conspicuously

Solid citizens with solid professions
And with family circles supported by their toils.

Though never quite relinquishing the mores
                              of our golden cenacle,
I spurned the overtures of my former comrades,
Refusing to face all reminders of loss.

My life grew liminal, vexed, covert,
            relegated to the margins
Of worlds in which, never outgrowing the boy
I once was, still subject to his fears, desires,

Ambitions, I could never feel at home.
                              I labored at my verses
But no longer gladly anticipated an immediate
Response, discerning and sympathetic;

Instead my good works were entrusted
            to my own purview, to an audience of one,
Becoming increasingly hermetic,
Dead to a world in which they had no place.

I kept seeking, my friend, but never met
                              a chosen other in whom
I might lose and find myself–a fruitless ideal
That my love for you had led me to envisage.

It was as though I kept approaching
            a threshold that kept receding
Or vanishing as I grew near, impossible to cross–
Or perhaps, again, I was fearful of crossing it;

Perhaps I unwittingly chose the sole,
                              habitually estranged self
That possessed me, feeling increasingly unreal,
Unreachable, unredeemable, cut off

From the vibrant energy of life itself,
            the wellsprings of grace from which
We once drank, not knowing how lucky we were

Or that they could ever dry up.

Decades later, I am in irrevocable exile.
                              Our brief time together
Feels like ancient history, unchronicled, effaced,
Living only in the shadow house of memory.

Insouciance, wit, intelligence, beauty—
    all have now thoroughly deserted me.
Specters of *age, pain, despondency, madness*
Are my constant, unwanted companions.

Each morning, my friend, it is as though
                    I receive an envelope,
Must extract a page upon which no characters
Appear, upon which I can no longer write

Either poems or the barest outline
    of some new chapter of a life
That now feels effectively over, yet refuses,
Adamantly, to relinquish me,

A page that remains as empty
                    as these leaden hours
That seem to last forever, tending nowhere,
Toward no imaginable, redemptive end.

My will exhausted, I can feel nothing
    but terror and the terror of nothingness;
Whatever word or image arises in my mind
Prompts only a scalding regret.

Yet sometimes I struggle to hold to the notion
                    that the whole of a life
Cannot be judged by any one segment of it,
That its end is no more definitive

Than all that has preceded it,
    that my life has been not only a catalogue
Of errors leading to an intolerable impasse,
That I have performed some acts of dignity, of worth.

And, if time, though felt by us as diachronic,
              is also synchronic
And can be spread out before us like a map
After we cross life's final threshold,

Then somewhere still our little group
    is reconvening, its members all young again,
Laughing, remonstrating with each other,
Their lives lying before them;

Then somewhere, my friend, you are still
              suavely holding court,
Exchanging ripostes with the best of us, or saving,
With a fine generosity, a friend from himself;

Somewhere still we are running exultantly
    on a beach at night, reveling
In our bodies' impossible freedom, not thinking
Beyond ourselves, not thinking at all,

Merely listening, hypnotized, to waves
           surging and retreating,
Their emphatic pulse commingling ecstatically
With the rhythms of our breath and blood;

Still, still we are plunging into the sea,
    waters from which we rise naked, restored,
Recovering a moment, endlessly suspended, in which
We lie together beneath a blazing sky

8.

ROADS TO DAMASCUS

1.

On November 7, 1974, my life took a sudden and irrevocable turn. I had spent the previous summer in Boulder, Colorado at The Naropa Institute, which sponsored a freewheeling Buddhist summer school. The Institute was the brainchild of a controversial Tibetan Buddhist teacher, Chogyam Trungpa Rinpoche. I was not particularly drawn to either Trungpa or his lengthy spiritual disquisitions, but I was searching for inspiration for my fledgling poetic efforts—for an inspiration or stimulus other than that fitfully supplied by alcohol, which I had recently renounced. I decided to try to turn to meditation instead, and each morning, under the tutelage of one of Trungpa's devotees, I spent four hours "sitting." I began quite quickly to feel the beneficial effects of these sessions, effects augmented by the beauty of the environs of Boulder, which, set in the foothills of the Rockies, then had the quality of a smallish Western town. I had never spent time at even a moderately high altitude, and the sky had a kind of ubiquity, and a depth, brilliance, and radiance, that I had never before experienced.

The following fall, I enrolled in an MFA program at Brown University in Providence, Rhode Island. For my first two months there, I was rapturously happy. I was writing freely again and had even embarked upon a love affair that promised to be an additional source of joy. I continued to meditate, and began to feel it would be helpful for me to find a teacher. A friend of mine recommended that I attend an "Intensive," a weekend retreat, sponsored by an Indian guru.

I should stress that at this point I did not consider myself religious. My parents were nominally Presbyterian—indeed I was related on both sides of my family to Puritan divines—but I had never attended church. I considered myself agnostic. I was hoping that the retreat would help to deepen my meditation and perhaps supply me with a spiritual guide more congenial to me than the aforementioned Trungpa.

And so it was that I found myself on November 7 in a small, packed meditation hall in midtown Manhattan. The Intensive was conducted not by my soon-to-be guru, who was then residing in his ashram in India, but by one of his disciples. The Intensive included teaching talks and sessions of chanting, but the highlight was four periods of meditation during which all of us, we were told in an introductory talk, would receive *Shaktipat*, an initiation that would awaken in us an inner spiritual energy called *Kundalini*. Though of an inveterately skeptical cast of my mind, I decided to willingly suspend my disbelief—at least for a weekend. Things proceeded pleasantly enough until, about midway through the last session of meditation, something entirely unexpected occurred. I felt arising within me a sudden and overwhelming upsurge of love of a kind I had never before experienced and began to sob uncontrollably. Several minutes later, my diaphragm began, involuntarily, to expand and contract at a rapid rate like a bellows. When the session ended, I asked a hall monitor about this phenomenon. He explained that I had been experiencing *pranayama*, a kind of rapid yogic breathing, the spontaneous manifestation of which was a sign of the awakening of the kundalini.

I returned to Providence in a euphoric and slightly disoriented state. I sensed, or rather knew, that my life would never be the same, that much had been given to me and much would be asked of me. I knew that I would have to suspend the love affair that had so recently and promisingly commenced: those living in my teacher's ashrams were required to be celibate. At the same time, for well over a month, I was in an altered state. I felt in some way reborn and felt, too, particularly on the long walks I began to take, an extraordinary state of loving unity with all that was around me, as though all things were suffused with an inner light, were one with each other and with me, while at the same time they seemed more radiantly, uniquely, and distinctly themselves.

I, of course, connected all of this spooky action at a distance with my guru, who was considered by his disciples to be a saint, a realized master of yoga. In India such figures are regarded as tantamount to God in a human form.

I did not know that for much of the next decade and a half, after graduating from Brown, I would live a celibate life in my teacher's ashrams in India and in upstate New York, nor did I know that I would become an assiduous student of a tantric tradition called the nondual Shaivism of Kashmir. Its chief exponent was a medieval philosopher/saint, Abhinavagupta, whose theological treatises had, until the early twentieth century, been little known in the West, but whose writings on aesthetics, from the time of their appearance until this day, have been in India the canonical works on the subject, far surpassing in prestige that of Aristotle's *Poetics* in the West.

My intent here, however, is not to expatiate on yoga but to redress the relative absence of any account of Christian mysticism and other forms of Western mysticism in my prior book, *Some Segments of a River*, subtitled *On Poetry, Mysticism, and the Imagination*, which explores the resonances of Eastern spiritual traditions, chief among them Kashmir Shaivism, with literary texts both Eastern and Western. Among the Western poets I discuss at some length are Stevens, Keats, Shelley, and Blake, none of whom, with the exception of Blake, were Christian. Thus the reasons for the lack of anything but a passing discussion of Christian mysticism in my prior aforementioned book is too obvious to state.

2.

It somehow always surprises me to recall that I have spent a considerable amount of time in graduate school. Shortly after having received spiritual initiation from my guru, at the beginning of my two-year stint in the MFA program at Brown, I took a course in "The Bible as Literature." Previously, during my life as a non-militant agnostic, born into a family of non-militant agnostics, I had neglected seriously reading the Bible almost as successfully and assiduously as I had neglected going to church; neither, during brief instances of exposure, had managed to stir my imagination.

But after I had received initiation by my guru in my early twenties, both the Old and New Testaments, which had seemed dense, opaque, and distant from my concerns as a fledgling poet, suddenly opened up to me. My attention, when turned to the Gospels themselves, seemed to me to reveal, in the figure of Christ, one who was much like my own guru, and whose teachings, particularly those purported to be transcriptions of his own words, seemed entirely consonant with my preceptor's. The Old Testament, with its fundamental myth of exodus and return, and with its continued episodes, post-exodus, of estrangement and recovery, likewise spoke to me in a new and compelling way as providing metaphors for the spirit's struggles on the spiritual path.

During the fall semester of my second year at Brown, I attended the most inspiring seminar in which I have ever participated. Conducted by a brilliant young associate professor named Jack Irwin, it was entirely focussed on Michelangelo's frescoes in the Sistine Chapel and on *King Lear*. The excitement of attempting to decode Michelangelo's theological program as reflected by the images on the Sistine ceiling awakened in me a fascination for the complexities of interpretation and hermeneutics in general. I began to become engrossed by iconography and read Irwin Panofsky and others on the subject. At the same time, *King Lear*, read with scrupulous attention to its biblical context, began to disclose some of its darker mysteries to me, which was a devastatingly moving experience. Thereafter, I found myself reading Shakespeare with a deeper awareness and sensitivity. Finally, I was at that time ardently reading Blake as well, which involved attempting to decode not only his densely allegorical prophetic poems but also the engraved images that accompany them.

During a subsequent break or sabbatical from the ashram, a brief abortive year as a graduate student at Penn, I had the chance to continue my study of iconography in general and of Michelangelo in particular. I took a course with the brilliant and controversial art historian Leo Steinberg, whose interpretation of the panels of the

Sistine ceiling and of the Last Judgement trace vectors or lines of significance not only within but between or across its frescoes. His essays on these subjects were revelatory and entirely convincing to me.

Steinberg's analysis of the "Conversion of Saul"— an extraordinary depiction of the almost violent *suddenness* of conversion—called to mind with particular directness my own powerful, likewise transformative experience of spiritual initiation. I conceived of the idea of writing an ekphrastic poem on the painting and wrote the two opening lines in iambic pentameter. I soon realized that I was not yet up to the task of writing a long poem in blank verse, but as it turned out, I would take it up again and complete it years later.

Crucially, and most importantly, while at Penn I took a year-long course on Dante, which was a rapturous experience for me. I found the *Divine Comedy*, and in particular the "Purgatorio" and the "Paradiso," enthralling, and was drawn to Dante's balance, in his peerless poem, between the sweetness of divine love and an uncompromising spiritual and intellectual rigor.

In seeking to come to a deeper understanding of Dante, I read Augustine's *Confessions*, which I found not only moving, but somehow contemporary, in no way dated or a relic of the past. It is a particularly remarkable example of a text in which, as in Dante, the way of love and the way of the intellect are almost perfectly balanced. Augustine's discussion of his mother Monica's intercession leading him to the love of Christ is deeply moving; she becomes a kind of figure for the Virgin Mary. At the same time, I found Augustine's discussion of time and its relationship to eternity both intellectually brilliant and spiritually profound.

In *Some Segments of a River*, I have touched upon the distinction between apophatic mysticism, which embraces a conception of God as utterly transcendent, devoid of any definable qualities or attributes, and cataphatic mysticism, which ascribes some positive qualities to God and regards Him as at least to some degree immanent in the phenomenal world. Among Christian authors with an apophatic bent, I was particularly struck by St. John of the Cross—whose *Dark Night of the Soul* takes the form of exquisite commentaries on verses that he himself wrote, verses that are deliberately reminiscent of the *Song of Songs*—as well as by the remarkable sermons of Meister Eckhart.

But I was particularly drawn to the writings of medieval Catholic authors with a more cataphatic bent, works that stress God's sacramental presence in the world. I found the works of Saint Bernard of Clairvaux ineffably touching in their combination of simplicity, clarity, and understated lyricism. Bernard was himself not only a preacher but also an occasional poet. His writings stress in particular the central tenet of Christianity, the incarnation of God as man, the ultimate instance of the presence of the transcendent in the immanent as not only memorialized but actualized in the Eucharist, which is the lynchpin of Christianity's cataphatic bent and the source of its antipathy to all forms of dualism. They stress, even more strongly, the essential role of Mary as a divine intercessor through whom both divine grace and the vision of God can be attained. Thus in the very last cantos of Dante's "Paradiso," it is Bernard who replaces Beatrice as Dante's guide, leading him ever more deeply into an apprehension of the mysteries of his final visions, first of Mary, the Queen of Heaven, then of the triune deity itself. Bernard's exaltation of Mary recognizes, of course, a feminine energy instinct in the innermost recesses of the divine that is an essential aspect of other spiritual traditions as well, and which would otherwise be lacking in Christianity—as it is in Protestantism, in which the figure of Mary plays a far less prominent role.

I found myself drawn, too, to the writings of St. Bonaventure, to his loving enumeration of the ranks of the angels who represent stations on the soul's way to God. Bonaventure's cast of mind seemed to me to be profoundly poetic and imaginative, and his writing, like that of Bernard, to exude both an elegant simplicity and an ineffable sweetness. In some ways, I felt closer to writings of these mystics, which have not only a spiritual but also a specifically Western literary quality, than to the sutras, the pithy aphorisms, often followed by lengthy philosophical commentaries, which constitute the form of many of the Eastern mystical texts over which I have pored.

In the process of further augmenting my understanding of Dante and of Christianity, I encountered a critical work that had a more profound and visceral impact on me than any other I had yet read, with the possible exception of Northrop Frye's *Fearful Symmetry*, a brilliant and inspired examination of Blake's thought. I am referring to a seminal essay, "Figura," by the great German scholar and philologist Erich Auerbach, in which he traces the origin and development of typological readings of the Bible, a mode of reading adopted by Dante which became a key structural principle of the *Divine Comedy*.

The subject of typology and of its fourfold scheme is far too complex for me to adequately broach here. In the simplest possible terms, the four levels of the typological scheme adopted by Dante, which he appropriates under the rubric of "the allegory of the poets," are the literal; the typological proper or the figurative; the moral or tropological; and the anagogic. Typology became a means of relating *figures,* characters or events from the Old Testament and in the case of Dante, figures and events from pagan antiquity as well, to their *fulfillment* in characters or events of the New Testament—most centrally to Christ and to the events of his life, including his death and resurrection. The literal or first level in typology's fourfold scheme is the foundation of the others, though in itself it is inadequate. The second level, the figurative, involving the relationship of figure to fulfillment, is key to the understanding of scripture. It involves a recognition of the conjunction of the eternal and the temporal in the unfolding of God's providential plan as it works itself out not only in history writ large but in the history of the individual soul. The third level, the moral or tropological, involves as well the reader's ability or inability to understand the characters and events of the Old and New Testaments both literally and figuratively; it stresses that the ultimate disposition of the soul and body is at stake in the reading or misreading of the Bible. This final settling of spiritual accounts, at the apocalypse foretold in the *Book of Revelation*, is the final or anagogic level, which is fundamentally oriented toward the future—a future, however, in which the final synchronic identity of past, present, and future, and the final, eternal fate of those whose have become one with God, will ultimately be realized. Those who are able to read scripture with the eye of the spirit and to conduct themselves accordingly are assured of salvation.

The fascination typology held for me involved its revolutionary revision of the nature of allegory. The transcendent does not merely float abstractly above the literal, whose primary function is to offer a series of narrative counters which point to it, and which having performed this function are dismissed as of little account. Rather, both figure and fulfillment are concrete, historical events in which the transcendent spirit is fully present both physically and temporally. Through its unfolding in time, the transcendent is ultimately, with the return of Christ promised in the *Book of Revelation*, immanently realized. In typological readings, the immanent and the transcendent are intimately related in a way in which they are not in simple forms of allegory, which, as a kind of two-tiered system in which the significance of events on the literal level is exhausted by pointing to abstract truths, to the argument of a conceptual meta-discourse, seemed to me essentially, structurally dualistic. It is precisely typology's insistence on the intimate relationship of the immanent and and transcendent in the concrete unfolding of history, as well as its intricacy, subtlety, and complexity when employed by Dante as one of the structuring principles of the *Divine Comedy*, which was and is the source of my interest in typology.

In the two years immediately following my guru's death, during which I pursued a master's degree at Columbia, I took several courses on my beloved Romantics but focused primarily on typology as a structuring principle in various works of English literature. In some forms of Protestantism, typological readings of the Bible were influential. I ventured typological readings of Spencer's "Epithalamion" and of Milton's "Lycidas." Several other such essays written while I was at Brown or Penn followed: on "The Drunkenness of Noah," one of the panels of the Sistine ceiling; on a canto in Dante's "Purgatorio;" on Blake's "Milton," and on the relationship between Shelley and Milton. All—stacked in one box in my assigned bin in the underground storage room of my parents' apartment building—I carelessly and all too typically managed to lose.

In the course of my studies on Christian poetry, I read Auerbach's magisterial *Mimesis*, which chronicles the fruitful tension in Western literature between the allegorical, whose ur text is the Bible, with its relative paucity of foreground details, with its gaps and lacunae suggestive of a metaphysical background, and the mimetic, whose ur texts are the *Iliad* and the *Odyssey*, which concentrates on the meticulous filling in of the foreground details of the phenomenal and human worlds. *Mimesis* tracks, chapter by chapter, the increasingly sophisticated syntheses of these two modes.

I also read Frye's *The Great Code* and *Words of Power*, his two late works on the structure of symbol and myth in the Bible and on the subsequent poetic expressions of this structure in literary texts. These books seemed to me a bracing recovery—after the categorical doldrums of his *Anatomy of Criticism*, and several other books in which the urge to generalize trumps sensitive attention to minute particulars—of the power and impassioned argument of *Fearful Symmetry*. Finally, I encountered Kenneth Burke's remarkable and too-little-read last book *The Rhetoric of Religion*, likewise a brilliant excavation, from a literary point of view, of the rhetorical structure of the Bible.

Of course, I have felt and still feel a deep affinity with many specifically Christian English poets, from the medieval author of *The Pearl*, to the seventeenth-century metaphysical poets, to Christopher Smart, to Bake, and to Hopkins' ecstatic, or in some cases anguished and *darkly* ecstatic sonnets, and finally to Eliot's "Four Quartets," to whose charms I confess I am not entirely immune.

Christianity, until the age of the Victorians, has been a constantly flowing stream in English poetry, though it has occasionally run underground in periods when Neoclassicism becomes prevalent, as it does in the poetry of Ben Jonson and Alexander Pope, and in the later eighteenth century the work of somewhat lesser luminaries such as Oliver Goldsmith and Thomas Gray.

The Victorian era was also the era of Charles Darwin and of an overweening empirical science that seemed to have no place for God and to leave man at sea, bereft and disoriented. Matthew Arnold's "Dover Beach" is the most condensed and most moving expression of this predicament, but his longer verse dramas feel studied and dry. Browning was primarily a secular poet, as was Tennyson, apart from his "In Memoriam," which although it has Christian overtones, in essence seems to be an obsessively reiterated, numbingly pious, secular canonization of his beloved Hallam. Swinburne, a poet of great ingenuity and formal skill, developed his own decadent, daemonic form of Neoclassicism, while the more roughhewn Hardy was famously agnostic, the apostle of a natural world whose immanent will is either hostile or indifferent to man. Gerard Manley Hopkins, whose work I will discuss in the subsequent essay in this volume, is singular among the great Victorian poets in his wholehearted embrace of Christianity.

Of course, in our own era the death of God has become old news; it has been occasionally thematized, even by poets, like Wallace Stevens, who otherwise seem sensitive to spiritual concerns.

The seventeenth century, in contradistinction, was the great age and flood tide of religious poetry in England, the epoch of John Donne, George Herbert, Andrew Marvell, Richard Crashaw, Henry Vaughan, and Thomas Traherne. These various members of the so-called metaphysical school seem to me, however, to be yoked by violence together; their dissimilarities are as notable and instructive as their similarities.

Marvell had the most secular temperament of the aforementioned, canonical six, though, of course, his great poem "The Garden" has resonances to the garden of Eden. There is a peculiar mix of urbane smoothness and mysterious uncanniness in this poem, as in others of his, that I find compelling and mysterious.

Strange to say, I find Herbert the least congenial of the Metaphysicals. The elegant regularity of his meter; the perfection of the many forms he assayed; the relative lack of any kind of spiritual struggle in his poems, as well as a sweet assuredness in the of the efficacy of God's grace, at least as it pertained to him; his strict adherence to harmony and unerring sense of proportion, with each of his poems finding its due place within the architectonics of his book *The Temple* as a whole—all somehow, despite myself, leave me relatively cold.

I feel most drawn to Donne and to Vaughan for quite disparate reasons. The immediacy with which Donne addresses his erotic partners in his early love poetry, and us, his readers, in his later devotional works; his strenuous yet playful use of logic and argument that somehow, at the same time, subverts and transcends logic; his love of paradox; the frequent roughness and irregularity of his meters, for which he was chided in his own time, but which seem to me to reflect a kind of vigor of thought and feeling—all draw me to Donne, as does the sense of continuity between his early amatory and his late devotional verse. "The Ecstasy" seems to me not only one of the greatest lyric poems in the English language, but one of the most profoundly mystical.

I love Vaughan's poetry for other reasons. His lyrics lack the strenuous rhetorical argument, playful or otherwise, found in Donne's poetry, and the meticulous architectonics of Herbert's. They sometimes seem to meander, after promising beginnings, at midstream, then to trail off. Still, they have their own peculiar directness and sweetness, and how strong their powerful beginnings are, of which the first stanza of his poem "The World" is a justly celebrated instance:

> I saw Eternity the other night,
> Like a great ring of pure and endless light,
>   All calm, as it was bright;
> And round beneath it, Time in hours, days, years,
>   Driv'n by the spheres
> Like a vast shadow mov'd; in which the world
>   And all her train were hurl'd.

Vaughan seems to me, among the Metaphysicals, the purest type of the mystic. When after finishing my final year at Brown I prepared for my first year-long stint in my guru's ashram in India, I resolved to give up reading Western poetry for a time and to begin the process of studying Indian scriptures, the only book I brought with me was Vaughan's *Collected Poems*. I don't recall how often I actually consulted it, but I do recall that having the volume in my possession was somehow comforting, a reminder of a world I had at least temporarily left behind.

I would be remiss not to mention Milton's great epic here, though the concerns of "Paradise Lost" are more polemically theological than mystical. One cannot adequately grasp the accomplishments of the major Romantic poets without taking Milton's influence into account. Though put off by his theological program, they, at least in their youth—with the exception of Keats, who was relatively apolitical— were sympathetic to the tide of revolution that swelled in their day as in his. The largeness of Milton's ambition, if not of his views of the divine, were reflected in the scope and power of their poems. His influence on Keats' first attempt at an epic, *Hyperion*, was perhaps too strong. Later, taking Dante as his model, he was able to overcome that influence in his revised but likewise unfinished *The Fall of Hyperion*.

Blake famously wrote that Milton was of the devil's party without knowing it, responding no doubt to the dark sublimity of Satan's rhetoric, and his feeling that Milton's prowess as a poet is particularly on display in his depictions of the angels' revolt—far more so than in his account of the the archangel Gabriel's attempts, later in the poem, to "justify the ways of God to man." The great Milton scholar Stanley Fish would only partly agree with Blake. Granting the sublime persuasiveness of Satan's rhetoric, he deems it as an essential instance of Milton's strategy throughout the poem, which is to impart to the alert reader an awareness of his or her susceptibility to being duped by demonic temptation, to being—and I am quoting here the title of Fish's book on Milton—surprised by sin.

Dante, of course, as has often been pointed out, deploys a similar strategy in his "Inferno," which includes many instances in which he, and through him his readers, feels a kind of natural sympathy for many of the the damned, only to be sternly rebuked by his guide Virgil. I have mentioned, however, that Dante combines as a poet both great rigor and surpassing sweetness. The latter becomes more and more powerful as *The Divine Comedy* progresses, at first in "Purgatorio," then in "Paradiso," in which Dante's rhetoric is every bit as persuasive as, if not more persuasive than, it is in "Inferno." Milton possessed Dante's rigor, but not his simplicity of diction and sweetness, and as a result seems a less than persuasive apologist for God and for his heavenly order.

I have mentioned above that when I first received spiritual initiation from my guru, I instinctively, and almost immediately, felt that much had been given to me and much would be asked of me. I probably sensed that the road ahead would not be easy, as indeed it was not. I instinctively resonated with the notion that self-sacrifice was a key part of spiritual life, and that this notion is closely aligned with the Christian notion of redemptive suffering, the key instance of which in Christianity is, of course, God's incarnation in the form of only begotten son for the benefit of mankind, as well as Christ's crucifixion, the ultimate exemplification of both divine and human self-sacrifice.

The concern with the wages of sin is a cardinal concern, though less hypertrophied, of Catholicism as well as Protestantism. The recognition of suffering as connected with the problem of evil, as well as the possibility of redemption, can be seen as more pointed than that of any Eastern mystical tradition. Kashmir Shaivism and other tantric traditions that I have discussed in previous books scarcely touch on the subject of evil and its attendant suffering at all. Vedanta, the most mainstream, orthodox school of conventional Brahminical Hinduism, speaks of ignorance—and its attendant illusion and delusion—rather than evil as the source of suffering. Even Buddhism, in which suffering is seen as the essential fact of the human condition, a recognition from which all else follows, likewise has no notion of evil or sin as a force, though it ruthlessly anatomizes illusion.

I will not dwell at any great length here on the role of Satan and of the notion of original sin in Christianity, and of the inevitable dualism that the notion of Satan as a very real force, as the source of evil and suffering, seems to imply, the overall monistic thrust of Christian mysticism notwithstanding. Nor will I discuss the notion of Adam's transgression as resulting in a *felix culpa* or fortunate fall which mitigates the apparently dualistic implications of Satan's role, revealing him, ironically, despite his assuming the mantle of an independent agent, as an actor in God's providential plan. Such concepts are doubtless familiar to those with even a cursory familiarity with Christianity and need not be belabored here.

What does deserve some mention in this context, however, is the *Book of Revelation*, which seems to me a pernicious psychotic revenge fantasy appended to the New Testament, and which is thoroughly dualistic in its thrust. To Christian apologists, the era of the *law*, associated with the Old Testament, has been supplanted by a new dispensation, the era of *grace*, associated with the New Testament, but John's wrathful apocalypse seems to return to the era of the law on steroids. I cannot help but wonder how the history of the West would have unfolded had this strange text not attained canonical status as the last word of the New Testament. Though, of course, the Christ of the Gospels recognizes evil as a real force, his primary focus is on at-one-ment, both with the Father with whom he is one, and with the indwelling divinity that is present, and which cries out to be recognized, as a principle and power inherent in man.

The Christ in John's apocalypse, with the *logos* as a double-edged sword grotesquely protruding from his mouth, is a kind of avenging angel intent upon separating the vast legions of unredeemed souls from the the sparse ranks of the redeemed. The *Book of Revelation* has the preternatural clarity of an hallucination—again, a psychotic hallucination somehow granted canonical status. Its undeniably brilliant vividness renders it a genuinely terrifying text.

It seems to me that one of the cardinal aspects of Protestantism, particularly in its more extreme forms, has been an obsessive concern with the *Book of Revelation* and an attendant focus on the ultimately unknowable status of the believer's soul, a focus that has led to equally obsessive and fraught forms of introspection. In the more extreme dissenting forms of Protestantism, first in Calvinism, with its notion of predestination and its stress on the belief that whether the souls of believers were destined for heaven or hell would be revealed only upon their deaths, and later in the Puritan sects that established a beachhead in the New World, Satan seems to be not merely subordinate to God, but almost his equal, and a particularly vexed introspection becomes terrifying in its intensity.

Again, Christianity's, and particularly Catholic Christianity's, propensity toward dualism has tended to be checked by a focus of God's sacramental presence in the world, on Christ's role as *logos*, and on the Holy Spirit's identification with divine love, a love that is also embodied by Mary as a kind of divine intercessor. The Christian mystics upon whom I have focused tend to gravitate toward a non-dual notion of the divine. This is as true of St. John of the Cross as of St. Bonaventure.

In what might be called normative Christianity as it developed in the centuries subsequent to Christ's death, any tendencies, gnostic or otherwise, toward extreme forms of dualism were rigorously suppressed. In the writings of Christian mystics of a cataphatic bent, though man may be fallen, nature, when apprehended with the eye of the spirit, is not. God is apprehended as fully present in nature, which becomes a kind of sacrament writ large, and nature's beauty cannot help but seem miraculous.

Of course, the central sacrament in Christianity is the Eucharist. The Catholic understanding of the Eucharist is that Christ is fully, bodily present in the bread of the Eucharist, as is his blood in the wine, and that in ingesting them the believer becomes incorporate in Christ and can thereby be assured of eventual resurrection. This identity of the blood and wine of the Eucharist with the body of Christ is one of the many scandalous paradoxes that are rife in the New Testament, more scandalous even than the notion that God has assumed the form of a man.

In Protestantism, this identity is, of course, denied, and the Eucharist becomes a kind of similitude or concrete metaphor of Christ's presence in the world, and a remembrance, not an actual reenactment, of the rite as practiced by Christ and his disciples in the New Testament. Man's embodiment and his senses are celebrated in Catholicism in a way that becomes attenuated in Protestantism, in which the written words of the Bible become more important than the sacraments, thus engendering, in my view, a kind of schism between the head and the heart, the head and the body. An indication of the tendency of which I am speaking is the notion, common to a number of prominent twentieth-century theologians, of God as "wholly other." A further symptom of this trend of thought, with its relative devaluing of the body and the senses, is the hostility of much Protestantism to visual art in particular, and the austerity of Protestant churches, in which an appeal to the senses is seen as a dangerous distraction.

3.

I will conclude this essay where I began, with my own experience of initiation or conversion. I mentioned above that not long after my experience of conversion I studied, under the tutelage of Leo Steinberg, Michelangelo's great fresco in the Vatican's Capella Paolina, "The Conversion of Saul," and conceived of the idea of writing a poem about it. I managed, as mentioned, to write only the first two lines of the poem. They were in iambic pentameter, and I had never before written anything other than free verse. It was only ten years later, when I had mastered at least the rudiments of writing in form, that it occurred to me to try to finish the poem. It emerged, in an experience that was unusual for me, all in a rush.

What I have written above is somewhat embarrassingly free of close readings of any kind. The poem that follows, by way of compensation, is itself a kind of close reading—though of a painting, not a poem. It is reflective of my many years of informal and entirely unsystematic reading of Christian texts.

It includes a few quite scandalous liberties, chief among them italicized passages that, because of the exigencies of the poem's meter, take the form of loose paraphrases, rather than direct quotations, of Paul. I hope in this case that poetic license is not too licentious.

In any event, I shall append here, without further apologies, the poem in question.

THE ROAD TO DAMASCUS

After Michelangelo's "The Conversion Of Saul"

His horse rears up. Sharp light is breaking down.
Thrown to the ground, he shields his blinded eyes,
His own name ringing strangely in his ears –
Saul, Saul, why do you persecute me?
His subjects see. Most can't hear what he hears –
The more than natural light bears no clear word
To those who in their terror, too, are strewn
In broad confusion on the barren ground
That tilts as though earth pitches on its axis.
While some stand frozen, others turn and flee,
Exposed rumps rhyming with the horse's rear
That shares, with Saul, the center of the frame –
Shall such humiliation ground humility?

Some twist toward the light, raise useless shields,
Or raise their hands, beseeching, at the glare
(Their arms rudely compressed, thick digits splayed)
While others run, hands clapped against their ears.
Their faces, stunned, reflect awe, wonder, fear,
Or stupefied disbelief, eyes vacant spheres,
Twin zeros trained on infinite emptiness
Like those of the sentry in light's line of fire,
His head turned by the threat it blindly seeks,
Fixed in fierce misdirection athwart Christ's beam.

Beneath him, in yellow vestments, bending low,
A nameless comforter half absorbs the blow
Destined for Saul upon his broad, curved back.
His face is tender, etched with care, concern,
Or with that simple unconcern with self that seems
Maternal, stoic amid reflexive throes of pain.
His arms transform the force that they convey,
Encircling the buckled form of his felled master,
Upholding a torso Saul's arm fails to prop,
But cannot wholly temper love's clear wrath.
Its force annulling distance, Christ's right arm
Alone is straight, extended, impossibly long;
His hand, though high above, still seems to press
Saul's once stiff neck until it bends, gives way,
Tilting his agonized face toward the light,
His martial features softened, suffused, aglow,
The outward sign of some internal vision
That flickers beneath the lids of his hooded eyes
While his midriff, forced by more than gravity,
Is driven toward the fresco's freighted frame.

Just here, at his being's unimagined nadir,
A voice breaks forth from from Saul's exploded core –
Lord, what would you have me do? – Me do? –
You, whose preposterous truth I have fought to deny,
Pitting my every step against gross superstition,
The Lord of ghosts my every word decried
And that Lord's vassals too, his scandalous minions,
The whole detested crew I would have routed
Til not one mongrel upstart shared my field.

But I now lie upon the frozen ground –
Conversus sum, my powerful form contorted.
Meanwhile, it is my host you have scattered,
My indecorous retinue who flee toward the hills,
Disbanded, cloven by one furious moment
Repeated, now, with each beat of my heart,
My captivated heart, each throb no fainting echo,
But bearing the shattering force of Your full charge.
My mind's wings blindly thrash against their cage.

Lord, what would you have me do? And the reply –
Arise now, arise and hasten to Damascus;
It is there that you will hear what you must do.
You, whose life has turned in a moment's compass,
You, with your capsized pride, with your will overthrown,
Your fine intentions blown like whirling sand;
You, who have become my chosen vessel,
Your foundering wisdom destined for this strand;
You, who once imagined you knew who you were
Now find yourself fixed at fate's extremity.
Know all is changed now never to be the same;
Henceforth you will be known by your new name.

Look closer. Paul's rapt face becomes the artist's.
High brow, determined eyes, pugnacious nose
Above a jutting jaw, a cleft grey beard,
The great head rising from a massive frame,
Proclaim a born aristocrat, though roughly cast
As out of common clay. Yet what great force
His whole aspect conveys! Mere painted flesh
Now seems transformed to marble, hardened, set,
As stubborn and obdurate as the hand that carved it.
Arrogance, ambition, grandiosity, pride
Still lurk within that face, recall the godlike man
Whose thought his art ordained to tame the world
And hold its gorgeous forms within his sway,
Forms perfectly proportioned, self contained,
Forever poised within their peeress beauty;
Whether patriarchs, idols, kings, or simple types,
His figures were all classic, made his name.

But now, nearing the limit of life's term,
His face reflects the ravages of his years,
Years filled with vanity's wages, trials, setbacks,
Great projects uncompleted, dreams elided,
His labors bent to the whims of lesser masters,
His fierce will mortified almost unto death.
Regret at others' actions, still more at his own
Have left him, in old age, a man of sorrows
With cause to repent until repentance grows
And, self-accused, he steps before God's bar,
Yearning for God to turn his stubborn soul
By grace or force towards love's elusive end.
He paints in lonely penitence, finds in Paul
The type of his innermost self until both merge
And the artist's face engenders the apostle's,
The past and present fusing beneath Christ's hand.

Behold Paul's ruddy coat, a leathery shroud
That parts from him, an old skin almost sloughed
From which, in vernal colors, he half emerges
As though to rise toward Christ's wheeling sky.
Behold again that face! It could be dreaming
The vision that now contains it, the teeming scene
Still glowing on the chapel's ancient walls.
Perhaps that dream engenders, too, Damascus,
The distant town that crowds the frame's far margin,
Itself a type of the future, a type of that Rome
In which the painter paints, lost in the present
Whose presence guides his brush's every thrust
Toward its mark, the heart that longs to see.

For centuries, pilgrims, artists, we have flocked
Beneath this frame that cannot quite enclose
Its warped, concussive space, it's canted ground
From which Paul's figure seems about to topple,
His tortured face drawn closest to our own.
(But not quite face to face. Our stiff necks crane
To view the impending titan loom above us).
We, too, grow rapt, involved in a design
That draws what's inside out, what's outside in,
That forms, unlike the mind, no false distinctions,

But only love's fretted, vexed continuum.

Christ renders a skewed triangle, inverted;
His left hand points behind him toward the future,
The moving ground on which all viewers stand,
Toward the dim, recessive outpost that shall shelter
His cruel judge dealt a saving reprimand.
Yet all still stand before him. His right arm
Still fires its fierce diagonal, fixing Paul,
Then finds us, its sunk apex, from whence rise
Two humble pages marching toward Damascus,
Proxies through whom we climb the bruited slope
Toward what fragile hope fate holds in store.

Just there, in Paul's near future, our far past,
His captive soul will waken to its plight,
Three endless days lost to an inner night
Refiguring his master's cruel internment,
Faint portents flickering on his mind's dark glass.
Buried within his flesh, both womb and tomb,
Now deaf as well as blind, he cannot hear
His helpless minions whispering in his ears.
A fast, constraining space past all convulsion,
Disconsolate, withheld beyond reprieve,
Shall hem him within its barren straits until,
Reborn to Christ's estranging word within him,
He sloughs his wasted years: behold the man
Delivered past extremity, barely stirring,
Whose outward aspect, calm, betrays no sign
Of that transforming sentence love has wrought,
Whose life, expiring, finally breathes life in.

Impossibly the same, yet wholly changed
As though freshly created, trumping time,
The world floods back, miraculous, to his eyes
From which a subtlest film has been withdrawn.
In the midst of his life journey a new dawn
Sheds potent rays that prime the yielding ground.
His heart's wick flares. It vital flame declares
Arise now and attend the voice within you.
Its light shall spread before you, show the way

That you must follow, even through those days
That seem all darkness. Persevere and praise
The mark that gathers all whose flight is true.

Once having turned, he never once turned back
Like that great word that is both will and act,
An incipient spring forever overflowing
From love's clear moment, changelessly renewed,
In which we live and move and have our being.
His deeds were eloquent, his words were acts
For which he suffered, patient past all telling,
An exile pledged to exile's distant end.
Time and again, while still he boldly tracked
Light's nuances, his inner eye's inflections,
Shadows took shape. Impostors blocked his way.
Mocked, rebuked, imprisoned, brutally wracked,
His flesh a text, a Testament to love's pride –
Let those who boast boast only of the Lord –
He soldiered on. No sophist's tricks could curb
The marshaled prowess of his strenuous tongue
That struggled to uphold, campaigned to serve
The grace in which all hearts are reconciled.
Time's prodigal, his fine, prodigious mind
Wrought transforming tropes that cured the blind,
The progeny his wisdom taught to see
Through paradox love's lucid mysteries.

Fierce, ruthless, brave, untiring, patient, kind,
He travelled every path, left none behind -
Jerusalem, Athens, Corinth, Paphos, Rome
Received his steps, his matchless ministry,
His words sown in no longer barren ground,
His time grown ripe, his hour close at hand.
The letters he sent still reach us to this day;
Though many, we, one body with the Lord
Are grafted each to each, each serving all.
What if some single member should be shorn,
One limb cut down, although most fully flowered?

At last betrayed when finally he reached home,
He prophesied his coming martyrdom.

The time of my departure now has come;
I have fought the valiant fight. My race is run.
I have not broken faith, await the crown
My Lord, a righteous judge, shall proffer me
And all who love him on love's destined day.
Fear not, remember me, and stay the course;
His grace shall guide you to its source and end.

Creator, painter, poet, pride of Rome
Whose ground absorbed Paul's apostolic blood,
The artist scanned his work (few called it good).
But could not rest. His race was not yet run.
His soul, still anxious, still at war within,
Wrestled with doubts his model seldom named,
With galling sins his rigorous poems abhorred.
No demigod, no conquerer, a mere man,
He struggled to submit, not to command;
Humbled, abashed, he dreamed the promised land
His years deferred, still stumbling, on his way,
Until his long life reached its final term.
At last to be human was his proper glory,
His history the epitome of our own.

Jerusalem, Palestine, Syria, New York
In which I write, my hand smoothing the page
From which your handiwork still speaks to me –
All suffer the fretted, vexed continuum,
All share the warped, concussive, gutted ground
Your brave work still conveys. As for the shock
That makes us shudder, shall it be our end
Engendering nothing but blind after-quakes,
Rote, literal echoes, endlessly the same,
Or shall it balk our vengeance, until like Paul,
A shattered vessel that love's wrath would mend,
We wake, newborn, to follow our brightened way
As light floods back, presaging a new day?

Through Michelangelo's fresco we still yearn
To shed, like Paul, despondency's stiff shroud.
The wrenched heart turns, in pain, toward itself
And still keeps turning, and discovers there,

In its own orphaned depths, a depthless clearing,
Love's inward opening opening without,
Love's wordless Word still summoning its answer
That claims its only world, transparent, healing,
A world transformed and endlessly transforming,
Responsive to that consummate life that flows
Within itself and yet keeps overflowing;
His soul, baptized in grace, becomes that body
Forever gathering, vaunting love's excess,
Enshrines that urgent voice that still proclaims
To our long-ravaged ears that yearn to hear:
At last, though yet the same, all shall be changed;
Henceforth you shall be called by your new name.

9.

Hopkins' Ecstasies

1.

The facts of Gerard Manley Hopkins' life are too well known to be rehearsed here. Nonetheless, the most singular, decisive, dispositive act of his life, his conversion, at the age of twenty-two, to Catholicism, deserves mention. During his time at Oxford, that venerable institution was awash with theological controversy. A wide array of theological positions were entertained by Hopkins' fellow students, ranging from those who wished the Anglican Church to institute reforms similar in kind, if not in degree, to Protestantism, to those who were tempted to, or in the end did, "go over to Rome."

Those who converted to Catholicism were frequently called "perverts," not converts. All manner of institutional preferments were denied them, and they were the objects of opprobrium. Hopkins' beloved father was appalled by his conversion, and thereafter Hopkins was estranged for some time from him and from his family, though the breech was never entire and was eventually healed. Thus Hopkins' conversion was in a very real way an act of self-sacrifice, one that, for all the hardships of his life, would ultimately prove redemptive.

Hopkins almost certainly did not consider himself a mystic. He was a Jesuit priest, and he chose to enter that order rather than become a Benedictine monk because he felt what he regarded as too great an affinity for a purely contemplative life and wished to counter that affinity by pursuing the more active life espoused by the Jesuits.

Hopkins, of course, was well and arduously schooled in Scholastic theology. All dogmatic religious systems, to varying degrees, have felt a tension with the mystical tendencies and the individual mystics flowering within their ranks. Subjective religious experience can be seen as putting too great an emphasis on the self rather than on God, and tends to be seen, from a dogmatic point of view, as potentially unruly and capricious. Mystics have typically been reined in and corrected, conformed to sanctioned religious doctrine, by their religious superiors—when not condemned altogether and banished as dangerously heterodox.

Hopkins' poetry, however, and particularly the great works of his early poetic maturity, which will be my subject here, has marked mystical tendencies. The master trope of mysticism in particular, more even than metaphor or analogy or paradox, is identity or the anagogic. The anagogic, as Northrop Frye has pointed out, has two aspects: identity *with*, and identity *as*. The more we identify *with* the things of this world, the more we participate in the living continuum that includes both us as nominal subjects and the things of this world as nominal objects—and the more, furthermore, we experience those things as uniquely, clearly, and positively what they are—the more, as a result, we will experience ourselves as uniquely and clearly ourselves, and the more we will experience others as uniquely, clearly, positively themselves.

Which is to say, also, the more clearly we experience the unique quality of things, of our selves and of others, the more we will experience what Buddhists call the unique suchness, or what Scholastic theologians call the quiddity of all phenomena. To paraphrase Paul Valery, the great miracle is not *that* things are, but *what* they are. When we apprehend with reverence the unique and unimpeachable *thisness* or *suchness* of things, or indeed of human beings, an experience that can be granted by mystical experience and by artistic creations that are sensitive to and suggestive of the unique quality of things, any propensity to do violence to them simply does not arise. When people or the things of this world or works of art are experienced qualitatively, they are seen as invested with a radiant clarity.

The aesthetics of Thomas Aquinas are, of course, of particular import to Catholic poets and writers. Stephen Daedalus famously riffs on them with characteristic humor and brio in chapter 5 of *The Portrait of the Artist as a Young Man*. Aquinas focuses particularly on the aesthetic ideal of beauty. The twentieth-century Catholic theologian Jacques Maritain, in the fifth chapter of his extraordinary book *Creative Intuition in Art and Poetry*, glossing Aquinas, cites his triad of the criteria proper to beauty: *integritas, consonantia,* and *claritas*. There are, he writes,

> three essential characteristics or integral elements traditionally recognized in beauty: *integrity,* because the intellect is pleased in fullness of Being; *proportion or consonance,* because the intellect is pleased in order and unity; and *radiance or clarity,* because the intellect is pleased in light, or in that which, emanating from things, causes intelligence to see.

Though in what follows I shall be emphasizing Hopkins' sensitivity to *claritas*, to the radiant particularity, the qualitative nature of man, language, and the objects of sense, I would be remiss were I not to point out that their ontology, their rootedness in being, corresponding to what Aquinas calls *integritas,* was also of cardinal importance to Hopkins.

From his undergraduate years onward, Hopkins was fascinated with the pre-Socratic philosopher Parmenides, for whom all things are one in their unchanging being, for whom change is an illusion, and for whom any distinction between subject and object is likewise illusory. It is their common rootedness in divine being that results in the identity of things with each other and with man. For Hopkins, it is the characteristic of being, while remaining transcendent, to express itself, to actively enter into man and the things of this world. As logos, *being* also inheres in and constitutes words and the significant patterns of words. Hopkins felt that individual human beings, individual words or patterns of words, and individual objects or patterns of objects are all not merely analogous but bound together, identified as one by their essential rootedness in being. Maritain writes:

> It was obvious to Aquinas, as to Dante, that, as he put it, the "beauty of anything created is nothing else than a similarity of divine beauty participated in by things," so that, in the last analysis, "the existence of all things derives from divine beauty."

It seems to me that the Hopkins, particularly in the work of his early poetic maturity, is the English poet most sensitive to the sacramental beauty of the natural world.

For Hopkins, the most essential sacrament is the Eucharist. For him, as for Catholics in general, the bread and the wine of the Eucharist are not merely a similitude of the body and blood of Christ nor a remembrance of the prototype of the rite as enacted in the New Testament, but rather they *are* the body and blood of Christ. Here, once again, the trope of identity or the anagogic is central. Without this crucial tenet of Catholicism, in Hopkins' view, Christianity becomes a mere shadow of itself. For Hopkins, the incarnation of God as man in the particular person of Christ is at the core of his faith. Christ's presence inheres not only in man but also in the radiant particularity of the variegated forms of the natural world.

After his conversion, Hopkins devoted himself to the long and arduous course of study and contemplation required of those who wish to be ordained as Jesuit priests. In the second year of his formal Scholastic study, Hopkins came across the medieval Franciscan theologian Duns Scotus' *Sentences* in the stacks of his seminary's library, and felt himself

> flush with a new stroke of enthusiasm. It may come to nothing or it may be a mercy from God. But just then when when I took in any inscape of the sky or sea I thought of Scotus.

Hopkins was particularly struck by Scotus' term *haecceitas*. In Paul Mariani's moving biography of Hopkins, he glosses Scotus' term and suggests the impact it had on Hopkins:

> *Haeceittas*, thisness, individuation—that which makes this oak tree this oak tree only, or this rose this rose only, or this person this person only, and not another—something unique and separate, God's infinite and incredible freshness of Creation every nanosecond of every day, world without end. Thomism is fine for understanding the unity of all things—being, species, and so forth. But *haeceittas*—thisness—the dappled distinctiveness of everything kept in Creation. With that he can certainly identify.

Hopkins coined two terms, *inscape* and *instress*, to express his sense of the thisness, the claritas, of the things of this world. These terms as they are used in various contexts accrue a range of related connotations, but they always include a sense of the luminous particularity and clarity of things as actively informed, patterned, and expressed by their mysterious, indwelling radiance. *Inscape* refers to significant patterns beheld in the objects that comprise the natural world. *Instress* refers to the impingement of such patterns upon the mind and to the highly charged energy or force field that draws and holds together the nodes of any particular pattern or inscape, whether of things apprehended in nature, of words in a poem, of notes in a symphony, or of brush strokes in a painting.

In his diary Hopkins declares: "I do not think I have ever seen anything more beautiful than the bluebell I have been looking at. I know the beauty of our Lord by it." This seems to me tantamount to a Buddhist saying, with regard to observing natural objects immediately, free of the intervention of conceptual thought, or indeed of thought of any kind, "when looking at a bluet I find Buddha nature." In a later passage on a whole field of bluets, Hopkins writes of bluebells "in Hodder wood, all hanging their heads one way. I caught as well as I could while my companions talked the Greek rightness of their beauty." He sees a radiant blue light "beating up from so many glassy heads," impressing "their deeper instress in upon the mind." There is a delicious irony in Hopkins' companions discoursing abstractly about the Greek ideal of beauty while Hopkins is intent upon apprehending the concrete suchness or quiddity of things in themselves.

Hopkins also refers to the inscape of things as their "self-being." In his fine study of Hopkins, *Gerard Manley Hopkins and The Poetry of Religious Experience*, Martin Dubois writes of Hopkins that:

> His idea, as he put it in notes of 1882, "Self is the intrinsic oneness of a thing," and so not accidental, but essentially and indivisibly singular.

Human nature, for Hopkins, was "more highly pitched, selved, and distinctive than anything in the world." Thus in "That Nature is a Heraclitean Fire," man is nature's "clearest-selvèd spark," the most intensely individuated of all created things.

It is, then, not merely physical objects, sentient or insentient, nor poems, nor the individual words that comprise them, but preeminently man himself who expresses an ineluctable, essential thisness or suchness.

The more intensely individuated a man or woman is, the more he or she will exemplify this quality, and the more he or she will apprehend it in nature. Hopkins writes:

> ...nothing else in nature comes near this unspeakable stress of pitch, distinctiveness, and selving, this selfbeing of my own... searching nature, I taste *self*, but at one tankard, that of my own being.

Among men, we can assume, Christ, who, of course, was man as well as God, possessed self-being to the highest degree.

Hopkins, as many passages in his notebooks make clear, delighted not only in his own unique self-being but also in that of others, including his monastic brethren, according full respect to their unimpeachable otherness even as he felt they were all united in Christ, each in their own often quirky and endearing ways participating in His nature.

2.

In Aquinas' view, the aim of the work of art is to induce in the viewer or reader a contemplative state of repose, an analogue of the peace that passeth understanding, and thereby to satisfy and still the restless intellect and to subdue the involuntary, reactive, appetitive, purely sensual part of man's nature, including carnal desire. It is to induce in the viewer, listener, or reader what Joyce calls, in the *Portrait of the Artist As a Young Man*, "stasis."

In *Some Segments of a River,* I discuss contemplative and ecstatic forms of mysticism. Thomist aesthetics, with their stress on unity and wholeness of being as paramount criteria of beauty—with what Mariani calls, dismissively, "being, species, and so forth"—and on the general, the static, and the categorical, seems allied with the quietism of the contemplative as an ideal. Hopkins, on the other hand, though certainly practiced in contemplation, in his early poetry in particular seems essentially to be, like Theresa of Avila or, among poets, like Christopher Smart and Walt Whitman, a type of ecstatic mystic. He was often, as in his encounter with

Scotus, struck with enthusiasm. Indeed, his early notebooks and diaries are brimful with enthusiasm—with enthusiasm and with an incandescent ardor.

Nature for Hopkins is never apprehended as merely static, in repose, but is at the same time ever-changing, dynamic. Thus he was as drawn to the Pre-Socratic philosopher Heraclitus, for whom all things are a continual transmutation of an ever-changing fire, as he was to Parmenides. The two together, for Hopkins, comprise complementary aspects of one reality.

The triune deity, of course, encompasses not only God the Father, and God the Holy Spirit, but also God the Son, through whose creative act all things, participating in that act, come into being. Thus the suchness or thisness of things involves not only the qualitative nature of the being of things, but their characteristic mode of action. This action, for Hopkins, is not merely random but purposive. When the inscape of a thing or a scene or a sentient being is perceived with the eye of the spirit, the sometimes chaotically apprehended welter of experience "falls into an order as well as purpose."

The sense of the indwelling being of things as vitally expressed in their ever-changing, significant, purposive pattern or gestalt falls under the second of Aquinas' criteria for beauty, *consonantia*, variously translated as order, harmony, symmetry, or proportion, which involves the proper adjustment of the parts of a work of art to the whole. Interestingly, in *The Portrait of the Artist as a Young Man*, Steven Daedalus views rhythm as a vital aspect of proportion. Hopkins was attracted to "all things counter, original, spare, strange." His "sprung rhythm," which I will later have occasion to discuss, was initially—at least to most readers—original and strange, and was counter to any standard metrical practice.

For Hopkins, asymmetry as well as symmetry is characteristic of the inscape of things. Hopkins' poems tend to be formally eccentric. Among the many sonnets he wrote, several, like "Pied Beauty," which contains only ten lines followed by the abrupt imperative "Praise Him," are abbreviated. Hopkins called these "curtail sonnets." Still others, like "Spelt from the Sybil's Leaves," which he called "the longest sonnet ever made and no doubt the longest making," overflow their prescribed, confined bounds.

To Hopkins, the apprehension of the inscape of things involved the perception of order as significant. The natural world, when seen aright, is replete with signs of the indwelling, sacramental presence of the divine. It is not surprising, then, that from his boyhood onward Hopkins was a constant, close, inveterate observer of nature. The notebooks he wrote until his early thirties teem with ecstatic notations. Hopkins was as sensitive to the visual arts as he was to poetry and spent much time, from his youth to his early adulthood, sketching natural scenes in which he attempted to catch the inscape of things, ever fugitive, ever changing, on the fly. In his youth, Hopkins learned to play the violin. Later in life, he became engrossed in formulating a theory of musical composition as novel as his notion of "sprung rhythm," and he set many of his poems to music.

The poems of Hopkins' early maturity are to an extraordinary degree sensuous. His poetry in general is sometimes faulted for its lack of conceptual content, particularly when compared with the metaphysical poets of the seventeenth century. But the sensuous immediacy of his poetry is perhaps its greatest strength. Bypassing the categorical niches of the conceptual intellect, it touches upon the quick of consciousness or of pure awareness itself. In Hopkins' poetry, the suchness of the concrete and the particular, even in their very evanescence, grants access to the ineffable, as to the logos itself. His poems, in attempting to capture the inscape or instress of the sensory manifold, are attuned not only to the objects of sight but also to smell, touch, taste, and particularly, of course, to sound, which is preeminently the medium of poetry as it is exclusively that of music.

Hopkins instinctively cultivated habits of attention that were not merely passive but strenuously active, leading to states in which the beholder and the beheld are one in the act of attention, or in the act of a consciousness that is neither subject nor object, but subsumes both. In a particularly pregnant passage in *On Creative Intuition in Art and Poetry,* Maritain writes that we awaken to ourselves and to "the inner side of things" simultaneously, by an intuitive experience that "has no intellectual framework." This, of course, first happens in childhood, a fact that Wordsworth touches upon in his great "Ode: Intimations of Immortality."

Most of us lose, as we grow older, this sense of wondrous intimacy between ourselves and the world. But Hopkins' poetry reminds us that through devotion and strenuous habits of loving attention it can be regained. We can reawaken, as adults, both to a profound sense of our own interiority and to the inner side of things, until, in the pure act of attention or consciousness, or what Buddhists call the awakened mind, we experience ourselves and the things of the world as one, and *both* as one with the divine. Indeed it is through God's, or the Holy Spirit's, loving grace that the unitive vision of the mystic and the stirrings of creative intuition in the artist occur. Grace, or its secular analogue inspiration, tends to irrupt, often in a kind of flash, to those who have long practiced spiritual or artistic discipline, the active, ongoing habit of attention to which I have referred.

What is a sense of the inner side of things but what Hopkins calls *inscape* or *instress,* which involves a quickening of awareness that draws subject and object together, granting what Wordsworth calls in "Tintern Abbey" the experience of seeing "into the life of things," a keenness of spiritual apprehension to which Hopkins testifies in his declaration "there lives the dearest freshness deep down things."

When things are seen afresh, with this sense of wonder, the least lily of the field, not to mention the whole sensory manifold, is apprehended as miraculous, making other miracles—flamboyantly supernatural signs of God's presence—pale by comparison. From this perspective, the senses are not to be bypassed or subdued, but they and their objects are to be gloried in and marveled at. Nor, again, are the active, or even the involuntary, reactive powers of man entirely to be spurned. The flight of a kingfisher or a windhover is instinctual, involuntary, both active and reactive, but is no less for that a sign of God's sacramental presence in the world.

There is, of course, a danger here of sentimentally valorizing the inarticulate state of the child, as Wordsworth comes close to doing. For Hopkins, however, the goal of man as of poetic speech is to become intensely, complexly individuated, whereas the inarticulate child is scarcely individuated at all.

It is with the arrival of speech that the infant's immediate sensuous apprehension of the world, his sense of wonder, is dulled and all too often dispelled. Words, too, can increasingly lose their uniquely lustrous vital lineaments, can become in effect disarticulated, can be dispersed into a mere Babel-like, indifferent welter. This is as true of the conventional effusions of bad or indifferent poets as it is, say, of the cries of the urban poor in Blake's "London." In one of his ecstatic, early sonnets, "God's Grandeur," Hopkins writes,

> Generations have trod, have trod, have trod;
> And all is seared with trade; bleared, smeared with toil;
> And wears man's smudge and shares man's smell: the soil
> Is bare now, nor can foot feel, being shod.

All that is rote, routinized, and habitually unconscious in man's life, abetted by industrialization and the urbanization of the poor, obscures God's grandeur. Language too—and not only, of course, the inarticulate speech of the poor and disenfranchised, but the abstractions of their capitalist overlords as well—can become "bleared, smeared with toil," can lose its vital lineaments. Like the plodding metrical feet of "have trod, have trod, have trod," man's actual feet become plodding, shod like those of dray horses, their sense of touch dulled, unable to feel the denuded earth beneath them.

And yet while language can lead to the self's estrangement from the world, when its vitality is reclaimed, when the language of the tribe is not so much purified as reinvigorated, charged with the power of the logos, it can lead to a cleaving of self to world, of world to self, and can ease man's sense of self-estrangement with respect to the world he inhabits. The sense of immediate sensuous contact with the world can be restored at a higher level; one need not, as an adult, merely resort to the weak, compensatory solace of Wordsworth's "philosophic mind."

3.

It is past time to take a look at one of Hopkins' poems. I cite here the second of the ecstatic sonnets that Hopkins wrote after completing "The Wreck of the Deutschland," the great poem that broke his long, self-imposed, poetic silence.

As Kingfishers Catch Fire

As kingfishers catch fire, dragonflies dráw fláme;
As tumbled over rim in roundy wells
Stones ring; like each tucked string tells, each hung bell's
Bow swung finds tongue to fling out broad its name;
Each mortal thing does one thing and the same:
Deals out that being indoors each one dwells;
Selves—goes itself; myself it speaks and spells,
Crying *Whát I do is me: for that I came.*

Í say móre: the just man justices;
Kéeps gráce: thát keeps all his goings graces;
Acts in God's eye what in God's eye he is—
Chríst—for Christ plays in ten thousand places,
Lovely in limbs, and lovely in eyes not his
To the Father through the features of men's faces.

Hopkins here exults, more clearly than in any other of his poems, in the thisness of things, a thisness that is not so much instantiated by the being of things but by their characteristic mode of action. Indeed, we would have no tidings of being if it did not in some way express itself. Kingfishers do not merely, passively *flash*, nor do dragonflies simply *glow*. Rather, kingfishers actively *catch* fire, as dragonflies *draw* flame. After these initial two visual images, there are expressions of sound, the first the purely natural sounds of stones ringing as they fall into wells, then two instances of sounds produced by musical instruments devised by man: "...each tucked string tells, each hung bell's / Bow swung finds tongue to fling out broad its name." Again, the profusion of verbs and adjectives in which verbs are embedded in the first quatrain is extraordinary: *catch, draw, tumbled, ring, tucked, tells, hung, swung, finds, flings.* The sheer dynamism of the world as apprehended in the poem's first quatrain is entirely typical of Hopkins, for whom even nouns, adjectives, and adverbs seem to aspire to the condition of being verbs.

The succeeding quatrain is perhaps Hopkins' quintessential expression of the thisness, the unique quality, the essential, qualitative, splendid individuation of all mortal, evanescent things. Hopkins first states the one unchanging principle of which the first stanza provides the passing instances: "Each mortal thing does one thing and the same: / Deals out that being indoors each one dwells." Again, were it not for the active, creative dealing out by things of the mystery of their indwelling being, enabled by God or Christ as creative logos, we would have no tidings of that being, of what Maritain calls the "inner life of things" that corresponds to and calls forth the inner side of ourselves.

The dealing out of things, with respect to man, is also a kind of standing forth. I have mentioned that in his early nature poetry, Hopkins is a type of the ecstatic mystic and poet. The root of the English word "ecstasy" is the Greek *ekstasis,* which denotes a standing outside of oneself. The indwelling nature of the being of things and their active dealing out of themselves are the two sides of a single phenomenon, reflecting the unity of the transcendent and the immanent, of pure unchanging being and of the multifarious and ever-changing phenomena of the natural world. Through the incarnation of Christ, God, as it were, proceeds outward from his innermost nature, stands forth and becomes sacramentally immanent in the world. The final words of the quatrain, "What I do is me / For that I came," refers, among other things, to the coming of Christ, through whose creative act all mortal things likewise come into their being.

In the sonnet's sestet, we move from the things of nature to man himself as a "mortal being." Once again we have a noun transformed into a verb: "The just man justices." Such a man "Keeps grace: that keeps all his goings graces; / Acts in God's eye what in God's eye he is— / Christ." When he strives to surrender himself, to permit himself, like Christ, to be a vessel of God's grace, and when he *acts* in imitation of Christ, man becomes not only Christ-like, but in a kind of radical move by Hopkins, in keeping, again with mysticism's affinity for the trope of identity or the anagogic, he becomes quite simply "Christ"—the same Christ who is everywhere immanent in the world, who "plays in ten thousand places." When seen through the eye of God, such a man is seen as "lovely in limbs." His incarnate body as well as his indwelling spirit is seen as beautiful. Man, like Christ, is "lovely in eyes not his / To the father through the features of men's faces." Just as Christ is lovely to the Father, so men and women who keep grace, who keep all their goings graces, are lovely to Him, and in particular it is "the features of men's faces," what is most distinctive, most individuated, most recognizable in man, that is most lovely to the Father.

In "As Kingfishers Catch Fire," even insentient things are endowed with speech and address themselves to the eye of the beholder. Thus "each tucked string tells"; each "hung bell," when rung, "finds tongue to fling out broad its name"—with the ingenious suggestion here that the bell's clapper is its tongue. And finally, again, these two instances are subsumed under a general rule: each mortal thing not only "speaks" but, as in the case of written words, "spells" its own nature.

Language, when its freshness is renewed and reclaimed, as in the finely calibrated words of masters of both poetry and prose, is a bodying forth of the energy of things, and this is particularly the case when the marks on a page are vocalized in physical utterance. There is much to be said for speaking the words of any fine poem aloud, but this is particularly true of Hopkins.

Having briefly glossed the meaning of the poem, I have in fact barely penetrated its surface or said anything about this what makes this poem, or Hopkins' poetry in general, so distinctive, so intensely individuated. I am speaking here of the highly distinctive sound and rhythm of his poetry, and how both are inseparable from their meaning.

With respect first to sound, Hopkins, of course, makes full use of alliteration, assonance, consonance, internal rhymes, and end-rhymes, as well as words compounded of two or more words yoked together by dashes, thereby creating extraordinary skeins of interrelated sounds. I will not here point out instances in the poem under consideration. They are everywhere apparent in it, and the reader can easily trace their lineaments for him or herself. Hopkins writes:

> Poetry is speech framed for contemplation of the mind by the way of hearing or speech framed to be heard for its own sake and interest even over and above its interest of meaning.

In the series of ecstatic sonnets that Hopkins wrote upon renewing his vocation as a poet, his language is, for all its extravagance, denotative and mimetic, calibrated to accurately express both the appearances and the indwelling radiance of things. For Hopkins, true poetic language has no truck with airy fantasies nor with the mythological; nor is his use of language in any way symbolic. The conceptual, discursive, or abstract find no more place in the poetry of Hopkins than in that of William Carlos Williams. For him, poetic language must cleave to the literal, to the real, to the sensory manifold as it presents itself to the poet. Only then can the indwelling radiance of things be revealed. The American Modernist poet Hart Crane, whose finest poems rival those of Hopkins in the sheer exuberance of their diction, wrote with typical insight after first perusing Hopkins' poems: "It is a revelation to me—of unrealized possibilities. I did not know that words could come so near a transfiguration to pure musical notation—at the same time retaining every minute literal signification."

For Hopkins, the relationship between words and things is not arbitrary. Words, too, spring from the logos; individual words too, according to Hopkins, have their own inscape; and, finally, they too, when deployed with attentiveness, are charged with energy and form themselves into significant patterns. The highly patterned sounds of words is one with the highly patterned world of things when their inscape is beheld with the eye of the spirit. Thus the sound of words and the things they denote, their meanings, correspond to and reinforce each other. When either words or things, whether as observed in nature or as set forth by the poet, are drawn together by the logos into significant patterns, they are elevated, lifted up, and energized by a distinctive charge.

The literal, mimetic function of his poetic language was referred to by Hopkins' as its "over-thought," which corresponds to the poem's meaning. But again, for Hopkins, the soundscape of poems, which he calls their "under-thought," has an interest and power apart from and greater than their denotative meaning. The charged patterns of the sounds of words, and the affinities between them, which it is the task of the poet to body forth, grant access to the ineffable, to the highly charged power of the logos, to a kind of meaningfulness that underwrites any particular meaning.

In "As Kingfishers Catch Fire," Hopkins speaks of Christ "playing in ten thousand places." Play is endemic not only to children but also to the wordplay of poets. Hopkins was well-versed in Latin and Greek and taught himself Welsh because he was particularly attracted to its long vowel sounds. Like others of his learned brethren but perhaps more so, he was a master of etymological punning, an exercise in which he took great relish. Such punning, of course, is a kind of serious play, stressing as it does a sense of some unifying principle at the heart of language, or of languages.

Hopkins was instinctively a social creature, and his sense of fun as well as his conviviality endeared him to his ecclesiastical companions—as it had to his schoolmates and to his friends at Oxford. His fellow seminarians hailed from all over England and Ireland, and from several continental countries as well, and in his diaries Hopkins frequently makes note, again with a playful relish, of the differences in their pronunciations of the same word.

Hopkins thought, like Wordsworth, that poetic language should be demotic, should not depart from the common usage of native speakers. But unlike Wordsworth's, his language is a kind of intensification of speech in which words are pitched to an extravagantly higher key. Hopkins was as fond of the recondite as of the demotic. Nor did he shy away from archaisms, from words rescued from the past and revitalized in the present. Such words are close to their etymological roots, to their origins, to their source, as to the freshness of a spring, and often their inscapes have a peculiar vivacity. The roots of Hopkins archaisms are often Anglo-Saxon rather than Latinate. They are not a fusty species of the Parnassian, a reveling in an idealized past, which Hopkins saw as typical of Tennyson at his worst, but rather a reconnection of the past to a living present.

Moving on from the sounds of Hopkins' poetry and from his diction, it remains for me to glance at its rhythm, or rhythms, which I have briefly alluded to in my prefatory remarks above. Rhythm, of course, is an aspect of sound. It too draws words together into significant patterns. In Hopkins' case, it is perhaps that which is most idiosyncratically distinctive and individuated about his verse. He is known for what he called "sprung rhythm," which he defined as "scanning by accents or stresses alone, without any account of the number of syllables, so that a foot may be one strong syllable or it may be many light and one strong." Hopkins called sprung rhythm a "most delicate and difficult business." According to Mariani,

> sprung rhythm depends solely on the number of stresses in a line, like the underlying accentual beat in Anglo-Saxon verse, whether there are one, two, three, or even more unstressed syllables between accents. Or none.

To establish iambic pentameter, all that is necessary is that the second syllable of a foot be more strongly stressed than the first; the second syllables of some feet often *feel* quite lightly stressed, and the reader's expectation of the poem's meter is then required to provide the appropriate stress. When a given foot contains "one, two, three, or even more unstressed syllables, or none" the kind of scansion appropriate to iambic pentameter, or to any other conventional meter, is upended.

Hopkins attempted to aid the prospective reader of his poems by providing marks above accented syllables, in effect suggesting something like a musical notation or score. In his prescriptive poetics, Pound urged poets "to compose in the sequence of the musical phrase, not in sequence of a metronome." The metronome is, of course, a reference to the kind of standard, rote meter that Hopkins conspicuously does not deploy.

Whatever is meant by "the sequence of the musical phrase," in Hopkins' poetry the stresses are unusually strong, stronger than in regular accentual verse. The long vowel sounds that he found so attractive in Welsh and that he incorporated into his own poetry, their "duration," to use the technical term, in addition to their accent, resulted in syllables that are particularly strongly stressed.

In addition, the Anglo-Saxon words that Hopkins favored are disproportionately monosyllabic, and nouns, verbs, and adjectives of a single syllable, it seems to me, are intrinsically strongly stressed. When the proportion of such words in a poem is high, they have the muscular quality that Hopkins so prized in his poetry. Hopkins was drawn to Medieval English verse, and particularly to "Piers Plowman," with its four-stressed lines in which the first two stressed words, prior to their medial break or *caesura*, and their second two, after it, alliterate. Hopkins felt that this kind of alliteration also augmented the strength of its stressed syllables.

In "That Nature is a Heraclitean Fire and of the comfort of the Resurrection," whose lines contain three stressed syllables on either side of a medial *caesura*, Hopkins experimented with his own typically quirky adaptation of the twelve-syllable line of the Alexandrine, the characteristic meter of classic French poetry, which is based on the duration of syllables, not their accent. In "Spelt from Sibyl's Leaves," Hopkins placed four stressed syllables on either side of a medial caesura, producing some of the longest lines in English poetry.

Dubois helpfully notes another aspect of sprung rhythm's "capacity for variability." The fact that for Hopkins, a given foot can contain not only several unstressed syllables but also none, allows for several feet that contain only one stressed syllable to follow each other, thus contributing to a feeling of density and intensity. Moreover, as Dubois notes, there is another principle of alternation in Hopkins' poetry, "at one moment bunching its stresses and in another dispersing them again." This kind of alternation can be seen as a kind of meta-rhythm at work in Hopkins' most characteristic poems.

Pound famously wrote "to break the pentameter—that was the first heave." Hopkins' poems, with their highly variable number of stresses per line and with their disruption of a simple iambic beat, not only break but shatter the pentameter. This is one reason why, when his poems were finally published in 1918, he seemed to many poets an oddly contemporaneous precursor, a modernist poet who had written before modernism.

The poem of Hopkins that most extravagantly, exorbitantly displays both his dense patterning of sounds and his vaunting, vaulting, springing or leaping rhythms, whose diction is the most elevated, uplifted, and high-flown, yet whose overall movement is ultimately downward and earthward, is "The Windhover," which Hopkins declared was his favorite among his sonnets.

THE WINDHOVER

To Christ our Lord

I caught this morning morning's minion, king-
   dom of daylight's dauphin, dapple-dawn-drawn Falcon, in his riding
  Of the rolling level underneath him steady air, and striding
High there, how he rung upon the rein of a wimpling wing
In his ecstasy! then off, off forth on swing,
   As a skate's heel sweeps smooth on a bow-bend: the hurl and gliding
  Rebuffed the big wind. My heart in hiding
Stirred for a bird,—the achieve of, the mastery of the thing!

Brute beauty and valour and act, oh, air, pride, plume, here
  Buckle! AND the fire that breaks from thee then, a billion
Times told lovelier, more dangerous, O my chevalier!

   No wonder of it: shéer plód makes plough down sillion
Shine, and blue-bleak embers, ah my dear,
  Fall, gall themselves, and gash gold-vermillion.

The sonnet originated in Italy in the thirteenth century and was assimilated to the chivalric conventions of courtly love. "The Windhover" is a renewal and reconfiguration, or transfiguration in Christian terms, of this tradition. The Falcon is referred to as a "chevalier," a knight, and also as a "minion," as knights were the minions of a king. The poet's exclamation "Brute beauty and valour and act, oh, air, pride, plume" extols the martial virtues of valor and pride. The helmets of knights were, of course, adorned by plumes. Knights were known and prized according to their acts, both martial and chivalrous. It might seem strange for a Christian poet to extol these virtues, most especially pride, but Hopkins wrote several poems on soldiers as types of Christ, a not-uncommon Christian trope, and was drawn, as we have seen, by all things active and dynamic.

The poet's heart is stirred by the Falcon, and he addresses him in terms of endearment as "my chevalier" and later as "my dear." In a reversal of the courtly tradition, the poet's heart and spirit are feminine and the Falcon is masculine. But this kind of reversal is another Christian trope, with the soul of the believer often figured as the bride of Christ.

Some critics have wondered whether the windhover or Falcon is indeed a figure for Christ, citing the fact that Hopkins added the poem's dedication, "To Christ Our Lord," years after having written the poem. The fact that the Falcon is likened to a brute creature as well as to a knight in no way precludes his being a figure for the Christ who plays in ten thousand places and shines through the features of men's faces.

Over and over again, in his notebooks and letters, Hopkins stresses that just as Christ is really, wholly, and truly God, so as man he was really, wholly, and and truly man. Thus, though in one sense Christ is coequal with God, in another sense, as man, he is God's minion, or his servant, under his dominion, just as a chevalier or knight is the minion of a king, and as the Falcon is described as the minion of morning, of the kingdom of daylight, with God the Father being here analogous, perhaps, to the rising sun in a sky that is metaphorically a heaven. Additionally, the Falcon is referred to by Hopkins as a "dauphin," a term that refers to the firstborn son of a French king and is therefore analogous to Christ as the only begotten son of God the Father. Finally, Hopkins capitalizes the word *Falcon*, just as the names of God are capitalized.

Christ, however, is not only the servant of God, but in humbling himself by taking on a human form, he becomes the servant of man—albeit a servant who is also paradoxically a master. While the octave of "The Windhover" is primarily concerned with Christ as master, as coequal with God the Father, whose transcendent realm is figured, again, by the sky in which the Falcon ranges, its sestet enacts in its downward movement Christ's incarnation as man. Again, it is important to note that there is no rupture between Christ as coequal with the transcendent farther and Christ as incarnate man. They are two aspects of the same divinity.

"The Windhover" opens with two densely alliterative clusters, first of "m" sounds, then of "d" sounds, and with one of Hopkins' compound words, "dapple-dawn-drawn": "I caught this morning morning's minion, king- / dom of daylight's dauphin / dapple-dawn-drawn Falcon." "Dapple" is a key word for Hopkins, denoting spots of color or light that appear with an irregular regularity, often in motion, marking all manner of variegated things or phenomena, sentient or insentient. Another of Hopkins' early sonnets, "Pied Beauty," written in close proximity to "The Windhover," begins, "Glory be to God for dappled things...," and the poem itself is an ecstatic inventory of such things.

The Falcon is depicted as drawn across the sky by the dawn and, as the "king- / dom of daylight's dauphin," implicitly perhaps by its king, God the Father. The word "king," which is in effect extracted from the word "kingdom" by an eccentric line break that bifurcates it, is granted special prominence.

The Falcon is borne aloft, held "high" by the pressure, the stress of the "underneath him rolling steady air." "Pressure" is a word that is often associated by Hopkins with instress. In "The Wreck of the Deutschland," he writes of "a pressure, a principle, Christ's gift." The Falcon's "riding" is, typically for Hopkins, a "striding" and later a "gliding." He is likened to a skater whose "skate's heel sweeps smooth on a bow-bend," as though incising subtle marks, parabolic vectors of force, on the sky. The poem's speaker exclaims: "How he rung upon the rein of a wimpling wing / In his ecstasy!" "Wimpling," one of the archaic words that Hopkins characteristically mixes with colloquial ones, means, variously, to ripple, to fall or lie in folds, to bend or curve, or to follow a meandering course, all of which usages are richly drawn together here. "Rung," as Mariani helpfully points out, is a technical "term used in falconry, which refers to the bird rising through the air in spirals—circling upward." But it also retains its other meanings. I have mentioned that for Hopkins even individual words have inscape. The percentage of polysemous words in Hopkins is remarkably high, particularly when their etymologies and archaic meanings are taken into account. The various related meanings of a word also form the significant patterns that are characteristic of inscape.

The Falcon veers "off, off forth on a swing." The Falcon is both active, striding on the air, skating as though on ice, and passive, "reined" upon a "wimpling wing." The poem is everywhere alive, dynamic, replete with forces that are counterpointed by countervailing forces, just as its rhythms are counterpointed by countervailing rhythms.

There are only two references to the poet/speaker himself in "The Windhover." The first is the initial "I caught," which, in contradistinction to the more passive "I saw," emphasizes the active participation of the poet in the scene that he has been observing. The second, "my heart in hiding / Stirred for a bird,—the achieve of, the mastery of the thing," clearly registers the poet's active responsiveness to, his participation in, the scene that he is beholding, and his identification with the

Falcon, which again is a figure for Christ conceived not in his role as master but as servant. The phrase "the achieve of," rather than "the achievement of," is yet another instance of Hopkins' morphing of other parts of speech into verbs.

Why should the poet's heart be "in hiding"? Clearly, the speaker's heart is awed, overwhelmed by the sublimity of the magnificent scene that he is observing, and specifically by the "achieve of, the mastery of" the Falcon. It is as though the poet/speaker, in effect, dares not show his face.

The ecstatic stirring of the poet's heart highlights his identification with the ecstatic motions of the windhover and accounts for the insistently exclamatory language of the poem, a language that perhaps achieves its highest pitch in the lines that conclude its opening movement, "Brute beauty and valour and act, oh, air, pride, plume..." The sonnet's belated volta, beginning its ninth line with the word "buckle," occurs with an extraordinary, almost violent suddenness.

> Brute beauty and valour and act, oh, air, pride, plume, here
>   Buckle!

The word "buckle," due to its placement here, and to the intrinsic inscape of the word itself, has tremendous power. It announces the Falcon's abrupt descent as he is caught, no doubt, by a downdraft toward the earth. To buckle, according to one dictionary definition, is to "bend or give way under a weight or force." The sudden, almost violent downward movement of the Falcon here figures not only Christ's incarnation as man, but his final fate, his violent passion and crucifixion, his ultimate sacrifice as man and for man, in which his body buckled and gave way on the cross. The poem continues:

> ...AND the fire that breaks from thee then, a billion
>   Times told lovelier, more dangerous, O my chevalier!

The Christ of the incarnation and the crucifixion is "a billion times lovelier" in his loving sacrifice, enabling man's redemption, than he would have been had he remained wholly transcendent. To be lovely is to be loved, to be worthy of love. There are references to the Holy Spirit in the above lines, the Spirit whose nature is the ardent love of the Father for the Son, or quite simply love itself. The Falcon here is a figure for the Holy Spirit that descended like a dove and hovered over Jesus when he was baptized, and "the fire that breaks from Thee then" recalls "The tongues of fire" that "came to rest on each one" of Christ's disciples on their first celebration with Christ of the Pentecost, thus firing their hearts with love and zeal, filling them with enthusiasm, and inspiring in them ecstatic utterance.

The fire that breaks from the Falcon as a figure for the Holy Spirit is also a billion times "more dangerous" than is any mere raptor or heroic knight. The fire referenced in "The Windhover" is a frequently, almost obsessively, recurring motif in Hopkins' poetry, recalling not only Heraclitus' references to fire as embodying the flux and dynamism of all things, but also referring to the purifying fire and radiance of God's love. To be touched by the fire of God's grace, to receive Christ, is to realize that one's soul is radically, *dangerously* at hazard, subject either to salvation or damnation.

The next line of the poem effects another abrupt transition: "No wonder of it: shéer plód makes plough down sillion / Shine." The line is thoroughly characteristic of Hopkins. The alliterative pairs "plow, plod" and "sillion, shine" comprise an instance of Hopkins' borrowing, mentioned previously, from the four-beat line of early English poetry, where alliteration, as previously noted, adds additional stress to the stressed syllables. It also characteristically mixes plain spoken words with the exotic archaism "sillion," which is derived from the French *silon*, meaning furrow. In its rare English usages, *sillion* has referred variously to the plough, to the furrow, and to the soil turned over by the plow. In the context here, both the plow and the earth worked by it are seen as shining.

The sky has now been left behind, and the poem has emphatically descended to earth. The "striding" or "gliding" of the Falcon has been replaced by the plodding or "plod" of man at one of his humblest tasks, that of plowing a field. The circling, sometimes meandering, course of the Falcon has been replaced by the inscription of a straight line, like the inscription of a line in a poem. The work of plowing a field and sowing seeds in it, though humble, is also generative and regenerative, as it makes possible a later harvest and the conversion or transfiguration of wheat into the bread of the Eucharist. Here, as so often in Hopkins, the divine expresses itself as much in the ordinary as in the extraordinary. The plowing of a field produces its own shine, its own radiance, a radiance that is a humbler version of the fire that breaks from the descending Falcon.

The poem concludes: "and blue-bleak embers, ah, my dear / Fall, gall themselves, and gash gold vermillion." The downward, falling motion of the poem continues, and it finally moves, as well, from outside to inside, to the observation of a hearth, which is another recurrent motif in Hopkins' poetry, often signifying the comforting warmth of God's grace.

The poem's last line seems to me one of the most uncannily beautiful in Hopkins' verse, with its triple alliteration of "g" sounds, and with the heavily stressed, internally rhyming, monosyllabic "fall" and "gall," with their long vowels, placed emphatically at the beginning of the line. Again typically, the embers are seemingly endowed with sentient life, with the power to gall themselves. The noun *gall* signifies something bitter and cruel, but here the word is a verb, and thus the embers can be seen as actively submitting themselves to a bitter fate. Their galling of themselves results in a "gash," clearly another reference to Christ's crucifixion, and the shedding of his "vermillion" blood. That blood is, however, a royal "gold" as well as vermillion, and thus the "blue-bleak embers" are transformed into something, again, lovely, and wondrous to behold.

The ecstatic confidence of Hopkins' early sonnets would eventually erode over the forthcoming years, as Hopkins' always-fragile health deteriorated, as he was posted to often squalid, urban settings whose poverty overwhelmed and dispirited him, and as the exigencies and demands of his priestly duties taxed him almost to the breaking point. His focus on Christ's incarnation, and his apprehension of His sacramental immanence in the world, gave way to a long, dark night of the soul, to a sense of the incommensurability between God and the world, God and his desiccated self, and to a concern with final things and with his place in the afterlife.

In Hopkins' late "terrible" sonnets, the speaker's authorial "I" is more insistently and explicitly present, though God, who seems to have withdrawn completely, is nowhere apparent and no longer responds to his tongue's confessions. Hopkins, in the extremity of his suffering, turned inward upon a self that is paralyzed and sterile, is unable to feel Christ's grace, and his own ascetic self-sacrifice, modeled on that of Christ, results only in gall and heartache. His longing for apotheosis and oneness with Christ will not occur in this life but only, if at all, after death. These late poems strive to say "yes," to initiate, as in "The Wreck of the Deutschland," a dialogue with God, but ultimately fail.

Hopkins began to see the writing of poems and his affinity for the beautiful not merely as a distraction but as a type of vanity and self-love. Though his ecstasies were mostly a thing of the past, his faith never wavered. His last words, at the premature age of forty-four, were, "I am so happy. I am so happy."

10.

MALLARMÉ'S VIA NEGATIVA

I would like to touch upon a poet who followed a kind of *via negativa* in his adumbrations of what was, for him, a poetic truth analogous to, though not identical with, the existential truth sought out by mystics—a truth pursued, too, with the kind of rigor, discipline, and ardor that any genuine spiritual quest entails.

I am speaking here of Mallarmé, who deployed negative constructions more than any other poet of whom I am aware. These constructions were more than a mere trick, parlor game, or poetic tic. Nor, as I shall later discuss in more detail, were they the kind of life-destroying negations that Blake describes. Mallarmé's poetry betrays, no doubt, a kind of hermetic bent, and in this he may seem to have something in common with Yeats. But I would argue that Mallarmé came by his hermeticism honestly, discovering it first-hand as a result of a profoundly transformative experience of conversion akin to that of spiritual experience. His poetic expressions of this experience were in no way dependent upon a wife acting as amanuensis and channeler, as Yeats' had, nor upon a guru spouting dubious second-hand mash-ups, as Yeats' sometime spiritual guide Madame Blavatsky had, or indeed on any of the excrescences of prior hermetic schools. Nor do I consider Mallarmé an avatar of decadence, though both his work and his life, read superficially, can be mistaken as displaying some of its symptoms.

Certainly Mallarmé became a kind of magus to the many disciples who came to comprise a kind of cenacle around him, and who met regularly in the Mallarmés' drawing room, raptly attending to every word of the master. I can imagine Mallarmé, a supremely canny poet, as having, with a twinkle in his eye, a delighted and ironic detachment from the two explicit roles that he performed—that of a seer and latter-day oracle, and that of an *haute bourgeois* master of social ceremonies. On the one hand, Mallarmé was the author of "Un coup de dés," the most radical, revolutionary, and profoundly unsettling poem of his time, and on the other, of the witty, aphoristic, deliberately slight "Cartes Postales" dispatched, as invitations, or as notes embedded in gifts, to various households throughout Paris.

Regardless of whatever roles he assumed later in life, the essential core of Mallarmé as a poet was forged by a sublimely transformative experience that occurred when he was a young provincial schoolteacher. In 1866, in a letter to his friend the poet and physician Henri Cazalis, Mallarmé wrote that during the past year he had undergone a "terrifying" spiritual crisis involving a protracted "agony" and that he had become "perfectly dead." "I am now no longer a person," Mallarmé wrote, "no longer the Stéphane you have known, but a means by which the Spiritual Universe can see and unfold itself through what was once me." What Mallarmé is describing here is a profoundly destabilizing experience of the evacuation of the ego, a baptism in a nothingness, which he later explicitly recognized as having a family resemblance to the Buddhist notion of the void. The experience of the death of the self as one has previously known it is a hallmark of mystical experience. A liberating experience of rebirth, and a confident realization of the nature of his vocation as a poet, followed Mallarmé's dark night of the soul.

Mysticism and poetry of an apophatic bent involve the process of de-creation in which not only the manifest, articulate, unfolded realm of objects adrift in an apparently extended realm of time and space, but also the isolated, apparently internal ego, the putative subject that apprehends them, and the rarified idealisms of the categorical intellect, are all translated or enfolded back to their unmanifest source. This process is akin to the spiritual project at the core of Rilke's "*Duino Elegies*," man's task of making the visible and external invisible and internal, or, in a slightly more modest key, of Stevens' attempts to make "the visible a little hard to see."

In the several books of informal criticism I have written over the past several years, I have insisted upon the essentially dynamic, fluid nature of the imagination, of its enmity with the nominal and the categorical, of its reveling in the free flow of appearances of the phenomenal world understood as participating in an unbroken continuum encompassing dimensions both physical an spiritual.

But Mallarmé's poetry brings me up short, serves as a kind of corrective, reminds me that just as in apophatic mysticism no positive attributes can be appended to God, so in Mallarmé's apophatic imagination nothingness is the essential given, and in his poetry it often seems that nothing happens, or alternatively that one ultimately ungraspable thing keeps happening, or not quite happening, over and over again. In much of Mallarmé's poetry, time seems to be arrested or suspended, and individual poems seem to be cross-sections of a timeless whole later to be embodied, as he boldly and excitedly prophesied in his letter to Cazalis, in one great book in which each poem would find its appointed place.

Over the years I have found myself returning to Mallarmé as though scratching a poetic/spiritual/intellectual itch. The sonnet below, conceived just after the spiritual crisis referred to in Mallarmé's letter to Cazalis, has long fascinated me:

SES PURS ONGLES TRÈS-HAUTS DÉDIANT LEUR ONYX

Ses purs ongles très-haut dédiant leur onyx,
L'Angoisse, ce minuit, soutient, lampadophore,
Maint rêve vespéral brûlé par le Phénix
Que ne recueille pas de cinéraire amphore

Sur les crédences, au salon vide: nul ptyx,
Aboli bibelot d'inanité sonore,
(Car le Maître est allé puiser des pleurs au Styx
Avec ce seul objet dont le Néant s'honore.)

Mais proche la croisée au nord vacante, un or
Agonise selon peut-être le décor
Des licornes ruant du feu contre une nixe,

Elle, défunte nue en le miroir, encor
Que, dans l'oubli fermé par le cadre, se fixe
De scintillations sitôt le septuor.

HER PURE NAILS OFFERING THEIR ONYX ON HIGH

Her pure nails offering their onyx on high,
Anguish, the torchbearer, on this midnight bears
Many a twilit dream burnt by the Phoenix
and contained by no cinerary urn.

On the tables, in the empty room: no ptyx,
That abolished trinket of sonorous vacuity,
(For the Master's gone to scoop tears from the Styx
With the one object Nothingness uses to honor itself).

Yet near the empty northern casement, something golden
Dies, in accord, perhaps, with the decor
Of unicorns kicking flames at a nymph;

She, naked and dead in the mirror, while
Within the oblivion bounded by the frame,
Scintillations appear as soon as the septet.

Mallarmé has presented himself with a kind of arbitrary challenge in "Ses Purs Ongles...," which has come to be commonly referred to as "Sonnet en -yx." He adopts an almost improbably difficult rhyme scheme, which requires that he repeat one strand of end rhymes eight times, concluding appropriately with the word *septuor*, and another strand six times, including several words (onyx, Styx, ptyx) which include, in reversed order, as though reflected in a mirror, the two penultimate letters of the alphabet, letters that can also stand for any number of possible numbers in an algebraic equation.

Scholars have gone on hopeless treasure hunts in search of the origins of Mallarmé's troublesome *ptyx*. Some claim to have discovered its origins in the English word *pyx,* others look to Greek sources. Such ingenuous exercises aside, *ptyx* is, in fact, a French nonce word, a neologism, one whose meaning moreover cannot be guessed at from the context in which it appears. Mallarmé's sonnet explicitly refers to *ptyx* as a "sonorous vacuity" or in other translations, simply as *nonsense.* With a delicious absurdity, Mallarmé negates his nonce word at the very moment of its creation. Indeed, the poem as whole is a field in which a riot of Mallarmé's negative constructions, immediately annulling what they posit, are at play.

The typical reading of Mallarmé's sonnet, which is properly sensitive to its non-representational or fictive status, notes not only its play of multiple binary terms but also its Eucharistic images (images that I will not unpack here, but which can be found in any scrupulous explication of the poem) and its many allusions to death and rebirth, including that of the mythological phoenix. Such a reading suggests that the untidy reality of the phenomenal world of which we are a part can, in a sense, be redeemed and preserved as the constellated words, the sonorous vacuities, contained within the tidy confines of the virtual space of the sonnet itself. Thus the poem can be seen as suggesting that what has been lost by religion can be recuperated by art, a notion that, with a slight twist, can be seen—again, I think, mistakenly—as a variant of the enervated dogma of art for art's sake.

This kind of reading, however convincing, seems to me to risk trivializing and domesticating the poem. I would suggest, perversely, that one begin with a more literal reading, as if the scene that it presents to us were not merely fictive but actual, and as if the space which it represents is likewise not merely virtual but actual. What is missed or passed over too quickly in what I have called the typical reading of "Sonnet en -yx" is that the poem, in its depiction of a scene that is devoid of any human subject, of any possible observer, but that somehow nonetheless *has* been recorded even as it is continually negated—a record that includes as its crowning image a description of flares upon the surface of a mirror enclosed by a gilded frame and affixed to the back wall of a dimly lit room—is quite simply terrifyingly sublime in its invocation of the vast emptiness of the space which it subsumes.

This extravagantly strange poem that records no human observer does record the absence of a Master, presumably the poet as subjective "I" or ego, who is nowhere present in the scene that the poem records, but who is cited as trolling for nothingness in Hades. At least in the mythological realm in which the Master is nominally sojourning, something—the Styx—is moving, whereas in the actual space of the poem nothing moves except for scintillations that flare even as they fade on the reflective surface of a mirror—like Shelley's trope for the products of the imagination, which he likens to coals that likewise fade even as they flare, spectral reflections of some sublime original conception that begins to be lost even as it represented.

As for nymph and unicorns, they, of course, belong to a realm that cannot be registered by us as actual. They are mere chimerical inhabitants of a mythological realm that no longer inspires our credence, are allegorical figures that now stand for nothing, just as any deity formed in our self-image as a kind of subjective ego no longer, for many, inspires our credence.

The "Angoisse," the embodiment of existential dread or anxiety, that appears at the poem's outset, herself a frozen and immobilized object, is a very real, indeed an essential part of the poem, but to whom does her torment belong? The figure of L'Angoisse appears as a kind of blind sentry who is stationed as though at the mouth of some harbor. In her monumentality, one might imagine her blocking the reflections in the mirror in the room that appears behind her, reflections to which she is not privy. Her nails, likewise perhaps reflective, are also a part of the human anatomy that continues to grow even after death. Perhaps the anxiety she embodies is our anxiety, but if so, even our anxiety is immobilized and estranged from us.

One can imagine Mallarmé, in the midst of the terrifying crisis recounted in his letter to Cazalis, looking at a mirror and seeing, in effect, no one, or no one recognizable, an absence instead of a presence. Of course, mirrors are not conscious of the images that appear in them, unlike the symbolically reflective surface of the mind that observes them. But what if, when looking at one's face in a mirror, that image were to vanish, as though the observing mind and its sensory emissaries had themselves been somehow negated and annihilated? When one sees only nothing, does one see at all? Is one conscious at all, in an ordinary sense? When one's external senses, objects, one's mind, and one's status as subject are negated, who or what is it who observes the scintillation of the septet? When all else has been negated, does some kind of reflexive awareness, apart from that of any human subject, remain? But isn't the notion of some mind or consciousness other than or greater than the human likely to be a projection of the mind itself?

Again I am reminded of Shelley, in this case of the close of his own terrifying and sublime poem "Mont Blanc." Imagining the summit of Mont Blanc, inaccessible to his sight, as symbolizing the transcendent conscious origin of the power that manifests as a cascading river of ever-changing appearances roaring and pouring down the mountainside, he inquires:

And what were thou, and earth, and stars, and sea,
If to the human mind's imaginings
Silence and solitude were vacancy?

Just as the status as "real" of a transcendent "thou" and of "earth, and stars, and sea" are questioned in Shelley's poem, so too is that of the entire scene depicted in "Sonnet en -yx" and in particular the image of the septet reflected in the mirror, an image that presents the illusion of representing a discrete constellation of objects but is really no different from the blank surface of the mirror itself. Shelley leaves one with no definitive answer to his rhetorical question but with a vertiginous sense of disorientation similar to that produced by the series of questions that I have perhaps with too much license posed above.

"Sonnet en -yx," like many of Mallarmé's sonnets, seems to include within its apparently condensed form vast spaces only sparsely populated by the barest and most spectral of signs. The poem seems to present us with an abyss into which all possible meanings, indeed meaning itself, seem *almost* to be swallowed up, with only the slightest glimmerings, scintillations, or traces of that meaning or those meanings apparently left behind, though with no one to observe them. There are sometimes vast gulfs between between the constellated signs in Mallarmé's apparently slight poems.

This spaciousness of Mallarmé's poems coexists with their extreme compression and density, with their diamond-like brilliance. Mallarmé's highly condensed poems recall Hamlet's reference to the human mind as encompassing infinite space bounded in a skull as negligible a nutshell. The twin qualities of spaciousness and density seem characteristic of Mallarmé's many sonnets in particular, coexisting with their tendency to negate, moment by moment, what they posit, the ghostly and spectral phenomena that arise and subside within them.

And yet, though Mallarmé's poems are hermetic, though much is occulted in them, they do not traffic in the occult. Nor do they credulously indulge in the latter day mysteries that result, in Yeats' weaker work, and in Jung's more thoroughly misguided project, in the kind of mystification that is in fact antithetical to genuine forms of mysticism. Although Mallarmé's poems self-consciously include, with a sublime playfulness, mythological figures that no longer inspire belief, they do not worship at the altar of the archetype. They posit no gods with whom the poet (who, as in Stevens' poetry, never refers to himself in the first person) identifies, imagining himself to be deified. Instead, they have their root in the profound existential crisis alluded to above. Far from being merely mystifying, they exude the aura of almost preternatural clarity.

Moreover, Mallarmé's poetry in no way embraces a Gnostic or a Manichaeans' dualism. "Sonnet en -yx" was in its first version entitled by Mallarmé "Sonnet Allegorique de Lui-Meme." The three titles by which the poem has been designated constitute, appropriately, a kind of hydra-headed trinity. In that which is an allegory of itself, which is synonymous with itself, allegory as pointing to something other, paradoxically, is subsumed. Like all poems, "Sonnet en -yx" stands as an allegory, in achieved, synchronic form, of its own process of creation—or of de-creation. But what is true of all poems is a kind of truism, is essentially trivial.

The poem, synonymous with itself, is comprised of words that do not refer to an ulterior, abstract, conceptual order outside of or above them, nor to some material realm of objects extended in space outside of or beneath them. Nor are they merely the excrescences of some nominal subject, some sovereign ego. Nor, in a kind of endless lateral drift or relay, are they comprised of words referring endlessly and indifferently to other words. Rather, they organize themselves, or are rigorously organized, by the invisible, occulted hand of their self-effacing Master, into closed loops, repetitive motifs, constellations of signs that seem as much to arrest the movement of language as to indulge in it—an effect to which the often radically disjunct nature of Mallarmé's syntax also contributes. Though some residue of the referential clings to Mallarmé's words, they enact and constitute their own intrinsic orders. They are enactments in which both the subject and his habitual world are negated, disclosing a sublimely terrifying but ultimately liberating, or potentially liberating, abyss. Finally, there is neither anything inside the poem nor outside of it. Inner and outer dissolve, vanish into a kind of virtual, pure, phantasmagoric reflective surface in which only the glimmerings of a pure self-reflexive awareness remain.

Here I will simply state what I have thus far failed to mention: many of Mallarmé's poems conflate an awful sublimity with playfulness, with a gloriously extravagant sonic exuberance that is a subtle monument of or to a licentious aural excess, and with an ironic humor, which together constitute a rare and characteristic combination. This is especially true of "Sonnet en -yx," which adds to the aforementioned traits its over-the-top neologisms and playful use of mythology. The image of a mythological unicorn, symbol of chastity, rearing up (with what seems like lascivious intent) to kick flames at a nymph is a deliciously ludicrous and lubricious example. Though Mallarmé's poems are often terrifyingly serious, they are often detached, as well, from any form of self-seriousness on the part of their absconded author.

Of course, his poetry does not always exhibit such playfulness. Mallarmé's masterpiece, "Un coup de dés jamais n'abolira le hasard," roughly translatable as "A throw of the dice will never abolish chance," his most difficult and challenging poem, also seems in some way his most unremittingly serious one, a final risky throw of the dice upon which Mallarmé felt his reputation as a poet would ultimately depend. The poem is written in a bewildering array of typefaces of different sizes, each of which, as we follow their irregular course from page to page, represents a discrete narrative strand. Any single page, however, is filled with these variously constellated narrative glyphs, which together extend to all four corners of the page, anticipating the all-over technique of abstract expressionist painting. This practice also brings to mind Charles Olson's notion of "composition by field," likewise resulting in poems that extend to every quadrant of the page, as well as the experiments with typeface that became almost commonplace in later avant-garde poetry. The poem seems to invite us to take it in visually, synchronically, all at once.

The various narrative strands of the poem have as their most prominent theme that of a shipwreck. Strewn across the page, the poem's typographic characters recall Hart Crane's lines from "At Melville's Tomb": "The calyx of death's bounty giving back / A scattered chapter, livid hieroglyph," which themselves refer to the scattered remnants of the Pequod observed by Ishmael, the sole survivor of the wreck. Implicit in this notion of such scattered chapters and livid glyphs is that they remain ultimately mysterious, impossible to decode, to make cohere. Though we take in each page of "Un coup de dés" synchronically, visually, all at once, we, of course, cannot read the poem all at once. We must read it diachronically, but in so doing we are afforded a dizzying array of options. Does one isolate its various calligraphic strands and read them, one by one, across the poem's multiple pages. If so, we must read each strand separately and therefore partially, a partiality that is somewhat mitigated by multiple readings, but can never be fully overcome. Does one attempt to read more conventionally, but here more radically, down the page, a process that seems to yield only an increased disjunctiveness?

Of course, the more we read any given work of verbal art, the more we are able to apprehend it as a kind of immediate, synchronic whole, as a kind of spatial form. But "Un coup de dés" seems designed to resist the mind's tendency to succumb to the illusion of a totalizing synchronic comprehension. It cannot be domesticated, made to cohere; neither, however, is it entirely incoherent. Each throw of the dice, each reading, one of a dizzying array of possible readings, affords a glimpse or a cross-section of the whole, a whole that we will never satisfactorily comprehend, which will always remain essentially indeterminate. No one throw of the dice abolishes chance. Each throw is unique, atomistic, digital rather than analogue, exerting no occult influence on any other. Each is entirely momentary, non-sequential, discontinuous.

"Un coup de dés" is what Wallace Stevens might have called "the accomplishment of an extremist in an exercise." Certainly, even to Mallarmé's disciples, the poem seemed a magnificent dead-end or cul-de-sac, a path that is the closest possible approach to the kind of apophatic event horizon past which it is impossible, short of death, to travel further.

Finally, just as at the literal level "Sonnet en -yx" evokes a very real existential dread that is not simply cancelled by other readings of the poem, so "Un coup de dés" has at its literal core a shipwreck, an instance of the catastrophic. One wonders if indeed—like Yeats' "Slouching toward Bethlehem"—"Un coup de dés" was itself precognitive of the kind of ultimate cultural and social catastrophes that were to come in the century ahead. I am referring not only to the World Wars but also to the Holocaust that in a very real sense was a kind of abyss that seemed to swallow up, cancel, nullify, negate not only all particular cherished meanings, not only all coherent narratives, but meaning itself.

11.
Isaac Luria/Paul Celan

Just as I have not much touched upon Christian mysticism in my previous books, so too I have entirely passed over any discussion of Jewish mysticism or Kabbalah, which developed over many centuries. The doctrinal history of Kabbalah is an extraordinarily complex subject, which I have delved into far less intensively than I have delved into Christian mysticism, although over the years I have read virtually everything written by Gershon Sholem, the preeminent scholarly authority on the subject.

The fundamental Kabbalist text, the *Zohar*, was first published in the thirteenth century in Spain, a period that resulted in so many key works of various mystical traditions that I have begun to think of it as a renaissance before the Renaissance. The *Zohar* is among the most esoteric of mystical texts. It is impossible to read literally and has a suggestive, lyrical, impossible-to-fathom beauty.

According to Kabbalist teachings, the Talmud when properly interpreted comprises, like typological readings of the Bible, four levels of meaning. These are the literal; the allegorical; the *midrashic*, grounded in the rich history of rabbinical commentary on the Talmud; and finally the secret, inner, hidden meaning that is revealed by study of the Kabbalah, which includes as well the practice of meditation, often leading to ecstatic states.

The Absolute is known in Kabbalah as *En Sof*, which literally means the infinite or limitless. En Sof is the invisible, hidden, transcendent face of God, absolutely without qualities, devoid of any possible predicate. Its nature is that of pure negation or nothingness, a nothingness that is irradiated by an undifferentiated light. In early versions of Kabbalah, God is fully manifest in the world. His presence emanates through a series of ten stages called *sephiroth*, centers of energy that set up a kind of alternating current in which male and female energies, justice and mercy, are dynamically balanced and inextricably related.

The sephirot are associated with Adam Kadmon, akin to the primordial cosmic man, who Blake is referred to as Albion, the one regenerate man in whom all mortal men participate. The sephirot are operative as centers of energy both within the divine and within individual men and women. Thus, the microcosm, man, and the macrocosm are inextricably related.

The sephirot are also likened to an inverted tree of life whose roots lie in the higher sephirot and whose diverging and proliferating branches comprise the lower. Adam in Eden eats from the tree of the knowledge of good and evil, which is the antithesis of the tree of life, thereby inaugurating the fall of man.

Additionally, in Kabbalah the twenty-two letters of the Hebrew alphabet are associated with the energetic pathways between the ten sephirot. Each of the sephirot are also associated with various names of God. Thus Hebrew as a sacred language plays a vital, paradigmatic role in the unfolding of the sephirot. Finally, the Talmud itself as a whole is taken to be the name of God, a concept akin to the Vedic notion of the totality of the Vedas as the name of God, and is seen as replete with esoteric meanings which it is the endless task of learned exegetes to unfold.

Toward the end of the fifteenth century, Sephardic Jews were expelled from Spain. Many resettled in Palestine, where, in the context of this traumatic disruption, a seminal flowering of Kabbalah occurred in the sixteenth century, centered particularly in the town of Safed. Its two most influential figures were Moses Cordovero (1522–1570), who wrote an influential commentary on the *Zohar*, and Isaac Luria (1534–1572), whose teachings were later propagated by his disciples and eventually became the preeminent, normative strain of Kabbalah.

In Lurianic Kabbalah, the first movement of the divine is not one of creative emanation but rather what in Hebrew is called *tzimtzum* or contraction, as a result of which God withdraws into his innermost recesses and is hidden even from Himself. This inward movement opens up an almost infinitesimally small space within the divine in which creation can take place.

Something goes terribly wrong in the process of the creative emanation of the world. The space created by the initial contraction of En Sof is not entirely irradiated by divine light, the partial absence of which leads to a catastrophically unstable, chaotic state in which darkness is separated from light. The ensuing conflict between darkness and light gives rise to an overwhelming stress whose result is spoken of as *shevirat ha-kelim,* or the "shattering of the vessels." The term "vessels" refers to the lower sephirah considered as the repositories of the divine. Their broken shards, fragments to which some residual light adheres, fall into lower realms of a phenomenal world seen as in part demonic, estranged from the divine. It is within this equivocal context that man himself, with his propensity for both good and evil, is created by God.

Man's role is to gather together, to redeem and make whole, in restorative acts called *tikkun,* the sparks of light encased within the material remnants of their worldly shells, thereby rescuing God's light from its exile in the world, and thus redeeming man himself as well. Lurianic Kabbalah has, as well, a pronounced eschatological dimension; the promise of redemption, prepared for by man's restorative acts, will be finally and fully realized with the coming of the Messiah.

Lurianic Kabbalah comes perilously close to enshrining a kind of dualism. Monotheism is preserved by the notion that the potential for good and evil lie within the divine itself. The first three sephirot, which are prior to creation, exist in a dynamic, harmonious equilibrium. With the fourth and fifth sephirah—associated respectively with female and male, with merciful loving-kindness and power or wrathful judgment—the emanation of what will eventually become the created world begins. It is in the fifth sephirah in particular that the seeds of the potential for evil lie. Were it not for man, however, that potential would never have been been actualized.

In practice, the Kabbalah became the province of an elite, relatively learned few, of a privileged class of scholarly rabbis. In the eighteenth century, however, there arose within Jewish mysticism a phenomenon that stressed the way of love, of an immediate contact with God, over the intellectual rigors of the way knowledge. I am speaking of Hasidism, whose seminal figure was the Bal Shem Tov, a highly charismatic saint whose teaching gave rise to a popular uprising within Jewish mysticism. Many of the stories associated with his hagiography, which include both words and actions imputed to him, are deliciously humorous in their lampooning of the pretensions and hypocrisy of the learned elite.

In the aftermath of the catastrophe of the Holocaust, the Kabbalist vision of Isaac Luria, which as noted above was born of a period of traumatic exile and extreme dislocation, regained a particular relevance and resonance. God, or En Sof, seemed, as in the Lurianic process of creation/fall, to have retreated terribly into his innermost recesses, hidden not only from himself but from his chosen people. A terrible gulf seemed to open up between God and man.

During the Holocaust and in its aftermath, the dynamically interrelated forces of justice and mercy seemed to have degenerated into something like gratuitous cruelty and cowardice. Justice gave way to a barbarous wrath, which trumped mercy; the will to power trumped the will to love; the material trumped the spiritual. During such times of radical spiritual, moral, and spatial misalignment, language too is disrupted and debased, perverted by sophistry, propaganda, or racist conspiracy theories. To many post-war critics, Jewish and otherwise, the Holocaust seemed almost to invalidate language in general, and the German language in particular, as creative, generative matrices of meaning or meanings.

In one of my previous essays in this volume, "Voicing Orpheus," I point out that both individuals and states construct narratives whose aim is to invest experience with coherent meanings, and that particularly traumatic events invalidate these narratives, replacing meaning with a pervasive sense of meaninglessness, and requiring often quite radical revisions of such narratives by which meaning can be restored. The Holocaust is an extreme instance of such a traumatic event. In the aftermath of the World War II, it seemed to many that the project of recuperation of meaning through the construction of some new narrative was inherently falsifying and reductive, and ought not even be attempted.

Theodor Adorno asserted, that "to write poetry after the Holocaust is barbaric," a view shared by others. Adorno apparently sought, as did Plato, to banish poetry from the republic, though why poetry, which at best is free from ideological cant—instead of, say, volumes of Marxist social criticism—should be so singled out seems unclear.

In terms of Lurianic Kabbalah, with the advent and then the aftermath of the Holocaust, tikkun, the task of gathering together the broken and dispersed shards of a once-integral light—and of a primordial spiritual language that was once associated with that light—from their degraded material husks, thereby reconstituting some kind of coherent whole, seemed both well-nigh impossible and urgently necessary.

One poet who took up this impossible task was Paul Celan. Paul Antschel was born in 1920 into a middle-class, German-speaking, Jewish family in Czernowitz, a predominantly Jewish provincial city in Romania. He began to write poetry during his adolescence, but his education was disrupted by the rise of Nazism in Europe. Rounded up during the Second World War, he worked in a forced labor camp from which he was freed by advancing Soviet troops, though both his parents died in such camps. After the war, he returned briefly to the remnants of his hometown, then lived from 1945 to 1947 in Bucharest, where he adopted the surname "Celan." When the Soviets gained control of Romania, he fled to Vienna, where he lived from 1947 to 1949, then finally moved to Paris, where he was to remain for the rest of his life.

In Paris, Celan initially experienced a terrible loneliness. A brilliant polyglot who spoke seven languages fluently, he at first eked out a meager living as a translator. In 1952, he married Gisele Lestrange, a talented graphic artist whose aristocratic Catholic family opposed their marriage. He assiduously sought recognition for his poetry but for a long time toiled in obscurity, ignored by the literary establishment.

Celan's move to Paris was an attempt to situate himself at the vital center of Western European culture, yet he would never feel at home there. He came to be wracked by guilt over the idea that his move to Paris had cut him off from his Jewish roots; increasingly, he fretted that he was not Jewish enough. Further compounding his peripheral status in Paris was the fact that Celan chose to write not in French but in German, which was both his own mother tongue and the tongue of the Fatherland, of the Reich that had sought to efface and destroy him.

In the aftermath of the Holocaust, writing poetry in German was for Celan fraught with ambivalence. As a Jew born in a small town in the eastern-most reaches of Europe, he was an outsider with respect to German culture, just as he was an outsider in the Francophone world of Paris, which for over two decades became his nominal home. As a Jew displaced by the Holocaust, he was in fact homeless, in perpetual exile, an *other* with respect not only to both German and French culture but also with respect to his own past and to his past self; as a Jew he had been subjected to an unimaginably radical series of enforced dislocations, uprootings, severances. Much of his own mature poetry would be marked by elisions, ellipses, caesuras, unexpected line breaks, snippets of passages in quotation—in short, by all manner of fault lines, rifts that seem ever on the verge of opening out into a vertiginous abyss.

If the literary and philosophical culture of postwar Germany, typified by Heidegger's silence regarding his complicity with the Third Reich, was invested in forgetting, Celan's poetry was invested in the quintessentially Jewish project of remembrance and commemoration. As such his writing was in its own way an act of tikkun.

Celan's most renowned poem, "Death Fugue," written in Bucharest at the beginning of his poetic career, has as its refrain its opening lines:

> Black milk of daybreak we drink it at evening
> we drink it at midday and morning we drink it at night
> we drink and we drink

This refrain is followed regularly by stanzas of varying length that themselves involve repetitive motifs like variations on a musical theme. The poem, despite its horrific subject, still adopts the decorum of poetic form itself, a decorum which Celan came increasingly to regard as falsifying. Though early in his poetic career, Celan admired and translated Mallarmé's work, his later poems are not bound together by any conventional form. They do not reflect the kind of self-conscious mastery that is an aspect of Mallarmé's poetic project; to the contrary, they abjure any notion of such mastery. They are more radically resistant to a reductive coherence than are any of Mallarmé's poems, including "Un coup de dés."

If the apophatic bent of Mallarmé's poetry was inaugurated by an overwhelming personal crisis, that of Celan's was forced upon him in the aftermath of a still more overwhelming personal, societal, and historical crisis. Celan ultimately came to question, as Mallarmé did not, the category of the aesthetic as well as the poetic sublimation of reality, however sublime or terrifying that sublimation might be; rather, he addressed and attempted to name, if necessarily obliquely and in a broken language that is stripped to the bone, the all-too-real horrors of an historical epoch.

If silence, for Mallarmé, like the whiteness of a page, is that which makes both his written characters and his constellation of symbols or habitual verbal motifs legible and intelligible, silence for Celan is associated with the silence of voices forever muted and erased in the Holocaust, and is that which must remain illegible or unsayable in the midst of that what is written of said.

Celan's early poetry, influenced by Surrealism, was densely figurative, richly inventive in its use of metaphor; in his later poetry, language is disfigured, cleared of the detritus of outworn rhetoric, brought closer, even if only in scattered glimmerings, to the radiance, to the peculiar lucidity of its primordial spiritual roots.

Celan's late poems, beginning with his volume *Breathturn,* written at the midpoint of his career, seem like the fragments of some lost original. With a keen insight, in her book *Economy of the Unlost,* Anne Carson reads them in apposition to the surviving fragments of the lyric poet Simonides of Keos, a contemporary of Pindar, some of which have come down to us in the form of salvaged scraps of papyrus, fragments quoted admiringly by later poets. They are testaments to an irrevocably broken or sundered chain of cultural transmission.

Carson discusses Celan's poetry in the context of his preoccupation with nothingness and negation. She reads his "No More Sand Art" as a radical exercise in negation, reduction, and excision. The poem concludes with the lines, or with the fragments of lines, "Deepinsnow/ Eeepinnow / Ee - i - o." In Celan's lexicon, *snow* almost always suggests the winter in which Celan's parents died in a labor camp. "Eepinnow" is a neologism that references nothing and means nothing. It is fundamentally disarticulated, mute, suggesting the muting of those lost in the Holocaust. The poem's final term or limit enacts a still further reduction and excision, the vowels "Ee-i-o." Carson notes that "if this poem were translated into Hebrew, a language in which vowels are not usually printed, it would vanish even before its appointed end. As did many a Hebrew." Sounded aloud rather than read, however, the poem's terminal vowels suggest an inarticulate cry of terror.

Celan's poetry does not attempt to posit some new narrative in which what has forever been lost is recuperated by an illusory recovery of coherent meanings. He was, after all, a lyric poet, but one who deconstructed the generic notion of the lyrical, pushing it to extremes, subjecting it to pressures in which its formal properties are fractured. Celan's poems attempt something like a homeopathic cure of a degraded language by deploying that language itself in a particularly distressed form.

It is impossible to say, of course, to what degree Celan felt that his poems succeeded or failed in the work of tikkun. On the one hand, they seem to admit defeat at their outset and are testaments to that defeat. On the other hand, they never abandon hope, even if only an impossible hope. In his famous Bremen lecture of 1958, Celan speaks of language in the context of a Holocaust, or *Shoah,* that he nowhere in his writing calls by name, referring to it only as "that which happened":

> There remained in the midst of the losses this one thing: language. It, the language, remained, not lost, yes, in spite of everything. But it had

to pass through its own answerless-ness, pass through frightful muting, pass through the thousand darknesses of death-bringing speech. It passed through and gave back no words for that which happened; yet it passed through this happening. Passed through and could come to light again, "enriched" by all this.

To pass through the thousand darknesses of death-dealing speech, language is required to enter a kind of abyss in which it becomes mute, recognizing that there are no names for that which is unnameable, no answers to questions which admit of no answers. The ineffability of this abyss is analogous to the ineffability of God, corresponding to the infinite recesses of En Sof, who remains hidden not only to man but to Himself, and whose nature is that of pure negation or nothingness.

And yet, if Celan's poetry cleaves to despair, it also, again, though more tentatively, cleaves to hope. If language is seen as that which fails, in the context of the Holocaust, to recuperate or heal the fractures in experience, it can also be seen as holding forth, or even inscribing, as an act of tikkun, of loving attention, the promise of such a recuperation.

After a terrible muting, after suffering the thousandfold darknesses of death-bringing speech, this prospect of return to the light constituted for Celan not only a personal but an eschatological hope, one grounded in his extraordinarily profound and extensive readings in Kabbalah, in the Biblical prophets, and in other Jewish writers who were engaged in the seemingly impossible task of coming to terms, or trying to come to terms, with the Holocaust.

Toward the end of Celan's life, however, his impulse toward hope increasingly gave way to despair. He suffered a series of debilitating depressions, a number of which, in the last five years of his life, resulted in his being confined in psychiatric wards, sometimes involuntarily—as he had been confined involuntarily as a young man in forced labor camps. Among the cures to which he was subjected was electroshock therapy, which seemed to Celan as much an ingenious form of torture as a cure.

In 1969 Celan was suffering, yet again, from a profound depression. His marriage had failed, and divorce, yet another schism, seemed in the offing. He had no choice but to exile himself to a cramped studio apartment. Yet again he was afflicted by a profound loneliness.

Then, as though providentially, he was asked to give a reading by the Hebrew Writers Association of Tel Aviv. While in Israel, he met an old friend of his from Cernowitz, Ilana Schmueli, with whom he commenced an intense erotic relationship. Together they toured Jerusalem. An unexpected union with a beloved other, and through her with a remembered Cernowitz, and finally a trip to Jerusalem, the sacred city of the Jews, seemed to Celan to hold forth the promise of a much longed-for and desperately needed homecoming.

After he returned to Paris, Celan wrote and sent to Ilana a series of twenty poems, entitled *Zeitgehöft,* a difficult compound noun that has most often been translated as *Homestead of Time,* but which has come to be referred to as the *Jerusalem Cycle.* Many of these poems commemorate the various holy sites which Celan and Ilana visited on their trip to Jerusalem, and together they map out a sacred topology.

In the poems of the *Jerusalem Cycle,* Celan meditates, in the context of his erotic relationship with Ilana, on Kabbalah's mystical notion of the *Shekinah,* the tenth and last of the sephirot. *Shekinah* literally means *to settle* or *to dwell.* The Shekinah, a feminine energy aligned with the principle of mercy, constitutes God's continuing indwelling radiance in a fallen world. The Shekinah dwells with Israel and with its chosen people in exile. It is also associated with the light in the temple in Jerusalem and with Jerusalem itself, both with the actual city and and with promise of the heavenly Jerusalem to come in which justice, not as retributive wrath but as mercy and love, will prevail and the souls of the dead, no longer in exile, will be redeemed, all sharing in a heavenly community in which peace will reign.

In erotic terms, the Shekinah is figured as the sister/bride of Israel. Several of the poems in the *Jerusalem Cycle* refer to or are situated at the East Gate of Jerusalem, which is at once both a threshold or portal and a divide between the dead and the living, between despair and hope. Passing through this gate, which in erotic terms is the entry into the beloved, is also an entry not only into the temporal but also into the promise of a heavenly, eternal Jerusalem. It is through this gate that the Messiah, according to Lurianic Kabbalah, will enter Jerusalem when the time of universal redemption is at hand.

The tenth poem of the *Jerusalem Cycle,* "The Poles," has a singular beauty and incandescence.

> The poles
> are within us,
> insurmountable
> while we're awake,
> we sleep to the other side, up to the Gate
> of Mercy,
>
> I lose you to you, that
> is my snow-comfort,
>
> say, that Jerusalem *is,*
>
> say it, as if I were this
> your whiteness,

as if you were
mine,

as if without us we could be we,

I open your leaves, forever,

you pray, you lay
us free.

The distant poles that in the waking state separate Paris from Jerusalem are reflected in the internal schisms suffered by both Celan and Ilana as survivors of the Holocaust. In the waking state these divisions are experienced as hopelessly "insurmountable." But in the sleep of mystical/erotic union both Celan and Ilana are carried "across" the distance that separates them and "up to the gate of Mercy," once again to the East Gate of Jerusalem, a gate which both joins and separates the dead, including those lost in the Holocaust, and the living, the actual Jerusalem without and the heavenly Jerusalem within, the isolated individual and the community of the saved. The lovers are carried "up to" this gate but not through it as the longed-for Messiah will eventually pass through it.

At the liminal placeless place of this gate, portal or threshold, at the Gate of Mercy, the poem's speaker says to his beloved "I lose you to you." As an avid reader of Martin Buber, Celan knew that only by a loving accepting of the unimpeachable otherness of the other can any authentic intimate encounter, bridging the gap between "I" and "Thou," occur. Back in Paris, Celan wrote to Ilana: "It is my—passionate—wish: that you bring forth what lies within you, that you become what you are."

In his chapter on Celan in the remarkable book, *Thinking the Poetic Measure of Justice,* to which I am much indebted, Charles Bambach writes:

> Only through a loving union of souls...a union where the self is brought to itself through the other, in bearing the other to the self, can the hidden potencies of the divine bring about the possibility of justice.

Justice here is associated not with the juridical, not with any set of laws whose aim is retribution and the exactions of penalties. To the contrary, any human act of love is an act justice, of tikkun, whereby the light trapped in the material world will eventually be reunited with its source, and the dead, including those incinerated in the Holocaust, will be reunited with the living

In the ninth line of "The Poles," which, as Bambach points out, is the exact center of a poem that is itself situated at the center of the *Jerusalem Cycle* as a whole, the speaker exhorts his beloved to "say that Jerusalem *is*," to utter the expression of an eschatological hope, and to say it "as if you were mine," as if the hope figured by erotic union had already been realized—even though the qualifier "as if" indicates that it has not yet and may never be more than fleetingly consummated.

The word *snow* here, instead of conjuring up the season of Celan's parents' death, is linked to the comforting whiteness of the body of the beloved. In the Kabbalah, it is worth noting, whiteness is a sacred color associated with the light of the divine. The erotic/mystical union of God with the Shekinah as his bride, figured by the erotic relationship of the poem's lovers, holds forth the hope that the dead will ultimately be redeemed, gathered together in the heavenly Jerusalem, though once again that hope may never come to fruition.

In the heavenly Jerusalem, "without us we could be we." Lover and beloved, free from their earthly identities, could be one with a community of souls who have, finally, become who they are. Celan imagines leafing open the beloved's body "forever" as though leafing through the pages of the book of life. The poem's last lines "you pray, you lay / us free" are addressed to Ilana as his human lover, as the embodiment of the Shekinah, and as the bearer of eschatological hope. They once again conflate the spiritual and the erotic, and again hold open the promise—if only uttered from the conditional realm of "could," of what might or might not be—of an impossible / possible freedom.

The poem is as close to a prayer as any of the poems that Celan wrote. But prayers are not always answered. Implicit in the poem is the possibility that Celan and Ilana will be balked at the East Gate, never to pass through it; that in losing Ilana to Ilana he will lose her; that their erotic bond will be severed; that the conditional and provisional will never become actual, and that Celan himself will never become who he is but will once again be riven by irresolvable conflicts that will perpetually exile him from himself.

Bambach succinctly recounts the tragic events that transpired shortly after Celan's return to Paris:

> Soon after his return, the familiar themes of ambivalence emerge in both his personal correspondence and in his poetry. He worried about the frayed relations with his old friends and relatives after so many years of separation, about the reality of leaving Europe for a new life in Israel. He even toyed with the idea of living on a kibbutz, of starting a new life with Ilana, of living among other Jews and speaking mainly Hebrew. But the old fears and ambivalence would not let him loose from their grip. After his great hopes were dashed and the future receded from view, he realized that the one possibility he allowed

himself—the hope of a redemptive "homecoming" to Jerusalem—was shattered. Within a few months he committed suicide.

As his life drew toward its close, the world and language, we can surmise, despite Celan's best efforts, ultimately continued to lie in smoldering scraps all around him.

The fact that Celan, like Primo Levi, committed suicide should have no bearing upon our judgment of his work. To have simply taken up the task, to have assumed the role that he did, required a kind of courage that is worthy of admiration and is ultimately above reproach.

In closing, I will simply cite here one poem reflective of Celan's later style, "Ashglory," a poem which typically, seems to approach, and *almost* to breach, a kind of event horizon beyond which legibility becomes impossible:

ASHGLORY

Ashglory behind
your shaken-knotted
hands at the threeway.

Pontic erstwhile: here,
a drop,
on

the drowned rudder blade,
deep
in the petrified oath,
it roars up.

(On the vertical
breathrope, in those days,
higher than above,
between two painknots, while
the glossy
Tatarmoon climbed up to us,
I dug myself into you and into you.)

Ash-
glory behind
you threeway
hands.

The cast-in-front-of-you, from
the East, terrible.

No one
bears witness for the
witness.

Again, rather than comment on this poem—painfully raveled, scored, knotted, unrequitedly beseeching, triune as though balked at some fatal crossroads—a poem that is a barely-articulate bearing of witness, I will simply remark that I have perhaps chosen it because its references to ash remind me of a recent catastrophic event, which I am in no way equating in scope, significance, and power with the Holocaust, but to which nonetheless I, one among many, was forced to bear witness.

When the twin towers collapsed on 9/11, I was living in a walk-up apartment in Brooklyn about a mile away as the crow flies from the locus of the event. On the morning of September 11, 2001, I awakened in my bedroom to a sound like a bullet striking an aquarium. An eerie, unprecedented sound. I instinctively arose, turned on the TV, and saw, on the usually bland and indifferent screen, an apparition that all have surely now seen, and all too often: one of the World Trade Center towers defaced by a hole as ugly and menacing as a shark's mouth.

Later, of course, I saw both towers flatten in an instant. The wind was blowing in the direction of Brooklyn that day, sending a ghastly cloud of pulverized debris, including, no doubt, the nearly vaporized traces of human bodies, toward our roof. Upon its tarred surface surprisingly large scraps of burning paper, on which written characters were still legible, settled before definitively turning to ash.

The implosion of the towers seemed to me somehow metaphorical of a psychic implosion I have experienced a number of times during my lifetime. But again, of course, though experienced by many as a traumatic crisis, the events of 9/11 had a far broader cultural import. Justice, in service of a radically dualistic and perverse notion of good and evil, had become perverted into a terrible act of vengeance. In the American response to this event, justice, too, gave way to an excessive wrath, and there was scant attention given to mercy. Justice and mercy, as in the Kabbalist notion of creation that becomes a catastrophic fall, had become terribly misaligned.

I am currently writing during a particularly dark time in my own country, during a pandemic that is a minor plague, but a plague nonetheless, and just after the Capitol was briefly taken over by a violent mob. Fortunately, we seem to have escaped, whether temporarily or not only time will tell, the dark designs of a racist, fascist, would-be autocrat intent upon undermining democracy itself, as well as any distinction between truth and lies, lies and truth.

The subversion of this distinction, resulting in a proliferation of conspiracy theories, all of them almost unthinkably absurd, that stigmatize the other, and that have propagated a radical schism in the body politic perhaps more drastic than any seen since the Civil War, has, of course, been enabled by the internet. The internet has become a kind of open sewer wherein all content is subsumed by the bland, indifferent moniker of information that seldom informs, and in which a veritable Babel of debased scraps of language compete for the increasingly attenuated attention of those whom they in turn debase.

We live, as well, in a time of hopped up meta-evolution and of an artificial intelligence that grows exponentially, a time in which it seems our devices may soon become our masters not our servants, while meanwhile we, frail and embodied, despite our hubris, grow no wiser. Have we ever, as a species, for all our intellectual and technological progress, grown wiser? This question is perhaps impossible to answer.

.

APPENDIX: TALKING HEAD

TALKING HEAD

So many words have been put into my mouth
It's a wonder I've any left to call my own;
I mean those dreary rehearsals, poem after poem,
Of things that never happened, not to me—
Of my tragic, uxorious love for Eurydice,
Of my pitiful rescue mission, traffic with shades,
Of my foolish bargain with the Lord of Hell.
Well, when I look back, my agonized recollection
Is not of some dream of what could not have been
Dispelled by the cold light of sober day;
My affections had always bent the other way.
Are we all reduced to our legends in the end?
I never had a consort. Playing solo
Was all I'd done, all I'd been chosen to do.
Apollo sired me, bequeathed me my lyre,
Ordained me to be a priest of Dionysus,
To temper his savagery with my tremulous lays.
God, how I rue that summons, and that day!

It was D, of course, who had a knack for girls,
Outlandish rock star, face a mask, mere show,
His act all hollow percussion, driving beat.
It was he who started underground, made it big,
Emerged as from some source enticingly foreign,
Tossed on our white sands as by the sea,
A metaphor his crazed fans took literally—
Thus that lurid, odd, biennial argosy,
Their idol wheeled, shore to city, in a ship,
A painted prop, too fragile for any wave,
While they raved loud around him, a procession
Graced, too, by loutish goatboys wielding dildos,
Chanting his lewd dithyrambs, his punk anthems,
His solemn rite turned plain obscenity;
The advent of their hero—precious captive!—
Roused a mock greeting fit for a pilfered slave
Who slipped away, and headed for the hills,
Their capsized hearts left seized yet dispossessed,
By his daft abandon ravaged and enthralled.

His every appearance sparked the same sensation
That quickly spread, a sickening conflagration,
An epidemic—no, a plague, whose fever
Its victims gladly caught, and, mad, passed on.
Androgyne stroking his phallus and his tresses,
He teased our decorous virgins to a frenzy
Until they lost themselves and ran in packs,
Groupies, harpies, furies, fates, fierce Maenads,
Relentlessly tracking down that thing they loved,
Could never get enough of, like a drug
Whose simulated ecstasy trumped bright day.
And he, poor fool, could not, dared not control
The very force that he himself unleashed,
But threw his effigies into their roiling mosh pit
(Bulls, suckling calves, goats, lions, snakes—
How many bestial forms he wore and sloughed!)
Where they were torn, predictably, limb from limb,
The raw meat of his barbarous communion,
A god both of destruction and self-destruction,
The fate he feigned augmenting his fatal allure.

Blood brother to the dancing God, Lord Shiva,
(Ecstatic one who drank from the cosmic sea
The whole world's poison, transmuted it within—
Fierce alchemist whose crucible was himself—
To a quintessential nectar, and so survived,
His omnipotent lingam stirring in every yoni,
Lord both of death and conquering life, revived)
My wayward charge could never truly die.

Imagine the dreadful license exemption bred!
It was he, and he alone, who had compacted
With hell, disreputable mineshaft, and its Lord
And with his promiscuous father, god of gods,
As indulgent with his son as with himself;
Together, axial poles of the turning world,
They conspired, ever faithful, to secrete him,
Below, above, but safely out of bounds,
His limbs reknit, rebaptized in lake or sea,
Until, again, the earth quaked. Bromios roared
The blessing of his catastrophic word,

Braying his senseless name at the full moon
As, perched upon a high crag shagged by clouds,
A stream of golden light poured from his jaws,
Glowing like lava from some fresh eruption—
Prodigious prodigal that night adored.
Mysterium tremens! Their God's epiphany
Sent thrills of delirium through his votaries,
Expectant, who awaited his plighted return,
Yearning for their dance to begin yet again,
For their revels' entrancing, orgiastic rout.

Like his pale precursors, Osiris, Attis, Adonis,
The boy who never grows up kept showing up,
Forever unattainable, forever drawing near,
Still vacant behind the mask of his dazzling enigma,
Breaking the hearts of those who would be broken
Like him, yet live to break another day.
Like Elvis, worshiped at his shrine in Memphis,
Dionysus was ever a mama's boy at heart;
How he pined for Semele, his lost mortal part,
Vaporized by one bolt from a jealous father!
An aborted thing, snatched from her still hot ashes,
Peremptorily stitched into the God's hard thigh,
His cramped gestation yielded a second birth
Unnatural, unlaborious, still premature—
A tale to arouse any virgin's pity and scorn,
Inciting emotions half sexual, half-maternal
(An uneasy concatenation of roles at best).
And so at each least Dionysus-sighting
His devotees, convulsed, quit hearth and home,
Eloping to high wastes of snow-capped mountains,
Hair streaming, suckling wild calves at their breasts
While panting shrill cries anything but maternal
To the Corybantic clash of clanging cymbals
Until, swayed by an instinct blind within them,
They conveyed their charges, then their god himself,
Safe to the font, to the womb of life or death.

Dreamed consummation, then tragic dispersal—
A mess of limbs appalled their opening eyes,
Made worse by their implication in his demise,

A guilt that tore their world, rendered more telling
Their longing for his form, his fate's reprise,
As though his absence magnified his presence;
His death wore his more urgent life's disguise.

D, of course, kept laughing behind the scenes;
Through him the tragic turned toward the absurd—
Lord knows, at the start of a long, hard day
There's nothing quite like a rollicking satyr play!

No mere shape-shifter, he switched others' shapes,
Rearranging and deranging their forms and fates
With more than a director or a dramatist's skill;
The whole world was the stage, or the blank screen
On which he worked his magic, his special effects,
His miracles, his mise-en-scène, his Maya,
Or, assuming the actor's role, directed himself
(Above all, he loved to see himself being seen)
With special care to entrances, quick exits
So stunning his fellow actors blew their lines.
But D alone truly lived, disappeared in his roles,
Agent as well as actor, pained sufferer, too,
And in his masques the illusory and the real
Converged, with not a jot of space between them.

Zagreus constantly slain, D ever reborn,
And Bromios faithfully bellowing at His side—
His names were like concurrent incarnations,
Chords echoing through divergent universes;
Cropping up here, there, everywhere, and nowhere,
He seemed to play no part, yet played them all.

And so, crude tyrant, martyred liberator,
He came as a stranger, conquering foreign lands
Of which, in truth, he'd always been a native,
Possessing, repossessing hearts and minds
He blessed and blasted, plagued and glibly saved,
Brave exile reclaiming polis after polis,
Confounding their too rigorous paradigms.

He came from India, Persia, Arabia, Thrace,
His face in ruddy makeup, dread God of War,
After first tracing the same route in reverse
(A procession after which Lord Alexander,
Whose bent, ambivalent heart stiffened his will,
Would later style his straight, triumphal race).
A tempestuous male diva wreaking mayhem—
At once jack-booted vandal and femme fatale—
Upon his cowed, sycophantic retinue
Of would-be satyrs, aging boys in the band,
D imagined slights, exacted tribute due
To a demigod jealous of his name and fame,
His least or latest whim momentous law.

Such rumored antics proved a surefire draw.
Generalissimo who took each city by storm—
Heil promised *Ubermensch! Heil Zarathustra!*—
His feral, high-pitched, vaunting rhetoric
Buckled the sold-out stadiums on his tour;
All clamored to greet his strobe-lit apparition;
After years of anticipation, the throes of release
Convulsed his throng, a wild, protracted labor,
An hysterical pregnancy issuing in no birth;
Some fainted, prostrate at his prancing feet
While others jerked in spasms, jammed the aisles;
Still others froze, chills running up their spines,
Feared the crumbling temple would succumb,
Interring all beneath a spoiled brat's crown.

D saved his proudest gig for his home town.
Bandying lines with his dimwitted cousin,
A heart he'd hardened, blinded in advance,
He played an effeminate herald, a fey Hermes,
A hippie longhair whose guru's seductions
Corrupted matrons' morals, drove them wild
With Eastern notions (peace, love, back to nature).
What gall! He insisted Pentheus join the cult,
An insult framed to engender a fierce reply
The frantic, dumb-struck king failed to supply.

What better time to conjure a blind seer?
Tiresias knew which way the wind was blowing
(For him it used to blow both ways at once)
And so it was no great stretch to don a gown,
But Cadmus, too, was quick to ape the hipster;
Each young/old, male/female, neither/either,
These two, united, formed a winsome couple
As hand in hand they shuffled out of town.

How coyly, passively D accepted the shackles,
The cuffs by which he eagerly was bound,
A masked tyrant queerly glad to play the slave
Like a smug dominant acting the submissive
In the practiced, lascivious choreography
Of some choice, preauthorized rite of S&M,
A game not to be tried with rougher trade,
But in the right hands an enthralling masquerade—

Only to break free! More fleet than Houdini,
He performed his miraculous magic in no time flat,
Was almost as quick to level the whole polis;
Its palace, temple, walls—all toppled down;
At the apex of the sole façade left standing
He gleefully pegged Pentheus' headless crown.

His act, of course, was not confined to land.
For D, the wine dark sea was floating theater,
A protean stage for his outlandish pranks.
And so, a fetching youth, his comely feet
Printing the untrammeled sands of an ivory shore,
Soft zephyrs combing, uncombing his gold hair,
He caught the eyes of pirates, only too happy
After years of celibate toil, uncertain pay,
To ensnare, as sweetest spoil, such easy prey;
They stashed their trophy deep in the ship's hold.
But D, as ever, proved himself the pirate
As sprouts of profligate life spread everywhere;
Tendrils of ivy clutched the bellying sails
As thick vines snagged the oarlocks and the oars;
Wine, as though poured freely, but from no jars,
Exhaled its dank perfume, and kept on rising

Until it sloshed about the sailors' thighs;
A lion roared in the bow; in the stern a bear
Unbaited, crammed its maw with human flesh.
A basilisk wound about the stiff mast, miming
The serpent-twins entwined round Hermes' staff,
Or Moses' miraculous sign raised in the desert,
His rod-serpent-rod that with a salient tap
Released life-giving streams from penitent rock.
But D was a prophet of a different stripe—
The ship, enchanted vineyard, uncanny garden,
Would yield no promised land to its lost crew;
Sated, his sweet revenge almost complete,
In a grand *deus ex machina*, his ultimate coup,
He burst, glad day, in glory from the hold,
His wine, mixing with blood, soaking the planks,
And boldly seized the tiller, giving thanks
As his black vessel cut through cresting waves
That danced about it, in proud tumult raved.

Intimate with earth's depths as with high seas,
It was D, some said, at Demeter's behest,
Who descended, on cue, to rescue Persephone,
Hell's Queen, his second mother, virgin bride,
Abandoned her to the tender fields of spring.
It was he, nocturnal one, who burst the bonds
Of his ravenous hell hounds, the fell Erinyes,
Insatiable as the fiercest of Maenads,
Pouring through the earth's wide-yawning maw.
Requiting crimes that D himself incited,
Their vengeance, too, was its own sovereign law.
He summoned, from below, the riddling Sphinx,
Half woman, half lynx, devourer of men,
Sibyl reciting the lines of his cryptic script
(Rendering all but Oedipus stupefied and mute)
As a special prize to bedevil his closest kin—
Like death, no respecter of lineage, caste, or clan;
Thebes early had suffered his unfounded rage,
The keen stripes of his avid fennel whip.

Hades and Dionysus are one and the same,
Heraclitus, sage of paradox, proclaimed,

Who knew that *the way up is the way down.*
If not the same, then constantly trading places
In one of D's alternate self-mythologies;
Confederate, they harried uprooted shades
Who, shielding lidless eyes from the sun's rays,
Gadded about unhallowed on D's festal days—
For him yet one more play within his play.

All this was his force that I was bid to curb
Who could not help but feel his pervading charm;
I was, after all, his sworn priest, although bound
By a firm command to keep him within bounds.
O, endless indenture to a double bind—
I felt myself, day by day, growing more like him
Whom I was impossibly charged to civilize;
I sensed a fate like his growing within me,
Sensed, too, my own would be far more unkind.
My single father was no match for his
Dual patron-parentage, Olympian Zeus and Hades,
Lords of unspeakable heights, fathomless depths
I was taught to neither ponder nor traverse;
My melodious voice was trained to a middle range,
A golden mean, whole numbers, undistorted,
To chant of things familiar, not estranged;
But now I could faintly hear odd notes within me,
Dark intimations, brief, of a dissonance
That later would surge up, and then submerge me,
Would be my portion in life's troubled dance.

Before that cruel, humiliating summons
To play priest, apologist, publicist to a phantom
I had my own, my youthful golden time.
Uneducated in the world's deceptions,
My heart was almost as true as my perfect pitch.
I poured out my songs to the spontaneous pulse
That spoke within me, deftly plucked the strings
Whose resonance was the thrum of life itself;
And then I let my sweet words come unbidden—
No hunter, I had no need to track them down.

I seemed to move within a column of light
Whose radiance spread about me everywhere.
My senses, quick, engrossed their several objects
Not serially, yet distinctly—O all at once
They vanished, reappeared in that golden shaft
Expanding, contracting, humming with such speed
It seemed to annul all sense of time itself
And so not to move at all, still standing fast
Like Zeno's arrow, staying while it flew.
And yet my song's circumference grew wider;
Tall sentinel trees bent toward it, and wild beasts,
Quitting their lairs, grew tame within my sight,
Breathed softy as I stroked my lyre's strings—

Yes, like a virgin's fingers working her loom
Within her father's house, weaving, unweaving,
Suspending, prolonging the day with her reverie,
Dreaming (half hoping, half dreading) the hour
When a youth bold as Hector, fair as Hyacinth
Would cross her threshold, steal her heart away:

So I, too, played within my father's house,
Its dome the sky, its boundary the horizon,
The unmarked line he broached with his flaring robes,
Twice daily trespassing, touching earth's domain
That he, its prince, had long since made his own;
He kept his distance, yet kept drawing near,
Or seemed to, when, alone, I chanted his name
And meted out my measures in strict song.
I kept to my proper rooms within his mansion,
Oak-vaulted vales where, carelessly, I wandered
And listened to blithe fish plash in the streams,
The bobcat purr, fleet insects whir midair,
Paired doves coo, and the falcon, wheeling, cry,
My only fear the gross shriek of Pan's pipe,
Twin organs fashioned from a nymph he raped
When he came pillaging from his mountain lair,
Fanning quick panic through my reverent glades,
A priapic interlude far from mere comic relief;
Like one of D's cleft satyrs, half man, half-goat,
Coward, he skulked back to his sullen rocks

While I renewed the hiatus of my vows.

I hymned a living sum, a breathing cosmos,
The whole in each part, each part in the whole
Addressed to every other in just proportion,
In numbers that my instinctive octave sounded
And sounding, did its own part to uphold.
The stars and planets spinning in their courses,
Each root, trunk, branch, leaf, and winding vein
That flourished beneath the slow arc of the sun,
The rainbow parsing its colors in bright mist,
Constraining banks permitting streams to flow,
All spoke to my eyes a proximate symmetry;
O, only by being bounded were things free
To open outward toward light's unscored sea,
Forever unreachable, lost to my command.
I preferred the vocation, sweet, enjoined on me—
To be just where I was, and not to wander
In thought or act from work that came to hand:
To care for, cure my plots of native land
And find, in cloistered clearings, the green fields
Of Elysium, redeemed from distant shores.

Meanwhile, my vision frequented its stores;
A seer perhaps too enamored of sight itself,
Of the play of dappled shade on indolent limbs,
I cherished not only pristine things, self-sealed,
Forever turning into themselves, rapt spheres,
But the charged, immaculate spaces between them
Like the silence between words, its reticence,
The vibrant precondition of utterance
Or of its meanings, multiple yet coherent
Though intangible as a temple's atmosphere.
I sought an art, a life, composed, intact,
I never longed to pierce, nor to be pierced,
(Whether by Eros or by some warrior's arrow),
To strike beyond surfaces to the pith within,
Or to be stricken, like some wounded deer,
Or if I yearned to, was balked by an urgent fear
Somehow instilled in me from my first years.
No mere poet, after all, but a latent priest,

Clairvoyant in the simplest of senses,
My vision clear, my body modest, chaste,
I only wanted to gaze, no, never to taste.
And that is why my boys were drawn to me
Or to my songs (I almost thought them the same).
They knew that I would seek, ask nothing of them
Unlike their parents, lovers, girlfriends, wives,
And so they submitted to my words' designs
And lay about me, innocent, undefended,
Not thinking, for a time, of martial feats,
Of training in their unconquerable phalanx
Which melded all, incorporate, in one body,
A soldered file of soldiers, arm in arm,
A single faultless wall of brazen armor
Deployed to repel the brashest of attacks,
To shield their polis from all threat of harm
(The antitheses of Maenads' swarming packs,
Each feeling herself the sole spouse of her God,
Each reveling, proud, in all the others lacked).

But now, lost in my songs' untended moment,
The willing captives of its yielding spell
They laid their shining shields upon the grass,
Reclined, half-shut their softly lidded eyes.
Why, they seemed almost, almost feminine
And I, a mere poet, was their trusted captain,
Confederate in the arts of peace, not war.
I gazed on their rapt features like a lover
Who wakens first, and finds the face beside him
More lovely still in sleep's unvexed repose,
And felt the aching tenderness of a mother,
A vigilance more poignant than any dream.
Still cradling my lyre, I felt its subtle humming
Along my nerves, converging on my heart
From which, redoubled, then sent forth again,
It found its way into my burgeoning song;
Its words, though uttered singly, were blended
Like drops of water vanishing in a stream.
Perhaps I was not so different from my boys;
Well, I of the lyre, they of the heavy bow—
We both were masters of the tense, plucked string.

Nearby, in sacred groves, nymphs tended wells
Reflecting, in blue rings, unblemished skies,
Bright faces flashing in a liquid mirror
At which they gazed, their stray, cascading curls,
Submerged, half-hid, in mind's clear element
Unstirred by any ripple, its glass intact,
Its oases surrounded, screened by stately oaks
From any zephyr or stiff, sudden wind;
Those stillest pools were fed by buried springs
Whose urgent sources' bursting syllables
The nymphs alone, devoted, trembling, heard
Leaping like light beneath the placid pane,
Their tones too deep for my famed lyre to delve,
Their fleeting, abiding thrum enlivening earth;
O, they were beatified by their constant care,
So comely that satyrs, mortals, highest Gods
Profaned, by force, a grace none could possess—
A brute fate that had never threatened me.

It is true I shunned the company of women,
But I was still a youth. None would suspect
The thrill of pained perplexity felt within me,
Despite myself, despite my clear intentions,
Like an arrow fixed yet twisting in my heart,
A keenest wound half blessing and half curse,
Exhilaration strangely mixed with shame.
How could I speak what yet had no known name?
I scarcely knew what it was I felt myself,
Only that what now awakened in deep recesses,
Its echoes sealed in the caverns of the mind,
Was somehow dangerous, a dark foreboding
That cast first shadows on my lambent days.

Well, after all, I was my father's son.
Bright Lord of the bow, the lyre, of dire wounds
That he alone, great healer, had skill to cure
With his scented herbs, his compound remedies,
Sadly, when he himself was cruelly stricken
With love of a youth by his swift discus slain
He found no sure recourse to redress his pain,

Only the red-streaked flower he renamed
For his beloved, inscribing each petal 'AI, AI',
His distress unmollified by that silent cry,
Yet duly commemorated, then duly mourned;
A god, he dilated to full strength, moved on,
Returned to his high station, the resonant sky,
Resigned his staff to Asklepios; his roving eye,
Undimmed, again surveyed his broad domain.

But I was left to burn with an inward smart
He would not or could not see, a world apart—
I'd always known I was far from his chief care.
A desire as yet with no object, a parching fire
Kept wasting me from within. Only my lyre
Could quench its flames, and set me free to roam
In the placeless realm of sound, now my true home,
The self-forgetful trance from which I'd wake,
As always, balked and baffled, bereft, alone.

When at last I could not hide myself from myself
I vowed never to act on any goad's prompting,
To let my life's inner stream flow out in verse
And yet flow nowhere, gathering force within
To radiate through each nerve, fiber, limb,
Growing like some vast cloud-headed tree
Until I almost glowed like my fortunate father
With his solar roar, his voice at whim's command,
His sovereign words as feared as those of Zeus
Although he did not scruple to speak in riddles,
A sly trick I would not deign to emulate.

I had my pride. Should I have let it go?
Son of a God, should I have played the pilgrim
And slouched toward Delphi, jealous of a fate
I knew, in its ripe time, would be unfolded,
Neither a moment too early nor too late?
What need had I to ponder, parse, or study
The hermeneutics of the Pythia's hiss,
Her forked tongue always signaling both ways
At once, and so at once both right and wrong,
In retrospect ever true to her dazed throng?

Her words, whenever literal, proved a scandal—
It would take long years to rehabilitate
Her image, but she always bounced back strong.
What need had I for Dodona's fabled oak,
Its sibilant speech all rustling consonants
(Its eager priests supplied the missing vowels)
When nearer trees, far loftier, bent toward me
And keenly listened to my simpler song?
What need to read the random flight of birds?
Their veering chevrons, glorious to behold,
Spelled nothing but a flash of white and gold.
Should I, who shuddered at the sight of blood
And chafed at sanctioned rites of sacrifice,
The slaughter of the heifer, the conjugal feast,
The libations spilled for the unfeeling dead,
Have stooped to haruspication, poked about
The steaming entrails of some innocent beast,
Getting the lay of a torn and wasted land?
Let darkness bury darkness. Why invoke
Chthonic shades with charms best left unsaid?

Should I have played the initiate at Eleusis,
Have fasted, plunged in vapid thermal baths,
Have quaffed capacious draughts of unmixed wine,
Until, sufficiently weakened in mind and body,
Deemed pure enough to join a credulous mob,
I melded with its motley, licentious queue
Of slaves, priests, politicians, duped patricians
Who yearly trooped to Demeter's dreadful shrine,
There to meander, lost, in the soul's dark night,
Its labyrinthine cellars, its stifling caves,
Half-choking, gasping for a shaft of air,
Feet probing for the first step of some stair,
Ah, finally, one with all, to be ushered above
By a hierophant, a psychopomp in white,
To fiery tongues of light, to flutes' and drums'
Wild, palpating arias, spasms of delight,
To the painted props of a promised Elysium,
Vouchsafed, at the end of life's false path,
To those who fell prostrate before an ear of corn,
Reaped and upraised, a bold, pneumatic phallus,

A tender idol, lovingly lopped and shorn?
No need to change one's life, to pledge reform—
Sufficient, more than sufficient, to have seen,
Surrendered to a mystery, to stand forewarned,
To remember faithless Attis, his eunuch priests
Wailing faint praise to the mother of us all.
Humbled, should I have chosen to be reborn?

I had my pride. I should have let it go
Who dreamed myself to my sole self sufficient
Despite the pangs that roiled me from below,
Upbraiding me with my own mysteries,
The sprouting and hybrid flowers of my soul.
I never though to confer with my truant father
Who never, it seemed, sought out his lonely son;
I would not plead. I would not be undone
By the chill scorn I feared he might bestow
On one who, waxing, blushed with a carnal glow
Like Hyacinth, new-veined with stripes of red,
Conceived to be cut down before his prime.
In that very fear I felt a god draw nearer,
Though even now I cannot name which one,
Or if, in secret league, two gods conspired,
Only that I spied my prone, blank shadow
One morning as I strummed my serried strings
And heard, for the first time, their minor chords,
Odd tones for which I found no ready words,
Although I felt a wordless premonition
Sweep over me, untuning my shivering frame.

It was then that, suddenly, Apollo found me
(Or D dressed in my father's borrowed guise),
Enveloping me in a mist of occulted light,
And spoke the literal sentence that fixed my fate—
Henceforth, an exile, I must quit my glades,
Exchange my quiet paeans for dithyrambs,
Serve as a roving rhapsode for Dionysus,
Induce a truce throughout my father's lands
Who already shared, with D, his shrine at Delphi;
Now I would serve two masters, one command.
Impossible task! To utter my misgivings,

To tempt two gods, was dangerous and futile,
And so, mute though appalled, I bowed my head,
Resigned to follow where my ill luck led;
Tentative, I stepped from my loved clearings
Into a wood that pressed me from all sides,
Its choking thickets and its pricking brambles
Oppressing me, retarding the easy stride
By which I'd glided, free, from field to field.
Probing, recoiling, I slunk, snaking my way
On a pathless path I was bound to improvise,
And passed into a covert world of shadows
Bedazzled by glints of syncopated light;
I stroked my lyre, startled by what I played,
Its dithyrambic beat, bold, shifting shades—
By the rough new style Apollo had prophesied.

Like a tame folk singer forced to go electric
By recidivist, barbarous tastes of a New Age,
I shuddered at raw, rebarbative sound unleashed,
My lyre's amplified twang teasing my ears,
Both shocked and pleased by its fresh prodigies,
But, O, the beasts my dulcet hymns once tamed,
Fretted by foreign rhythms, seized by fear,
Fled the charged bearer of a word transformed,
Now ramified far beyond its former scope—
Those intimate precincts, empty and foregone,
Were faded memories of some foreclosed era
No troubadour could recapture or prolong.

How strange to become a stranger to my kind!
The flashing forms that vanished into the brake
Left only a fleet parting, a rustling behind
Like a sudden gust of wind riffling the reeds
Of my past haunts, their recollected streams
Still voluble within me, the voice of dreams
Still whispering soothing words within my heart.

Alone and unattended, I grimly tended
Toward Ida's cliffs and caves and stately pines,
The alpine faults D made his polar home,
The hideaways from which he ranged on high,

And felt like a common trespasser. The sky
Weighed down upon me like a leaden crown.
The eagle's lair, *uber alles*, the despot's eye,
Olympian, freeze-framing glacial vistas,
The hygienic vaults of aesthetes on holiday,
Bare, rifted rockscapes, fetishized, sublimed,
The self its own spectacle, the ego inflated
Beyond itself, beyond mere earthly bonds,
The spirit's vertiginous whiteout uplifting all,
Wagnerian high camp shot by Reifenstahl—
All these were tricks D saved for later times.

My cold, compulsory exile was less sublime;
I secreted myself, for shelter, in a cavern
Carved, or rather gouged, in the side of a cliff,
And daily clambered down to grub for food
From grizzled shepherds driving huddled flocks
Through narrow passes, used to solitude,
Not knowing kin, communion, the only good
That I had prized, been formed by, understood,
Whose praise I sang of in my former days
To my soldiers, a listening circle in repose;
Each casual limb seemed stationed in its poise,
The body's fixed proportions a timeless truth.

Trial-tempted hero, quester, ascetic, saint,
Or forager in the woods, forced mendicant,
Were never roles that I to myself assigned
Who dreamed I played no role, instinct with self,
So seamlessly were my self and role aligned.
But now I scarcely recalled who I once was,
My frail, parched body whittled to a stick
With which to prod some jackal or rabid dog,
My soul stripped bare, emaciated, craving
Some vestige, touch of company, human care,
While shut in my cavern, O, far from oracular,
An apprentice hermit, my hermitage despair;
But I was ravaged still more by the fear
Of what I sensed awaited—D's epiphany,
For surely the God whom I was taxed to praise
By my sometime father would appeal to me,

Though in what form I dared not speculate.

I knew, from the first, my civilizing lyre
Was no match for D's redundant, vital power
That fed on itself, and yet grew ever stronger;
Though self-consumed, its own endless supply,
D's substance never wasted in the spending:
Ravenous, rampant, ecstatic, teeming life,
Absorbed, through death, still greater potency.

O, I had tidings of what transpired here
One moonless night when Bromios appeared
As sleek as a panther, pacing these same cliffs
To goad, past distraction, proud sisters of Thebes,
Impervious, who rebuffed his claimant's ire.
The moment his feet rebuked too solid ground,
Dull earth, once dormant, spun into overdrive,
Hopped up, juiced on its own amphetamines,
As Bromios pounced, himself a natural high.
Sprouting, unfolding, maturing in less than a day,
Vine tendrils hung with clusters of ripe grapes,
All fit to be burst on palates less than fine;
Fermenting instantly, rich, unmixed wine
Soon raced through matrons' overheated veins
As earth's fecundity staggered past all bounds;
Tranced nurses suckled fanged beasts, pacified
By breasts that spouted jets of copious milk
That spurted, too, from the bare pinecone heads
That tipped the lifted thyrsi firmly gripped
By Bacchae whirled in self-transcendent dance.

Hysterica passio: up, thou climbing rapture!
A thousand eager staves now rapped the ground
From which oil, honey, water, ardent, sprung,
As though from bursting wells as yet untapped.
The Maenads' leaps grew bolder, fleeter, higher,
As each assumed their deity's restless power
And trampled hard rock into the oozing mire
That stained their feet as they still blithely trod
The winepress of their odd, capricious God.

Past mania, they reeled into psychosis
Whose syntax, voiding objects, yielded signs,
Self-constellating ciphers, occult designs
So full of meaning meanings were annulled
In stunned, vertiginous, scorched, vacated minds;
Clues, portents, glancing surfaces, turning, faced
One way, to magnify the I that scanned them,
Each a rapt God in whom a God confided.
Countless glyphs with only one translation,
Like thought retraced to the mute pulse of will,
All things were Dionysus, whispered "kill,"
And in the thrilling turning of that moment
Each tender nurse waxed strong as an Amazon,
Each fiercer than a tribe of pale male hunters,
Quicker to pounce, more competent to rend
Whatever gorged beast wandered in her way.
Black widows weaving flaring, tensile nets
With which to trip, ensnare their flailing prey,
With unkempt cries they hoisted phallic thyrsi,
Shafts oozing viscous seminal milk and honey,
An orgasm prolonged past paltry spasms;
Others lit torches, dancing with forked fires
Whirled into orbits, halos round their heads
As, scaling jagged cliffs in ardent bounds,
They sought the heights of D's inchoate night;
Each dreamed herself a queen, like Pentheselia,
Would happily have severed a sagging breast
To make her aim more true, her only quest
To be a peerless hunter, rabid as Dionysus,
Ruthless to rout, uproot his implacable foes,
Usurpers of chaste rites, unsanctioned guests,
Voyeurs hot to crash their secret show.

Their fevered skin grew dark with an inner glow
As they consumed raw flesh, ah, freshly torn,
Each like black Kali, teeth begrimed with gore,
Skulls, pelts swinging from her ample belt,
Or like Durga riding bareback on her tiger,
Her mace and trident wielded by multiple arms,
Dashing worldly dreams with unworldly alarms.

O, fiercest of that whole crew was Agave,
The king's queen mother, sad sister of Semele,
A skeptic forced to yield to D's stern charms;
Her cries, pansexual, tore through the chill night,
Shrill ululations, triumphing in his will.
How suddenly she turned when his full frenzy
Torched her, rolling back her rapacious eyes,
Far-spanning, that spotted Pentheus, a bold spy,
A lion perched, incongruous, in a treetop
That she and her fervid sisterhood brought low,
Reserving for her the right to rend her spoil.
Like Perseus brandishing Medusa's head,
Poor Agave, stricken, hexed, strode into Thebes,
Vaunting the trophy of her hunter's prowess,
A lion's mane impaled on her thyrsus-spike,
Until the fit wore off, and she awakened
To scan familiar features, broken, mangled,
Reduced to a trope, the synecdoche of her son,
Then wailed at what her bloody hands had done.

D's willing consorts, too, faced tragic ends.
Some fell in exile, others to self slaughter;
Still others like Agave, turned on their sons,
A compulsive, repetitive theme, scripted by D.
All were stalked by him, the stealthiest voyeur
Who, hidden, relished wracked, climactic scenes
As though he died, survived, with every one.

Pent up, constrained by close, familiar walls,
I played, replayed D's myriad thespian feats
On a tape that unwound, rewound within my mind,
Revulsion mingling with a queer attraction,
Perhaps the pull of destiny, long delayed,
Or of solitude that yearned for an encounter
That kept not happening, day by aimless day,
Each one the same, a dumb continuum,
No blessed break, the promised guest detained.
One morning as I paced, beyond distraction,
A sudden shade, cast inward, traversed my floor;
Startled, I swung around, sought out its source,
An icon staunchly stationed at my cave's mouth

(No ideal form, abstracted, no dream of reason)
Backlit by slanting rays it partly blocked—
D's dreaded, anticipated epiphany!
His mask uprose, fresh-dripping from the sea,
All head, no body, that head the height of a man,
And faced me, as others, fully frontally,
His face with a gentle smile like a Bodhisattva's
That seemed to cancel all desire and fear.
But O, that smile was nothing if not deceptive,
More like the Mona Lisa's, Madonna or vampire;
Sweet monster, posed before a rocky wasteland,
Her lips, forever sealed, conceal a rictus,
A laugh whose echoes, dumb, remain congealed.
How glibly the God accosted me: *I am here*,
As he conjured up his visage, ex nihilo,
Challenging me to meet his steadfast gaze
As the roar of raw chaos itself assailed my ears.
I could not evade, nor apprehend obliquely
Like Medusa's image, caught in Perseus' shield,
Seen in that mirror darkly, not face to face,
His eyes that raised me up, and laid me low;
Transfixed, my vantage was more like the Gorgon's
The moment she descried her own reflection—
O, impetuous act of self-despoiling love!—
Whose severed head toppled from its lofty perch,
As Pegasus, new born, pranced up the sky.
I felt like a soul who'd died and yet survived.
Then furtively, uncannily, D disappeared,
Plunging toward heaven, lunging into the sea,
Bipolar tropes that merged in the awful silence
Subtending the pandemonium of his reign.
How quickly all the shrilling pipes grew still,
The cymbals ceased to clash, the thunder-drums
Sank into the sanctum of the inner ear.

His mask turned inside out, turned outside in,
Was both yet neither, other to no other,
Created a space not space, a warped lacuna
Where here was always elsewhere, elsewhere here;
To gaze at him was to be displaced, unplaced,
To banish oneself completely, unless one hid,

Retreated behind his mask, saw through his eyes,
Beholding the absence where one used to be;
Strange ecstasy! Not even my shadow lay
Before me, although it was far from noon,
So wholly was I consumed by his disguise.

Like a lunatic swapping places with a cipher,
I reverted to my own form, his mask vacated.
I shuddered awake, as into a further dream
Until, beside myself with joy or terror,
I once again confronted his grinning façade.
His features seemed mere copies of themselves,
The copies of a copy, themselves a copy
Of which no lost original could be found;
Reveal to me your face before you were born
He seemed to taunt, a cruel simulacrum
Delighted to laugh at my too earnest state.
Neither kindly master nor fierce nemesis,
He vaporized as soon as I would oppose him
And left me, lost, with nothing to retard
My headlong fall through an abyss that opened
(Within me or without – I could not tell)
Until, in the splitting of an orphaned moment
I caught sight of his blank, unmoving eyes;
And then I was not plummeting, merely standing,
Still as a statue, balked and paralyzed,
That as by some undue miracle comes to life,
Breathes, moves, exulting in the morning air,
And feels the living sunlight gild his limbs,
A slight breeze rise and fall in his flowing hair.

At last, beside me like a lost twin brother,
I glimpsed D's human form for the first time:
O beautiful past beauty!—man, woman, God,
Converging, found the zenith of their spring,
Sap rising, in his lithe and tender limbs,
All golden light, and glistening as with dew;
He smiled at me, moist eyes blue as the sky,
And in that moment, lost to all I once knew,
I felt myself his consort. Dancing for me,
For me alone, his sole, his chosen peer,

He deployed himself before my enchanted eyes
In gestures free and playful, hieratic and grave,
Indulgence fused with awesome majesty,
Until I was ready to tender myself his slave,
Almost, almost... A doubt shaded my mind:
Was this, his revelation, his cruelest disguise,
Bright unconcealment his preeminent ploy?

Quicker than thought his features reified;
A mask upreared, not smiling as before,
Its broad mouth twisted into a ludic leer,
From which a tongue, rude, lecherous, protruded,
The face of Gorgo, love transformed to fear,
The sneer of a sniggering, petulant, ancient child,
Polymorphously self-pleasuring, obscene,
Thick snakes coiling, uncoiling in her hair,
Tusks sprouting from her forehead to impale
Some crude impostor not yet turned to stone
By her petrifying need to seize, possess.

The mask was lifted. In its place a skull
Flashed fast before me, the last shreds of skin
Unpeeling from its shut, marmoreal jaws,
The concavities of its temples a searing white,
The all-color color of nothingness. I peered
Through hollow sockets that once harbored eyes
At the wide and disarticulating sky
Supersaturated, stained one immaculate hue,
Engulfing and absorbing my stupefied stare
Until a strange vision rolled within my mind;

I saw the Ganges, torpid, dun-brown, flow,
Silted with eras of sediment, sifted earth,
Bearing, upholding all life in its drifting sway,
A Goddess, gentle sustainer, slow as time,
While light grew denser with a saffron glow.
The sun swelled, softened by diffusing mist,
A pervasive, pendent, breathing atmosphere
That hovered, fed the primordial clay below.
Red-robed initiates gathered on broad banks,
Attended by priests, coiled incense. Temple bells

Told vespers from all quarters, tolling AUM,
The no-tone at the heart of all resonant tones;
Ascetics, pilgrims, shopkeepers, young wives
Joined with devotees—come from how far?—
Hands folded, wading waist high in the tide
That eddied about them, currents deep, alive;
At last, drawn by the waters, they submerged
Their limp and yielding bodies. Hearts entire,
They prayed never to return to this near shore
But like the great swan hamsa to soar away
When spirit stole from flesh on its last day.

Fade in, fade out. My vision turned to black;
Burning ghats flared beside the flickering tide
That flashed entwining arms of tainted fire;
Smoke rose from narrow rows of funeral pyres,
A pestilent incense fogging the fetid air,
Shrouding a yellowed moon, blotting the stars.
The stench of rotting corpses, crepuscular, rank,
Clogged every nostril, sank into each pore.
Night crawlers slunk from culverts of the day,
Prostitutes, thieves, transvestites, out to play;
Vultures wheeled, then dove upon their prey.
Scavengers pledged to scare up choicest scraps,
Kapalikas followed their left-handed path,
Skeletal, brandishing their skull-crowned staffs,
Haunting creation grounds, begging for alms;
Having taken the hero's vow, their solemn oath,
In obeisance to Lord Shiva, their all in all,
Trained to behold in all the indifferent same,
To find nothing repulsive, nothing to disclaim,
Nothing polluted, impure, but words of blame,
All things His body, all acts His gleeful play,
Sworn to slay each reflex or instinct of shame
That binds, as fast as desire, soul to flesh,
Zealous ascetics, they performed their rites,
Their foul black mass in Shiva's holy name;

And so, triumphant, conquering all distaste,
They swilled their sallow wine from cranial cups,
Devoured strips, charred ashes, of human flesh,

And thus, they thought, consumed the God himself,
Then swelled as if infused with Shiva's power
But lost themselves. Did even their God disdain
Their sacramental logic, pure, deranged?

Zagreus, too, was torn, slain, and consumed
By Titans, rebellious, antinomian crew,
Who gorged on him, yet left his beating heart
From which great Zeus, industrious, refashioned
A selfsame form to clothe the God, reborn;
Meanwhile, one bolt reduced the giants to ashes,
Their shades dispatched to blackest Tartarus,
But from their charred remains he molded man,
Gross flesh redeemed by a trace Dionysian.

How easily D subverted me from within,
His cinema unreeled on the screen of my brain
(Quick cuts, dissolves, abortive scenes, surreal)
Although all appeared to haunt me from without.
O, far from my lyre, outmoded, taming him,
My mind by his unstopped force was colonized,
Became a blank zone where lurid pictures bred,
Bright simulacra, virtual, undimensioned,
All words, all finer tones, chased from a head
Benumbed by D, his ideologue's sick designs,
A tyrant still, though I was no common slave.

His smile, smug, mock-triumphal, taunted me
One final time before his mask dissolved,
Returned to the sourceless source to which it fled,
Or joined my father, perhaps, for a tête-à-tête,
While I with my shaken sanity conspired
To find some way to drive my thoughts away
From the utter disintegration threatening them,
Decompensation, in some shrink's cold phrase,
A word with which no soul should make amends
When fathomless horror would serve as well,
Existence itself a soundless, empty shell.

My long exile was over. No interdict
Could bar me from my green, my native fields;

What prison could be worse than to waste here,
What penalty more dispiriting, more severe?
And so, for one last time, I cursed the cliffs
That had lately been my inhospitable home,
And then descended. The way down was easy
Compared to my forced ascent, a fruitless errand,
A slave's obedience, the extorted, false assent
Of a son whom his own father had betrayed,
Had orphaned for his own equivocal gain,
No gain at all. I sensed the price of my rebellion,
But, mad for home, discounted every cost.

Ah, finally I happened on the field I'd lost;
I knew it by its great oaks, its winding streams,
But no boys lingered there. Where had they gone?
No doubt they missed my lyre's notes, missed me,
And so, once again, I plucked its tensile strings,
But not one single soul appeared to greet me
And even tame beasts crouched wary in their lairs;
All wind died down, and eerie silence reigned;
It seemed my world had frozen, globed in crystal
That no clear note could crack, no zephyr thaw,
More adamant than stone tablets of the law,
Until, again, some least branch, silent, stirred,
Although accompanied by no human word.

I waited. *Days.* Yet nothing, *nothing* changed;
My lyre grew still. It had no power to soothe me
When my black moods, imperious, came on.
In every shifting shade I sensed some end,
Some inconceivable end, toward which I tended
And which, at the same time, inclined toward me,
Stalking me just past the margins of my fear
Soon to be crossed: a monstrosity almost here,
Was waiting, as I waited, to pounce on me.
O, only come *home* could I be so estranged
From what I once felt, remembered, of myself,
An inner exile banished from my own source,
My solitude more sere than in the mountains
For which I almost pined, but no turn backward
Could unthink thoughts increasingly deranged,

Or ravel threads that time kept playing out,
Would play out to their frayed, discordant ends
As *worse* drove on from *worsening* to the *worst*.
The mind is its own place? Well, not entirely.
I'd become, as sophists say, *the contested site*
Of irreconcilable forces that now controlled me,
Converging from without, emergent within,
The self, self-scandalized, traduced, undone,
A gutted field, a text ripped, shredded, burned;
The strings of a lyre vandalized and slashed;
Half-finished figures cut from a shattered loom,
Meaning shorn of context, orphaned, misplaced,
Its butchered fabric dangling severed threads;
Disembodied echoes sealed in an empty room;
An effigy formed of straw stuffed in a tomb;
Bare substance, uncreated, poor, forked thing
From which—as something else--I was reborn,
Divorced from the plighted life I dreamed I led,
Blank legend that my name no longer named,
As insubstantial, lost, as the absent wind
That still refused to rustle through my glades.

It started: a sound at the margin of the woods
That startled me, the first clear sound I'd heard
For days, the crackling portent of no good.
Robed, stately matrons stepped forth one by one
Into my clearing, eyes glazed, hypnotized,
Their motions measured, forced into no dance,
The grave antithesis of the Maenads' frenzy.
All seemed the embodied soul of premeditation,
Like the mute chorus of some wordless play
That unfolds toward its preordained fatality,
As they strode toward me, and as I retreated,
Already ruined, to the Hebron's tufted banks,
My beloved rippling stream, too swift to cross.
O, what took place there had already happened
And I was its locus, torn by the premonition
Of my crouching form surrounded by a swarm
Of furious, grappling hands now grasping me—
I knew them well. Impossible to fight them;
I had long since, in truth, given up the ghost

Of Orpheus, had long since been impaled,
Nailed to the canceled horizon of what I was,
Collapsed to a famished point, a deadened star.
Forgive me. I have no heart to enumerate
The exquisite, painful stations of my slaughter,
To glibly parse my parts' savage dispersal;
I have no heart at all, quite literally. I recall
We poets are nothing if not literal. Forgive me
If I spare all the brute *AI* of my ruptured cries;
There are some things to be unsaid for modesty.
Suffice it to say: I *should* have died, did not;
No, I was entombed alive in my severed head,
Now blind, left to deduce the scattered body
Upon which my kind beasts voraciously fed—
Yet none exhumed the offals of my brain.
No kindly god reassembled my broken parts,
No penitent mother, no son (I never had one),
And my lost boys, embroiled in foreign wars,
Had passed beyond my pacifying compass;
They never knew me. They were never mine,
Were loaned me to abandon me in their prime
While I declined to depths beneath their ken.

My dark, post-mortal life, compared to D's,
Was a travesty, a sham, though Dionysian,
As if he were living his queerest role through me,
Enacting some mad, delighted self-parody,
While the phantom body that my brain filled in
Throbbed with a searing pain entirely real;
Its wounds, though cauterized, would never heal;
Regrets, redundant, carved grooves in my mind,
A circuit, closed, enclosed in a calcified sphere
That neither light nor sound could penetrate,
The silent rasp of my prayers all I could hear,
The stuttered blandishments of a blinded seer.

O, nightmarish *life-in-death* and *death-in-life*
Of which one later singer had heart to tell
Who became the mute Orpheus of his inner hell,
Though he at least was granted the grace to die,
His obsessive perseverations thereby stilled,

Distilled into the notes some remember him by,
You grant me no respite. I cannot wake and die
But eddy on like the Hebron in which my top
Was tossed like refuse by some bloodied hand.

I commanded myself: let *I* now stand for *head,*
Shorthand for the part still left of me, its pith
More corporeal, more real, than my abstract *self,*
A concept depleted of all its inherited wealth.
So henceforth shall it be. Thus I decreed it
Who had no further power to set the terms,
The rules for the misrule by which I was led,
Misled, launched on my false pilgrimage
Toward nowhere I had the knowledge to predict;
By rights my syntax, too, might have been mangled,
Though I was left, small solace, the gift of speech
Yet granted no audience for my protestations—
Which, had it assembled, would have spurned them
As if each tender ear were plugged with wax.

Besides, my father had trained me to be *meek.*
And so, no swan, I was borne swiftly onward
Past the spoiled precincts of my erstwhile dreams,
Its flattened fields, its indifferent flora, fauna,
Which I had no further privilege to see;
At last the gentle Hebron's mouth disgorged me
Into the world-circling, wild, unpastured sea.

Lone ark stalled on the dark, mercurial tides,
Orphaned, vouchsafed no second of my kind,
My pitchy head had become *un bateau ivre,*
Although, both bark and passenger, stone sober,
I had the will to command, but no possible way;
It tendered no tiller, and I lacked any hand
With which to stay the waves' tempestuous sway,
Unlikely protagonist of the *night sea journey,*
Its tests an *archetypal* phase of the hero's quest—
For what? *Reintegration? Salvation?* I forget.
My chaotic peregrinations spelled no end
And I, cast against type, was no Aryan hero;
I had never served as coxswain for the Argo,

Its manly crew, and my lyre's steady measure
Had never synchronized swift, thrusting oars—
A myth, like that of Eurydice, sadly untrue.
No, I had always distrusted the sea's livid flux,
D's rude dominion, soused with its own excesses,
Its ubiquitous, overlapping crests and troughs,
The hyperactive slough of my deep despond.
My head, as if set in some subtle gyroscope,
Kept turning right side up, facing a sky
That remained occult, an absolute zero to me,
Sunless, starless; night, day, space, and time
All merged with the lateral drift of my anomie,
Distance, direction, duration, all unmeasured
As the looping thoughts in my untethered brain,
Feedback reinforcing the same vexed question—
Who, if not I, was the author of my fate?—
Until, keeping nothing straight, I fell to raving;
The froth about my mouth was not my own
But might have been, my mind was so far gone.

Misogynist? No. Another myth. I'd never
Loathed women, only felt drawn to my kind;
A few chaste hours spent with innocent boys—
Had they forced gentle matrons from their looms,
Impelled them to such squalid handiwork,
Provoked from them a vengeance so unkind?
Implausible, if not goaded by D's whip,
But the solemn, stately troop that had assailed me
Had revealed no trace of the Maenads' frenzy,
Had displayed, in fact, an Apollonian poise.
Could my father have rescinded his gift of life,
Jealous of the lyre he had bequeathed me,
Its seductive influence breaching mortal bounds?
The archer, impartial judge, flayed Marsyas alive
For daring, fool, to challenge him in song—
But, diffident, I had never been one to boast.
Could D have silenced me for *seeing too much*,
My stalkers' steady gait his ingenious hoax?
Could Apollo, D, have broken my body's bread,
Small price to effectuate some solemn truce?
Why taunt me, then, with mock-immortal life?

Was it I, my emergent desire, that stalked itself?
O, these and cognate questions embroiled my head,
Unanswerable and never to be answered,
While, floundering on the self-besotted flood,
I bathed as if in my warm, spilling blood.

Between thoughts I was rapped, a sudden thud;
My minuscule ship had foundered on some shore,
A coconut fetched up far from its native palm—
O, moment of blessed stasis, just before
I was solemnly raised by massing, votive hands
Far kinder than those that last manhandled me.
A miracle! A sign! A talking head! All hung
And murmured, rapt, around my sunken visage
That the sun, the sea, had caulked to a stiff mask.
I petitioned for my life—for them to end it!
None paid the slightest heed to what I prayed;
No, they had other plans, those silken maids,
In solemn procession paced to Apollo's shrine
Where I was potted, enthroned, a sacred plant
Attended, with care, by a Lesbian hierophant,
High priestess of the island to which I'd come.

Was this, then, sweet Elysium? No, pure hell,
For them a blessed isle, but accursed to me,
Though from my gentle captors none could tell
That to be irreparably stopped and stranded here,
At the polar, antipodal outpost of my fate,
Was worse than to brave the maelstrom of the sea.
I knew there was no evading their intention
To domesticate me, prized like a sullen child
Whose least, precocious squawk presages genius,
While laying me, like a tyrant's corpse, in state,
A rank flame guttering, filming my blank eyes—
Tortures too clever for Hades himself to devise.

Lord, how I yearned for D's forced ecstasies,
To morph my vestal Nereids to frantic Maenads,
For his flickering, lurid cinema of derangement
To flash, again, on my mind's vacated screen,
But now a permanent blackout locked my brain,

One life, one death, cold solitude, one fixed frame,
No savior to spring me from the sacred gaol
Where I lay sequestered with my secret shame,
No name to cry out, except, in vain, my own--
Famed Orpheus tamed, reduced to an oracle!

Ah, to be less than human, and yet deemed more!
A monster, an unholy terror, yet duly installed
In their innermost sanctum, holiest of holies,
Rescued, yet damned to terminal self-internment,
Outcast, yet smuggled within tall temple walls,
My unique debasement prompting my elevation,
My cruel election a boon to my credulous hosts,
My fractured existence a riddle to stump the Sphinx—
From me the barest fact was its own disguise.

An impotent Pan decamped amid coy nymphs
(More willing, but to no end, than doomed Syrinx)
My only instrument was my severed windpipe,
My grating voice forced through a hollow straw,
No voice, but a hoarse hiss, a ghastly whisper,
The last recourse allowed me by Godly decree.
My lyre, my precious lyre. Where had it gone?
Down Hebron, swept to the sea's imagined floor
To consort with Morpheus on his ebony bed
While I scratched forth the noise within my head.

Perhaps I dreamed I *spoke*, but merely *mouthed,*
Like a hooked fish, an agonized pantomime;
If so, the Gods' joke, tasteless, was still on me;
But clearly my keen auditors thought they *heard.*
My every word of complaint, however banal,
Was gold coin new-issued from Apollo's mint,
Its figures tortured, conformed to grand designs
Far loftier than their progenitor had in mind,
Whose only intent, quite literal, was to die—
No mystical dark night, but extinction itself;
To be burned, packed in an urn, stuck on a shelf,
To annul my fool's charade, my cancelled self
Upon which counterfeit idols could be stamped
Was all I begged for with confounded cries.

My words fell not on deaf, but distant ears;
The more I repeated myself, the less they heard,
Until I vowed, hellbent, to *stop making sense,*
And spewed a gurgling stream of consciousness,
A wild glossolalia, post-Babel, a polyglot brew
My priestesses copied, coopted, sanitized,
Reframed into the corpus of *Orpheus' Hymns,*
Inspiring the vulgar cult of *Thrice-Born D,*
Yet another crude, world-despoiling, mystery
Ensuring all comers eternal incumbency.
                                    And *I*
(O, crowning irony!) was named its founder.

Like the wandering Jew, yet unable to wander,
Immortally harried, yet hammered in place,
An internal alien, foundling, the ward of no state
But my own, but my own, my stammering dreams
Congealed to unsoundable howls of disgrace,
Self-enclosed O's, frozen shocks of brute fear
I suffered my scrupulous nymphs not to hear;
How I longed to relapse into sod, to dissolve,
Atavistic, in primal muck stamped by no gods.

My jaws a gaping yoni, my tongue a lingam,
My face a leering death mask, more obscene
Than any Gorgon's, fixed in an abject grin,
Like Lear reduced to a zero without a figure,
I, memberless hermaphrodite, blinkered seer,
Was laved by obsessive ritual ablutions,
Pure torture to me, to my vestals a fond chore;
Yet still I endured, not hoping past all hope,
My vatic mouth washed out with votive soap.

Where was the boy within me, his firm trust
Displaced by the taste of terminal disgust?
Of him above all I dared not think to think
And of his harmonious numbers, so wholly slain
Not even a plangent trace of their ardor remained
To reverberate through that golden atmosphere
In which all objects rounded to their prime.

What of his verdant precincts, ripening glades?
Did no virtuous youth remember he had gone?

From time to time I heard D's truant laughter,
Far off, yet in the vault of my echoing mind,
Amid sophomoric quips (*no man is an island*)—
Mocking me, exiled from my body's mainland—
Disposable rhetoric, costing its speaker nothing
Yet leaving me destitute as a bartered son.

My graven tablets, forged in Apollo's temple,
Bore the clear, hard marks of his imprimatur
By which, at least tacitly, he legitimized D
Whose rage, in turn, was tamped, if not contained—
A pact, improbable, sealed at my sad expense.
Now neither god put stock in my spent voice
That had outlived its mandate. Had it had one?

My father, staunch upholder of the law,
Swooped down and stuck a lead bit in my craw—
While still, through later voices, I babble on,
None willing, at last, to shrive me, empty me.

So many words have been forced into my mouth:
Elegies, lyrics, soliloquies, sonnets enthralled
By noble panegyrics, proud poets' skilled
Self-flattery tricked out in my borrowed guise,
Their heads bay-crowned, my cruel fate falsified,
My ruptured flesh, my seasonless inner hell,
Atrocity's garbled shame, its torturous syntax,
Smoothed out in rolling numbers, tolling rhymes,
All forcing me to bear glib hymns of praise:
O Orpheus, O tall tree in the ear!—from which,
Bent low, dismasted, unmanned, cut down
I, too, like luckless Pentheus, was uncrowned.

Enough! Enough sublime, stentorian lines;
It is time, past time: I refuse to ventriloquize,
Charge all to heed the ultimate reprimand
That brave Apollo poured in my stopped ears:
Even now can you not curb your wagging tongue?

For God's sake, turn away, let me be silent;
I suffer blank, unspeakable, tractless days,
Each pinned to the ruined pediment of no future
As pain sifts through my brain as through a sieve—
O, sleepless nightmare, truth wracked past belief!

Quit me, now, be *quiet*—and dream that you live.

A NOTE ABOUT THE AUTHOR

George Franklin graduated from Harvard University, where he studied poetry with Elizabeth Bishop and Robert Fitzgerald, in 1975. He subsequently received an M.F.A. in Creative Writing from Brown University and an M.A. in English Literature from Columbia. He lived for over ten years in the ashrams of his spiritual preceptor in India and in upstate New York. He has published two books of poetry, *The Fall of Miss Alaska*, Six Gallery Press, 2007, and the chapbook *Contour With Shadow*, Frolic Press, 2016. A book of literary criticism, *Some Segments of a River*, was published by Nicasio Press in the winter of 2020, and a memoir/critical study *Portraits from Life* was published in 2022. His uncollected poems, including "Talking Head," a forty-page work in blank verse, have been published widely, most prominently in *Epiphany Magazine* and in *The Recorder: The Journal of the American Irish Historical Society*.

Lightning Source UK Ltd.
Milton Keynes UK
UKHW050841230123
415808UK00009B/1659

9 798986 410012